GENERAL PRACTICE MANAGEMENT

Dr. V. Subramanian

Copyright © Dr. V. Subramanian 2015

This book is sold subject to the condition that it shall not, by way of trade or otherwise, be lent, resold, hired out, or otherwise circulated without the publisher's prior consent in any form of binding or cover other than that in which it is published and without a similar condition including this condition being imposed on the subsequent publisher.

The moral right of Dr. V. Subramanian has been asserted.

ISBN-13: 978-1514790748

ISBN-10: 1514790742

DEDICATION

I dedicate this to all the new entrants to the healthcare industry.

From youngsters, joining the GP surgery to gain work experience, for part-time or full-time employment and to all other persons, when a change of career is envisaged.

This picture was taken while visiting a tiger sanctuary near Bangkok. Even though I was walking the tiger, this could not be accomplished without the trainer walking beside, along with scores of people around, should the tiger react to deer and pigs moving around in the vicinity.

GP surgery management rules and procedures are akin to a jungle and there are so many aspects to be aware of. Staff in the surgery need help from all those around, e.g. GPs, Nurses, Practice Managers (in case of receptionists and other staff reporting to him), Healthcare Professionals, PCT/CCG, Pharmacists, Health Visitors, hospital contacts, and scores of others. Once this is understood, appreciated, cultivated and nurtured then one can perform the tasks very well in this healthcare industry.

ACKNOWLEDGMENTS

My wife, Bala; our elder son, Sanjay and his wife Meera, who helped at various stages and finally in getting the manuscript to Kindle; my second son, Deepak, a Medic, and his wife Kashmira; my elder brother Mr. V. Jagannathan, a practicing Chartered Accountant in Chennai; my mentors late Mr. Ramachandran, of Pune and Mr. Dev Ganesan, an entrepreneur, who motivated me to use Kindle for my publication; my friend Mr. G. Viswanathan, accountant, who introduced me to GP surgery management; two practicing GPs – Dr. Siva Devaraj and Dr. S. Jaiswal; Kartik, who helped with issues on WordPress; the 10 GPs from the surgeries I worked at, and all the staff in the various PCTs in London, Birmingham and Manchester.

CONTENTS

Preface i
Foreword v
1. Introduction 1
   1.1 General *1*
   1.2 Organisation *3*
2. Operations 5
   2.1 Surgery Tour *5*
   2.2 First Time Arrival *10*
   2.3 Reception *18*
   2.4 Appointments *33*
   2.5 Immunisations *46*
   2.6 Telephones *57*
   2.7 Registrations *62*
   2.8 Prescriptions *78*
   2.9 Practice Manager *85*
3. IMT 101
   3.1 Tasks *102*
   3.1a Details of IMT Tasks *103*
   3.2 Procedures *107*
   3.3 READ Codes *107*
   3.4 Claims *109*
   3.5 Other Tasks *109*
4. Medical Secretaries 111
   4.1 Tasks *112*
5. Claims 114
   5.1 Background *116*
6. Patients 120
   6.1 Customer Service *123*
   6.2 Quality & Customer Service *125*

7. Premises 129
7.1 Rent 129
7.2 Rates 130
7.3 Heat and Light 130
7.4 Communication Systems 131
7.5 Out of Hours Services 131
7.6 Maintenance 133
7.7 Modifications 134
7.8 Security 134
7.9 Disabled Services 135
7.10 Insurances 135
7.11 Mortgage 135

8. Administration 136
8.1 Communications – Telephones 137
8.2 Computers 137
8.3 Post 138
8.4 Travel 138
8.5 Motor 138
8.6 Subscriptions 139
8.7 Accounts 143
8.8 Bank Charges 143
8.9 Sundries 144
8.10 Petty Cash 144

9. HR 148
9.1 Job Specifications and Job Descriptions 149
9.3 Job Appraisals 160
9.4 Staff References 168
9.5 CVs 170
9.6 Recruitment 176
9.7 Disciplinary Procedures 184

10. PAYE 190
10.1 Software Packages 191
10.2 Tax and NI 192
10.3 Employer Annual Return 193
10.4 Forms 193
10.5 NHS Pensions 196

11. Finance 198
11.1 Mortgage details 198
11.2 Loans and Interests 198
11.3 Hire Purchases and Interests 198

12. Superannuation 200
12.1 Superannuation 200
12.2 Seniority 201
12.3 CCGs and the Changes 203

13. Depreciation 205
13.1 Capital Allowances 205
13.2 Depreciation 206
13.3 Disposals 208

14. Nurses 209
14.1 Duties 209
14.2 Patients 210
14.3 Training 210
14.4 Emergencies 210
14.5 Medicine Management 213
14.6 Protocols 215
14.7 Clinics 216

15. GPs 221
15.1 Duties 221
15.2 Patients 223
15.3 Locum GPs 223
15.4 Triage 227
15.5 Clinics 229
15.6 Do's and Don'ts 230
15.7 Home Visits 231
15.8 Risk Management 231

16. Partners 233
16.1 Advantages 233
16.2 Disadvantages 233
16.3 Costs 234
16.4 Parity 234
16.5 Earnings 234

- 16.6 Contract 235
- 16.7 Management Miscellaneous 235

17. Outside Contacts 238
- 17.1 PCT 238
- 17.2 HMRC, NHS Pensions 240
- 17.3 Hospitals, Walk-in Centres, Carers, District and Community Nurses, Social Services 240
- 17.4 Banks 240
- 17.5 ACAS 241
- 17.6 Sales Representatives 241
- 17.7 Others – Professional, Utilities and Service Personnel 241

18. Accounts 242
- 18.1 General Principles 246

19. QOF 262
- 19.1 QOF Domains and Indicators 263
- 19.2 QOF Clinical Indicators 2012/13: Summary Lists 265
- 19.2a QOF Indicators for 2014-15 267
- 19.3 DES 267
- 19.4 2015-16 QOF Changes 268
- 19.5 Sites to Check 269
- 19.6 Target Indicators 269
- 19.7 Support with Clinical Audit 275
- 19.8 Patient Information 275
- 19.9 Access 276

20. New Set-Ups 277
- 20.1 Clinical Commissioning Group (CCG) 277
- 20.2 Care Quality Commission (CQC) 279
- 20.3 GPES and CQRS 281

21. Healthcare Professionals 283

22. Health & Safety 290
- 22.1 Legal Issues 292

23. Remedial Issues 293
- 23.1 Causes 293
- 23.2 NCAS Role 293
- 23.3 Investigations 294
- 23.4 PAG (Performance Assessment Group) Assessment 295

23.5 Complaints Procedures ... 295
23.6 Disciplinary Procedures ... 297
23.7 Gender Issues ... 304
23.8 Tidy-up Tasks ... 306
23.9 Look Back Exercises ... 307
23.10 Practice Manager Role ... 308
23.11 General Outcome ... 308

24. Health Issues ... 310
24.1 BMI ... 311
24.2 BP ... 312
24.3 GI Values ... 314
24.4 GL Values ... 316
24.4a Glycaemic Index and Glycaemic Load Chart ... 317
24.4b Food Values ... 323
24.5 5-a-Day Concept ... 326

25. Patient Information ... 328
25.1 Rights ... 328
25.2 Confidentiality ... 329
25.3 Whistleblowing ... 331
25.4 Clinical Care ... 335
25.5 Clinical Governance ... 336
25.6 Clinical Supervision ... 339

26. PBC ... 340

27. Impending Changes ... 341

28 Fraud ... 345

29. Practice Booklets ... 351
29.1 Standard Format ... 351
29.2 Modified Format (29.2a) ... 351

30. The List of Attachments ... 367

References ... 368

Contact Us ... 373

Thanks ... 37474

Postscript ... 37676

About Me ... 38282

Preface

This was originally written as 'blogs', which have now been converted to an 'eBook'. However, the writing will be referred to as blogs for convenience here.

These blogs on General Practice Management are about the management of a GP surgery, primarily in England. There is a void in publications in this crucial area covering the various aspects of Surgery Management.

There isn't a single book, dealing with all the areas covered here, to help the various personnel working in the GP surgeries and to assist them with their training, self-learning and being continually prepared for the demands of the job.

The eBook covers all areas of management which a Practice Manager (PMgr) has to deal with in order to perform his tasks effectively. These lay out the basic principles and points to know about if he/she has to be skilled in general administration.

The eBook is based mostly on my notes while working, with PCT and other organisations continually giving information on changes and how to process them.

The eBook does not deal with clinical aspects of the GP surgery responsibilities in detail as these are in the domain for GPs and nurses; the PMgr is not required to focus on these areas unless he is a Medical Doctor. The PMgr is required to focus on admin duties only and should not get involved in clinical duties, even inadvertently.

The scope of the eBook is to be helpful to all staff in knowing their tasks and how to deal with situations involving patients and outside personnel. A comprehensive perspective is given with suitable references for detailed study as appropriate.

With an engineering background and senior management experience for several years in multinational companies, at a very late stage in life, I was asked to manage a large GP surgery in London by an accountant friend, Mr G. Viswanathan, in London. I grabbed that opportunity as I always had a fascination with working for GPs.

With a staff of nearly 20 and two surgeries with 6 GPs for a list size of nearly 10,000 patients, I found the job quite stimulating and satisfying. There, I felt the need for helping receptionists who were young and new to this industry and were keen to learn and perform well.

In those days, and even now, the courses offered were very few and in the main, the courses were for the Practice or admin managers and special training for nurses. Apart from a few short sessions, the receptionists were generally side-lined.

Many years after that, when I was required to train a Practice Manager recently, I found the opportunity for using such courses was very scarce and very expensive. This made me write the eBook as an aid to the receptionists, practice manager, nurses, other staff and GPs for the admin areas.

I also felt that the book should be available at an accessible price for anyone embarking on a career in the NHS. Each one should be able to get a copy and refer to the eBook for self-learning and get familiar with the practices followed in GP surgeries in England. Rules are similar in Scotland, Wales and Northern Ireland, with some variations, should they wish to move to these parts of the country later in their careers. The eBook is intended as a 'reference book' for all employees of a GP surgery and a 'must-have' copy for each of them to possess.

Primary Care Trust (PCTs), BMA, NICE etc. have laid out the procedures in detail and help materials to use. The eBook makes only reference to those organisations and does not reproduce their lengthy publications. For example, Quality and Outcomes Framework (QOF) for 2011-12 runs to over 187 pages in PDF format. Only a sample sheet is attached to elucidate key points; this principle is applied to all the others in the document. The admin and clinical protocols with details cover over 200 pages; I have only included a list with short descriptions for some of them. Even though PCTs have become Clinical Commissioning Group (CCG), I have not changed the eBook from PCTs to CCGs. CCG details have been dealt with in Section 20.1.

I chose to write this originally as a book, (now as blogs), due to necessity for my immediate needs and also to help the staff in GP surgeries, working at present, and those who will continue to join. I have been used to writing operating manuals with Do's and Don'ts and felt compelled to author these blogs with eventual publication as a 'book'. With cash-strapped PCTs, the training courses offered are very limited now and the surgeries are sometimes so short of staff, in-house training is difficult and puts the junior staff under undue stress.

I learnt accounting from my elder brother, Mr V. Jagannathan, a chartered accountant, in Chennai, and have managed to do accounts in the early 80s for freelance operators like a songwriter, a fashion designer, a few hotels, and for small limited companies. In that process, I developed an Excel-based system for the surgery, whereby inputting the income and expenses, the rest of the accounts are automatically computed and displayed; this made the accountant's job a lot easier.

The GP partner need only spend about 30-45 min each month to input the income and expense figures. The Partner will have a feel for the surgery accounts each month and have the 'status' when clicking accounts. Nothing should come as a 'shock' at the year-end.

This system is used in one surgery and I still check the final account computation at the end of each financial year (more as a courtesy for setting up the system than as a necessity).

I sincerely hope that all readers find these blogs of great help, not only for knowing the jobs involved but also in assisting them to settle in quickly and make them want to make a good career out of the GP surgery work.

The references given later in a separate section are for the users of the blogs – for current practices and more detailed descriptions of each of the sections in the blogs.

In my opinion there is no better place to work than in the Healthcare industry and no finer place to work than in a GP surgery in the UK.

Having dealt with over 8 GPs, 5 nurses, 3 PCTs, and their staff, I must stress that these blogs would not have been possible without the help and support they provided to me while at work in the GP surgeries under these PCTs. Some may not even remember me or realise their contribution in motivating me but my gratitude is to all of them and I have also dealt with this in the 'thanks' section.

Foreword

It may appear unusual to have a foreword for 'blogs' but I decided to have my own, for personal reasons. For the eBook, I decided to keep it simple and use the same foreword as used for the blogs.

Initially, about 2 years ago, I planned to write a GP surgery manual in the form of a 'book' but due to various reasons, the project was horrendously delayed. There were mega changes in the NHS, as each minister wanted to make his mark, renaming various organisations, changing QOF, etc.

I told my close family friend, Dr. Shiva Devraj, a retired GP but still doing locums, about this book and gave the various chapter details. He was extremely encouraging and always kept in touch with me on the progress. I also told my son's GP friend, Dr. Sujoy Jaiswal, in whose surgery in Manchester I worked for a short period, and he was equally encouraging about this venture.

I researched the publishing market and found the publishers were brutally frank about the book – the topic was found to be quite interesting and appealing to them, but they were looking at money side, more than me.

The market I was hoping to attract may not be able to afford a high price for the book and the information in the book would be **'unread'**. That made me think and realise that all the hard work done in the last few years would be a complete waste.

Then it dawned on me that if I were to write as 'Blogs' then I would not have to worry about endemic changes happening to the NHS, QOF, funding, etc. The sections could be updated as and when needed.

I decided a year ago that I would not get this written as a book. It had to be '**Blogs**' and it should be available to all those who wanted to access the website.

I joined WordPress and Bluehost and this led to a long learning curve and a considerable time spent on learning about 'Posts' or 'Pages' and all the nuances of website design.

I had to tell the two GPs about the change from writing a 'Book' to 'Blogs'. The direction has been changed around. I have also turned around the 'Foreword' – instead of them writing about the blogs I decided to mention them in the Foreword.

My aim was to give something back to the society.

Despite my several years of working in Industry, in large corporate companies and in Senior Management positions, the few years I spent as Practice Manager (PMgr), working very closely with the GPs, nurses, Healthcare professionals, staff, HAs, PCT's, pharmacists and other allied personnel, had meant a lot to me, and I felt that the Healthcare Industry was the best industry one should aim to work for. Income may be modest but it would give mega satisfaction in providing quality service to the patients.

I decided to take the route of self-publishing using the Internet and made it available **'at an affordable price'** to all. I felt the reception staff, with such a meagre starting salary, statutory minimum hourly rate, should not be expected to pay a high price for reading the eBook.

The blogs are written as a manual so that at any point in their working career or even before joining, a person can refer to these, to have some idea of what the various roles involve while working in a GP surgery. It lists the areas, points to focus, procedures to follow, do's and don'ts, amongst many other things. It covers a wide range of areas to become familiar with. During the course of their working career, they can build up their knowledge base with further reading, using the vast resources available via the Internet. References are also given for them to search and learn.

Why Blog to Book?

The NHS is fast changing. The changes in the last 10 years, even the last 5 years have been phenomenal; some good, some cosmetic, and the rest bad. Nonetheless, changes are endemic with each government, when a minister is changed. The changes have been more since the government introduced an admin interface, e.g. Primary Care Trusts in between the minster and the NHS old hierarchy of consultants and GPs.

Consequently, if a book takes about a year or two to write, one is not able to keep up with the changes and the book would appear out of date even before it is published.

This posed a serious problem to me and I wanted to minimise this. Blogging gave an excellent opportunity as each blog could be updated with or without readers' input.

Several authors in the last 10 years have followed this route of **'blog to book'** for their own reasons and I felt that this was the route to follow for this management manual. Also, a book in the end would leave tangible evidence for the years to come.

Many people may prefer to have a book for easy reference than reading the blogs via computer or mobile iPhones or iPads. Books open doors for press coverage and speaking opportunities. Books make other people perceive the author as a serious writer.

I am fully aware that blogs and eBooks do not make money except for a very few reputable authors. I never considered making money from blogs as an option. In fact, the eBook might end up floating like a lead balloon – only time will tell.

One aspect of blogging is realising the crucial aspect and importance of social networking sites e.g. Facebook, Myspace, LinkedIn, Twitter, YouTube, Google, Yahoo and not to forget other bloggers. The more any author is familiar with and uses these sites, the better the opportunity to contact people when the blogs are published. I am a novice in the field of social networking too!

What the blog does and does not deal with is listed below:

- Covers most of the areas of admin. Responsibilities of all staff including GPs, nurses and Healthcare professionals; it isn't about the clinical responsibilities of the GPs, nurses and Healthcare professionals.
- General skills needed in areas of communication, assertiveness, management, human psychology etc. have been dealt with, but for greater appreciation on these aspects the readers are advised to use the web and libraries for specialist books.
- Only a brief mention about QOF points and how to deal with each is made, as these are brilliantly listed in other publications and the person can access these easily by looking through websites given in the Reference Section.
- Apart from how to access the sites of HMRC as regards to taxation, NI for various tables, the rest is left for the reader to source the information. Tax filing for partnerships etc. is also excluded. This also applies to the specific pay roll system used, as they are reasonably easy to use, and how to use them is excluded as well.
- The details of income and expenses, on which the PMgr has to focus and get the monies from PCT, are mentioned. The use of Excel sheets is shown, to have auto-preparation of accounts and to have an idea of the financial state of the practice at any given time. All aspects of financial accounting are left for the qualified accountant, who would be preparing the annual accounts.
- For computing and telephones only a list of providers and areas for search are included. The details of the specific computing system used in the practice are also excluded. The service provider would have trained key personnel in the practice at the time of installation and a trained staff in the surgery should be able to deal with new entrants.
- Regarding HR issues, only those pertaining to the surgery practice are mentioned. All general aspects could be sourced via Google search or using other references given.
- These blogs are meant to share the existing knowledge in every day operation in the GP surgery and is made available **FREE** to all who access the site. Case studies and preparing this as an e-learning book, have not been attempted, as this would involve a different emphasis with training in mind and there are several organisations that do courses for such training at a very high cost. I have been out of contact with surgeries for some years, especially when numerous changes were being introduced and for case studies one needs access to surgeries on a regular basis to get data for the book. Much

as I like to address the case studies' issues, I have no such access to surgeries, close to where I live, at present.

Remedial issues are so complex and detailed when an investigation starts, and there are several sources to obtain information (only the areas which the PMgr has to conform so that the practice follows all due procedures required in day-to-day operations are covered. These regulations and requirements happen to occupy the **'blind spot'** for focus, even for GPs).

All GP surgery staff – are 'heroes'.

Welcome to you all for reading the eBook to find out about the manual for General Practice Management.

This covers all issues – reception, admin. HR, payroll, accounts, claims, and fraud, amongst other crucial things that all staff should be aware of.

1. Introduction

1.1 General

In the last 15 years we have seen several changes in the National Health Service (NHS) due to political, economic, administration, and other factors like demand and accessibility. These changes have been costly, and resulted in mergers of General Practitioners' (GP) practices, new super Medical Centres and even opened the doors to private enterprises seeking Private Financial Incentives (PFI).

These days GP Practices have undergone major changes in the monitoring and delivery of services controlled by Primary Care Trusts (PCT) and each trust may supervise over 60 GP Practices in the area. These PCTs have enormous departments to serve the public, but are mainly set up to increase employment in NHS.

Presently, the NHS has over a million personnel on its payroll, mostly in administrative roles, swamping the number of Medical Doctors, nurses and other specialists.

The changes in the hospital sector have also been significant, often brutal, taking away the power base from the medically qualified and very professional consultants, to the hands of administrative personnel with questionable knowledge in medical field. Changes have been introduced for the hospitals to rely on GPs for the services they provide to the patients.

GP practices had mostly relied on the spouse of a Partner as Practice Manager (PMgr) and no formal qualification had been specified for the post. Due to diverse and complicated procedures involved in these changes, many practices had to appoint PMgrs with management experience in industry. Recently, however, due to various courses available and training set up within PCT in the early days and outside in colleges, Practices do specify a formal qualification for consideration when choosing a PMgr.

The Royal College of General Practitioners (RCGP), British Medical Association (BMA), and General Medical Council (GMC) provide, in most cases, a robust support to GPs, highlighting the areas to focus, how to do the jobs and even procedures, instruction leaflets and leaflets for patients to read and take with them when they come to the surgeries.

The Royal College of Nurses (RCN) provides training and support to the nurses for working in the hospital or GP practices, and they are very visible in their support for their fraternity. They also provide legal cover in various areas for the members.

Medical Defence Organisations (MDOs) are, mutual non-profit making organisations, owned by their members. All MDOs provide members with 24-hour access to advice and assistance on medico-legal issues arising from clinical practice, which fall outside the scope of indemnity provided by NHS bodies.

There are three MDOs: Medical Defence Union (MDU), Medical Protection Society (MPS) and Medical and Dental Defence Union of Scotland (MDDUS). As the benefits of membership of the MDOs differ, it is important that one considers each society carefully before making a choice.

The help afforded to reception and administrative staff, in terms of induction and training courses, is minimal both in PCTs and practices due to shortage of staff, funds and other factors. They have to rely on the PMgr to help, train and support them. They do not have any legal cover and they are not even recognised as a member of any institution which would provide cover. The PMgr can become a member of the above MDOs at a very nominal cost.

The author had been in GP practices, mostly in the London area but also for very short periods in Birmingham and Manchester surgeries, as a Practice Manager. Having had a staff of 20 people, in two surgery locations with about 10,000 patients, I had witnessed the plight of the reception and other admin staff, in terms of induction, training, salary levels, sickness and other privileges, which employees in other industries seem to enjoy more. Receptionists start usually at a basic minimum salary level but were expected to do a highly skilled job from the date of taking up appointments and in dealing with patients.

My usual philosophy, which was stated to the practitioners, whom I knew for some years, is that **'my empathy and loyalty is to the GPs but my sympathy is always with the staff, as they have little protection from external support organisations'**. GPs have generally concurred and applauded but, in reality, they have rarely shown any change in their management style and sensitivity to the issues.

The book is written as an aid to any person wanting to join the industry – as a new entrant from school or college, or a senior person from another industry with no exposure to the NHS previously. This is written as a manual for all admin staff, even for those at present in the NHS. There are several areas which they are aware of but do not usually focus on due to other commitments; also unaware in terms of significance when any error occurs and when procedures are not clinically and systematically followed. All the admin staff have to realise that they are working primarily in support roles to the GPs, nurses and other healthcare professionals and this principle is crucial for their effective functioning in their roles.

The author was not a staunch practicing Hindu but has stated to all the GPs and other personnel, that a GP Practice clearly elucidates the Hindu caste system.

The GPs are, the **'Brahmins'**, the high priests, and they are **'semi-gods'**. Never incur their wrath at any time. Nurses are like **'Kshatriyas'** – warrior class, in as much they, with their weapon of needles and injections, deal with patients. The reception and other staff are like **'Vaisyas'** – the traders, dealing with people and in this case the patients. Finally, the Practice Manager is like a **'Sudra'** – the working class, as the Practice Manager has to serve all the people in the surgery.

Even though he may be above the staff administratively the onus is on the PMgr to provide support, training and other crucial help for them to provide an effective service to the surgery and the community. As long as the Practice Manager realises and performs on this basis, the surgery will end up with a very effective team keeping the GPs, nurses and other Healthcare professionals happy.

1.2 Organisation

The structure is given for a very large and modern GP Medical Practice with over 20-24 GPs, with associate staff. From this, the structure for smaller practices with 2 GPs, as the minimum, to 6-8 GPs for medium is shown (See 1.2a). The staff list would include:

1.2a

Practice Size	Small	Medium	Large
List Size – approximate	To 3000	3000-8000	8000+
Practice Principals			Yes
Practice/Business Manager			Yes
Practice Manager only	Yes	Yes	
GP Registrars			Yes
GPs	Yes	Yes	Yes
Medical Student		Yes	Yes
Healthcare Professionals	Yes	Yes	Yes
Office/Admin manager		Yes	Yes
Receptionists	Yes	Yes	Yes
Other support staff (admin)	Yes	Yes	Yes
Trainees	Yes	Yes	Yes
Nurse Manager			Yes
Nurses	Yes	Yes	Yes
Enrolled nurses			Yes

Nursing students			Yes
Financial support (PT accountant)			Yes
IT support			Yes
Medical Secretary		Yes	Yes
Ancillary staff (cleaner, caretaker)	Yes	Yes	Yes

These are general guidelines. Small practices may employ some on a part-time basis to cover areas listed for 'medium' practices above. In several instances, for small to medium size practices, the Practice Manager may also look after some parts of the day-to-day accounts, property issues, loans and mortgages etc.

Very busy inner city GP surgeries usually have 2-3 receptionists to deal with patients, appointments, registration, prescription, telephone answering, etc. for the all surgery GPs and might have one Medical Secretary for the secretarial tasks.

In many surgeries in leafy suburbs, due to more orderly and different clientele, there might be only one receptionist for general enquiries. All other enquiries would be dealt by phone by the GP's secretary for appointments, registrations, nurses' appointments, emergencies etc. – all pre-booked. In such surgeries, each GP may have a dedicated secretary; sometimes 2 GPs might share one common secretary. Such a set-up has a tremendous advantage in that the surgery is not full of patients at any given time and the staff can attend to other equally pressing duties.

The structure for any practice ultimately rests with the Partners and there are no strict rules about how to manage the practice and the type of structure it should have.

2. Operations

The Practice Manager or a senior receptionist may receive the new entrant and after a welcoming brief about the surgery, the introduction of various personnel would begin: Introducing Existing Staff, Nurses and GPs followed by a Tour of the surgery premises.

The person designated to take the new staff on the tour should be an experienced member of staff and should devote adequate time to take around the premises, explain and answer all queries the new member may have and allowing the person to make notes as the tour proceeds.

2.1 Surgery Tour

2.1.1 Main Entrance

Highlight the presence of a sloping pathway for disabled entry (if not, it must be provided ASAP).

If some parking is allowed, specify who should and should not park.

The entrance would usually be by using keys in some surgeries and use of keypads in others.

The door opening should be automatic rather than 'PULL' or 'PUSH', for the convenience of disabled persons.

Surgery opening hours for the week, including lunch break and contact telephone numbers for an Emergency and Out-of Hours service should be displayed near the doors with preferably the names of GPs in the practice.

2.1.2 Entrance Hall

There may be one or more consoles, with keypads to register the arrival of patients in the system.

Simple input for this screen would be –

Gender, month, date and year of birth; name of GP/nurse to be seen.

The next screen would then display any delay time for waiting.

There usually would be a telephone to talk to the GP's secretary or the nurses in case of any queries; contact telephone numbers would be displayed.

Various circulars from outside organisations and various Healthcare organisations, surgery notices, along with others would be displayed.

The door opening to the Reception area should be automatic or by pressing, preferably, a large button.

2.1.3 Reception Area

Key tasks for the receptionists would include:

- To serve patients, answer telephone calls, register the patients and prepare repeat prescriptions.
- GP and nurses' queries.
- Prescription – collection by patients, pharmacies.
- Receptacle for empty sample bottles for collection and for patients to place samples for blood and urine tests.
- Collection of test results by patients.

Key facilities in the room:

- Seating for the patients during waiting.
- Small area with toys for mothers bringing children.
- Magazines to read.

Displays:

1. Display of various circulars – in-house and from outside sources.
2. Surgery times.
3. Names of GPs, nurses and Healthcare professionals working in the surgery.
4. Local pharmacies and their opening/closing hours.
5. Box for storing all keys to the surgery – located so as not to be visible to patients and visitors.

2.1.4 GPs' Rooms

Receptionists would have to ensure that the GP has:

- Adequate number of different forms, which a GP might require during consultations.
- Patients' notes kept before surgery starts and removed at the end of each session/clinic.
- Fridge should be used for medicines only and is for sole use by the nurses; other staff may access only with express permission of nurses or GPs.
- The desk, sink and patient resting/examination bed are kept in a tidy position before and after each surgery.
- Adequate roll of paper to cover the bed for patients to lie on prior to each examination, and a spare roll should be provided. The use of the roll of paper is advised for all surgeries as it keeps the bed clean, addresses MRSA issues, and the paper is disposed of after each use.
- All the equipment a GP would use – BP monitoring, syringes for blood samples for tests, weighing machine etc. should be checked for cleanliness and recent calibration. Adequate stationery should also be provided.
- Ensure the panic button is operational and routinely checked.
- Bins used for disposal of syringes and clinical wastes are kept separate from normal waste and periodically emptied.

As these are the consulting rooms where patients are seen, it is preferable these are located downstairs; if not possible, then disabled patients should be given an alternative GP appointment downstairs unless the surgery has a lift.

2.1.5 Nurse's Room

Receptionists would have to ensure the nurses have:

- Adequate number of different forms, which a nurse may require.
- Patients' notes kept before surgery starts and removed at the end of each session/clinic.
- The fridge should be used for medicines only and is for sole use by the nurses; other staff may access only with express permission of nurses or GPs.
- The desk, sink and patient resting/examination bed are kept in a tidy position

before and after each surgery.

- Adequate roll of paper to cover the bed for patients to lie on prior to each examination, and a spare roll should be provided. The use of the roll of paper is advised for all surgeries as it keeps the bed clean, addresses MRSA issues, and the paper is disposed of after each use.
- All the equipment a nurse would use – BP monitoring, syringes for blood samples for tests, weighing machine etc. should be checked for cleanliness and recent calibration. Adequate stationery should also be provided.
- Ensure the panic button is operational and routinely checked.
- Bins used for disposal of syringes and clinical wastes are kept separate from normal waste and periodically emptied.

2.1.6 Healthcare Professionals' Rooms

Receptionists would have to ensure the Healthcare Professionals have:

- An adequate number of different forms, which may be required.
- Patients' notes kept before surgery starts and removed at the end of each session/clinic.
- Fridge should be used for medicines only and is for the sole use by them and other staff may access only with the express permission of nurses or GPs.
- The patient inspection section with the bed and the covering with the paper roll are in pristine condition.
- All equipment for use – BP instrument – electronic or mercury type (now being replaced due to Health & Safety reasons) is calibrated periodically.
- Bins used for disposal of syringes and clinical wastes are kept separate from normal waste and periodically emptied.

2.1.7 Admin Room

This is the main domain of the Medical Secretary and Computer Specialist along with room for receptionists to work on an ad-hoc basis.

For patients having queries with the medical secretary, they have to be directed to this room, only during specified times and with her permission.

This might be the common location for the Medical Secretary and IT specialist, and serve as the main room for fax, copier and scanner.

All files of patients – insurance claims, hospital results etc. would be located here and these should be securely kept in cabinets, which should be closed at all times lest patients tamper with any files or notes.

Access to patients and visitors to this room should be strictly monitored due to stringent rules of confidentiality.

2.1.8 Practice Manager's Room

The accountant might also occupy this room, if he works part-time.

All files in this room regarding staff matters, accounts etc. are all confidential and without express consent of the Practice Manager should not be seen by others without supervision.

Other staff should not use the computers here without the Practice Manager's permission.

2.1.9 Kitchen

This room is designated for making coffee/tea etc. and for lunchtime use.

Fridge should be for the sole use of food/milk etc. and should not be shared with medicines.

Very strongly flavoured food should not be consumed on the highly clinical premises of the surgery. Food should not be consumed in offices for fear of MRSA issues; areas near the kitchen should be used exclusively for consuming food or drinks.

2.1.10 Storeroom

All consumables are stored here, along with folders of previous years (surgeries have to keep the records for at least 7 years before shredding any of them – recommend 10 years). Computer equipment, accessories etc. may also be kept here.

This room must be kept locked when not in use.

2.1.11 Toilets/Washrooms

There should a disabled toilet with suitable facilities.

It is preferable to have a room with suitable facilities for changing babies.

All toilets kept in a clean state and circulars posted to request users keep it tidy at all times after their use.

All essential items – toilet rolls, liquid washing soap, air dryers or throwaway paper towels should be stacked each morning and checked frequently to ensure they have not run out.

Must ensure adequate ventilation is provided and is in good working order.

Ensure the flush system is also in good working order.

Ensure the caretaker and cleaners check each of the facilities daily and call for a plumber in case of any issues to be dealt with.

2.1.12 Outside Yard

If there is a gate facility provided for the outside yard, it should be locked at the end of surgery.

If there is a designated parking area than it has to be rigidly adhered to.

The rear doors for entry should be locked normally and checked again at the end of the surgery.

It is preferable to have a keypad for inputting the alarm code to deactivate it in case some members of staff enter the surgery using the rear door.

2.1.13 Safety Issues

There should be provision of fire extinguishers located in 3 or 4 key areas of the surgery for use in case of small fires.

Fire safety procedures should be well displayed and posted in each room for staff, patients and visitors to follow.

Exit doors in case of fires to be clearly shown in the Reception area and in all rooms and staff periodically trained on the drill on evacuation procedures.

2.2 First Time Arrival

2.2.1 Main Entrance

New staff and particularly young receptionists coming to work for the first time in their working career in a GP surgery may find several issues daunting, and it is best to take things slowly and systematically. They should never be afraid to ask questions and should always write it down in their notepad that was given.

2.2.2 Keys

Ensure you have received the keys to enter the premises for both front and back doors, and that you were allowed to keep them.

Check each key is opening and closing the respective doors.

In case of any problem, let the senior receptionist or Practice Manager know and get the correct keys. Check once again that these keys are right.

Find out the place the keys are cut for future requirements. However, no keys should be cut without the prior permission of the PMgr or Senior Receptionist.

2.2.3 Alarm Systems

Find out the security code – four or six digit code or alphanumeric, write it down, without referring to it as the security code, and keep in a safe place. Do NOT discuss with outsiders and do not reveal the code to any new employee in presence of patients or visitors to the surgery.

Find out the location of the alarm keypad to type in the codes.

Find out the time within which you have to type in the codes – usually set for 1 minute.

In cases, when the alarm could not be deactivated in time and it sounds continuously, find out procedures for what to do to STOP the alarm.

Find out the name and address of the security system provider, address and contact telephone numbers daytime and after hours (24/7 number, if available).

If the alarm system provider or central monitoring office respond following an alarm, carry out instructions to stop the alarm.

In case of 'false alarm', and, if system is connected to the police, then inform them ASAP to save their time from coming to the surgery.

It is worth noting that in case of 3 false alarms, police would not provide their cover for 6 months and during this period the incidences of false alarms should be 'NIL', before they restart cover for the surgery.

2.2.4 Telephone Numbers

The Senior Receptionist or Practice Manager should give you or show you the booklet or sheets containing the key telephone numbers for the surgery staff – (GPs, nurses, other staff) – and all outside contacts.

Table 2.2.4 lists the typical contacts needed for each surgery and this has to be replicated to suit.

DR. V. SUBRAMANIAN

The telephone numbers should not be shared with anyone and the personal numbers, particularly those of GPs, nurses, staff, should not be given to patients or others including PCT or hospitals, in the interests of personal security.

No	Name	Home Tel	Mobile	Work Tel
A	GPs: < Do not give to any one including Patients >			
1	Dr A	020 8888 9999	077 8888 9999	020 8888 9999
2	Dr B			
3	Dr C			
4	Dr D			
5	Dr E			
6	Dr F			
Use Pager for GPs if permission given by the GPs				
B	Hospitals		Tel	Fax
1				
2				
3				
4				
5				
6				
7				
8	ENT			
9	Eye			
C	Emergency			
1	Ambulance			
2	Local Police			
3	Primecare			
4	Oxygen Concentration			
5	Strand Nurse			
6	Macmillan Nurse			
D	PCT/CCG			
1		Finance		
2		Registration		
3		Patient Service		
4		Main Contact		
5		General Waste		
6		Clinical Waste		
7		IMT/Comput.		
8		Presc. Advisor		
9		Complaints		
10		Child Immun.		
11		PCT/CCG Head		
12		CHD Facilitator		
13		Sr. Nurse Admin.		
14		Prac. Co-ord.		

GENERAL PRACTICE MANAGEMENT

E	Computer System			
1		Sales		
2		Support		
3		Accounts		
4		Trainer		
5		Training Dept		
		020 8888 9999	077 8888 9999	020 8888 9999
F	Support Personnel: < Do not give to any one including Patients >			
1		Health Visitor		
2		Dietician		
3		CPN		
4		Chemist A		
5		Chemist B		
6		Chemist C		
7		Newsagant		
8		Midwife		
9		District Nurse		
G	Services			
1		Handyman		
2		Electrician		
3		Plumber		
4		Carpets		
5		Furniture		
6		Builder		
7		Roofer		
8		Architect		
9		Lawyer		
H	Property Insurance			
1		Company		
2		BMA Services		
3		Loss Assessor		
4		Alarm		
5		Owner		
6		Locksmith		
7		Windows		
8		Insur. Co. A		
9		Insur. Co. B		
I	Banks / Accountant			
1		Bank 1		
2		Bank 2		
3		Accountant		
4		Auditor Co.		
J	Staff			
1		PMgr		
2		SR		

3		Receptionist 1		
4		Receptionist 2		
5		Receptionist 3		
6		Receptionist 4		
7		Receptionist 5		
8		Receptionist 6		
9		Nurse 1		
10		Nurse 2		
11		Med. Sec		
12		IMT Specialist		
13		Cleaner		
14		caretaker		

2.2.5 Computers

The use of computers would necessitate a very elaborate induction period involving training, usually by a computer professional.

Make sure your details have been set up in the system and you are given log-in procedures. Check you can log in easily.

Ensure that you are aware of where an operating manual is kept for the computers.

Also, after all training sessions, rely on self-help by referring to the manual continually.

2.2.6 Printers

Basic principles of operation and locations should be explained with a handout of operating instructions.

Essential elements pertaining to:

- Switching 'on',
- Loading of printing papers,
- Storage of copier papers,
- Printing multiple copies with stacking,
- Removing paper jams,
- Replacing cartridges

Need to be learnt within a few days of joining the surgery.

2.2.7 Fax

Basic principles of operation should be explained with a handout of operating instructions.

Systematic procedures of scanning documents should be explained after working in the surgery for a few days.

2.2.8 Scanner

Basic principles of operation should be explained with a handout of operating instructions.

Systematic procedures of scanning documents should be explained after working in the surgery for a few days.

2.2.9 Computer Systems

Different types of computer systems used by the surgeries in UK are:

(They are all Windows-based systems)

1. EMIS PCS/LV/WEB
2. ISOFT Synergy
3. INPS Vision
4. Micro test
5. Torex Premier/System 6000/ITS
6. TPP SYSTM One.

Coding clinical problems correctly is absolutely crucial for the effective use of the system. Information that has been coded can be searched for and analysed. Information that has been coded incorrectly or entered in free text will never be found.

http://www.emis-learning.com

All systems are very interactive in self-generation of:

- Computation of data
- Generating reports
- Highlighting shortfalls in service
- Highlighting patients missed for checks

- Highlighting actions to take for reaching targets
- List of patients by gender, surgery (if two or more locations within the same practice), GP
- Pathlab reports

Computer Systems would do the following operations, and a lot more:

1. First Time Users
2. 2nd and Subsequent Time Users
3. Patient Search
4. New Prescriptions (Only GPs to prescribe)
5. Repeat Prescriptions (GPs and Receptionists)
6. Prescriptions – Do's and Don'ts
7. Registrations – New and Re-registrations
8. Re-Authorise Drugs
9. Issue Repeat and New Drugs (already prescribed by Hospital)
10. Re-Print Prescriptions

Cancel Prescriptions

- Edit Drugs
- Finishing Drugs – Details in Patient History
- Changing Patient Details
- Add a Family Member
- Start UP
- General
- First Time Users
- 2nd and Subsequent Time Users
- Patient Search

Appointment Screen Access

1. Appointments
2. Booking
3. Booking – Clinics and Practice Nurse
4. Booking – Operation and Cancellation

Prescriptions:

- Prescriptions – Dos and Don'ts
- New Prescriptions (Generally GPs to prescribe)
- Repeat Prescriptions (GPs and Receptionists)
- Issue Repeat and New Drugs (GP/Hospital approval)
- Prescriptions – Miscellaneous
- Re-Authorise Drugs
- Re-Print Prescriptions
- Cancel Prescriptions
- Edit Drugs
- Finishing Drugs

Registrations:

1. Registrations – Do's and Don'ts
2. New Registrations
3. Re-Registrations
4. Changing Patient Details
5. Add a Family Member

Patient Records and Lists:

- General
- Receipt of Records from PCT
- Receipt of Green Cards from PCT

Daily Obligatory Tasks in System:

1. General
2. Deductions
3. Amendments
4. Claims
5. Registration
6. Maternity
7. Contraceptive
8. Minor Surgery
9. Child Health Surveillance
10. Reports

General

- Patient Lists
- Claims Paid/Unpaid

All staff including New GPs, nurses, and HCPs should try to use the system and learn more about navigation to get various data. In case of queries or problems the IMT specialist should be contacted and issues resolved.

2.3 Reception

Reception is the area, particularly in urban surgeries, where most of the administrative work pertaining to patients for the surgery is done.

Receptionists are the key to the good name of the surgery as their approach and communication reflect on patients' perception and judgment of the surgery.

All good work done by the GPs and the nurses may be totally eclipsed by one bad receptionist.

It is all the more important that they are suitably prepared mentally, dress sensibly, and communicate clearly to meet the patients, and respond sensitively to their queries and concerns.

For the first few days new receptionists are advised to do clerical work away from meeting the patients. They can understudy other receptionists, observe and make notes of procedures to follow.

2.3.1 Opening Letters/Posting

These tasks used to be in the domain of the Medical Secretary but due to the Med. Secs working shorter hours or a few days a week only, the responsibility has fallen to the receptionists.

This job may take about 30 min. or so daily and to do this effectively the receptionists given this responsibility have to be trained by the Practice Manager. To do this job effectively, surgeries usually train a receptionist who had been working for 3-6 months and also allow that person to be understudy for the Medical Secretary to find out what she expects when letters are opened and before being posted in relevant boxes.

Criteria to bear in mind for posting letters:

To place in relevant boxes e.g. GPs, Nurses, Healthcare Specialists, Medical Secretary, Practice Manager (PMgr), Journals and Miscellaneous.

All hospital, private clinics, insurance letters etc. to be posted to Med. Sec. even if addressed to GPs. She will then forward to respective GPs by internal mail.

Personal confidential letters to GPs alone should be posted to their respective boxes **unopened**.

Non-clinical staff should be instructed not to give the surgery address for their correspondence.

If any mail comes as confidential to any non-clinical staff, such mail will always be opened and then kept in the Miscellaneous box for collection

In exceptional circumstances, with prior permission from the Practice Manager, such mail can be left unopened for non-clinical staff.

2.3.2 Patients' Responses

Patients' responses:

- Differ considerably when they see a receptionist as opposed to a Medical Secretary.
- They perceive the Medical Secretary would do a lot more for them in terms of copies of letters from hospitals, insurance queries and the like.
- Also, when they see a youngster their attitude is different to seeing an older person.
- These aspects of perception can never be regulated by rules or procedures, however well-meant they might be. It has to be accepted as part of day-to-day reactions and the surgery has to deal with it in the best way they can.

2.3.3 Receptionists' Demeanour

The importance of appearance, dress, etiquette, tone and manner of speech, along with non-verbal communication must be stressed at the outset.

All these affect the response they get from the patients.

At all times, even under intense provocation, they should remain courteous and should a situation deteriorate, they should refer the patient to the senior receptionist or the Practice Manager.

The reception area is not for shouting or animated arguments with the patients.

The patients in the waiting room and other staff should always be treated to a quiet and professional atmosphere at all times.

If patients become violent or abusive then bring it to the attention of the senior receptionists or the PMgr for immediate attention.

2.3.4 Dealing with GPs and Nurses

Receptionists' dealings with the GPs and nurses are crucial for the smooth operation of the practice. Receptionists have to know their responsibilities and diligently carry them out without being reminded often. GPs, nurses, and other clinical staff want the surgery sessions to run smoothly and do not want any unnecessary delays. Their expectations would include:

a. Their desks are in a tidy state and any records from the previous sessions are not still left lying around.
b. Records for the current session are kept in readiness for them to refer to, if necessary.
c. The patient arrivals are notified by logging in the computer, but these days patients log in on arrival and the computer is updated.
d. Receptionists or other staff should not disturb GPs during the surgery sessions. It is expected of them not to refer calls to GPs during surgery hours except in case of emergencies, when even the PMgr is not able to sort it out.
e. The paper roll used to put over the bed, to examine the patients, is clean and a spare roll available, if needed.
f. Receptionists are in presentable outfits, fitting in with surgery and clinical conditions.
g. Receptionists are not heard shouting at the patients even if the patients are shouting, and expect the PMgr to sort out these issues.
h. Receptionists behave in such a way that the GPs and nurses do not ever want to hear complaints from the patients about the reception area personnel or facilities.
i. They expect the receptionists to contact hospitals or other people, as GPs and nurses require, so that they can complete their queries when dealing with the patients.
j. Receptionists should always address them with professional respect and do not allow any familiarity to influence their behaviour. It is not the time or place for jokes and laughter.
k. Receptionists should ensure that there is an adequate supply of forms that the GPs and nurses may need during their consultations.

2.3.5 Errors

The errors due to receptionists will not only affect a GPs performance but also earn the surgery a very bad reputation. Not all surgeries have gone paperless and use computers only. Inner city surgeries rely still on paper records and it means old issues still apply to patient arrival and waiting, paper records not given for appointments, etc.

The types of errors are detailed below (See 2.3.5a):

2.3.5a List of Errors in Service to GPs

(Affecting GPs performance and earning the surgery a bad reputation)

Date:
Day:
GP:
Surgery:
A/BL
Morning/Evening
Details:

- **Very Serious Errors** – liable for giving warnings to Receptionists on reaching count of three.

Prescription: Incorrect dosage, quantity, drug; wrong patient, not checked prior to seeking signature from GP; immediate supply not conforming to 48 hours' notice without prior approval of GP; wrong dosage information recorded in notes/on computer.

Records: Patient present but records not found; lab results/letters not filed; incorrectly filing another patient's details

Service: Not booking ambulance pick up for patients thereby causing delays/inconvenience; arguing with patients; being rude; any issues where patient has been proved to be correct and has a very justifiable grievance

- **Less Serious** – nevertheless, Receptionists must watch out for persistent errors.

Appointments: Multiple appointments for one appointment slot of 10 min; clinic appointments in normal surgery hours; unregistered patient given normal appointment; more than 4 appointments for clinics (max 4 each for 30 min).

Records: Patient present but wrong records given to GP causing delay; not providing health band cards or hospital results/letters; not giving emergency patients' records to GPs on time.

Service: Not informing GPs about patients' arrival and waiting for booked appointment

- More training to be given to Receptionists.

Appointments: admitting patients after 11 AM and after 6.15 PM; giving appointments beyond 10.00 AM in the mornings and 5.45 PM in the evening for normal surgeries; more than 8 emergency appointments for each GP in the morning and more than 5 in the evening surgeries; un-registered/not yet approved/removed patients given appointment with or without 'Temporary Services' forms; emergency appointments for non-emergency reasons; giving appointments for insurance, passports etc. during normal surgery hours.

Records: Not filing records/letters; giving too many continuation cards to GPs as records are not found or checked; not having records in time for GP to start surgery.

Service: Not having set of forms for GPs to deal with various requests from patients; not entering patients' details in computer within 48 hours of health check and GP seeing the patient and approving; giving incorrect payment amount details for vaccinations.

Note: GPs to fill in the forms for each surgery and leave it on the table for receptionists to collect SR to put the names of persons responsible for appropriate action. Copies of forms will be on the pack along with other forms on the GPs table

Action points will be notified to GPs during monthly meetings or as appropriate.

The PMgr from time to time could do a status evaluation of receptionists' performance by giving GPs the above list and requesting GPs to circle those where errors had occurred with date, day and time of surgery session.

Receptionists should collect these forms and give to the senior receptionists to fill in the names of the receptionist responsible for appropriate action.

Action points to be notified to the GPs during monthly or at other meetings as appropriate.

Favourable changes that have taken place in surgery operations in recent years:

- Online path lab reporting
- Patients registering arrivals to surgery by logging details in the entrance hall
- More use of computers by GPs, nurses, HCPs etc. has minimised issues due to wrong paper records being given to them
- Life has now become a lot easier for all concerned in the surgery.

2.3.6 Path Lab Test and Results

It is not uncommon in surgeries for a trained receptionist to see the Path Lab report and then log these into respective patients' records so that the GP, during the consultation, can access the results easily. The receptionist is expected to come 15 min. or so early in the morning and do this important work, saving GPs' time. When the results are abnormal, then they have to highlight these in the records and also make a special note in the pad and let the GP know about the result to take immediate action.

2.3.7 Various Tests

Receptionists will come across various requests for blood tests, diabetic checks etc., and it is useful to have some rudimentary appreciation of some of the diseases and a brief outline is given below. For any detailed study they would have to access Google for further relevant information. Whereas some details are given, receptionists are warned that they should not second-guess ailments by looking at ranges only. Please leave it to the GPs and nurses for the diagnosis and corrective action.

Blood Tests

Blood test results, made possible by the taking of blood samples, are one of the most important tools that your doctor uses in evaluating health status. It is important to realise that a blood test result may be outside of what is called the 'normal range' for many reasons.

A large number of laboratory blood tests are widely available. Many blood tests are specialised to focus on a particular disease or group of diseases. Many different blood tests are used commonly in many specialties and in general practice

Most blood tests fall within one of two categories: screening or diagnostic.

Screening blood tests are used to try to detect a disease when there is little or no evidence that a person has a suspected disease. For example, measuring cholesterol levels helps to identify one of the risks of heart disease. These screening tests are performed on people who may show no symptoms of heart disease, as a tool for the physician to detect a potentially harmful and evolving condition. In order for screening tests to be most useful, they must be readily available, accurate, inexpensive, pose little risk, and cause little discomfort to the patient.

Diagnostic blood tests are utilised when a specific disease is suspected to verify the presence and the severity of that disease, including allergies, HIV, AIDS, hepatitis, cancer, etc. (For further details refer to NICE publications).

If a person suffers from anaemia their haemoglobin level will always be less than normal.

Full Blood Count (FBC)

A full blood count (FBC) is probably the most widely used blood test. It is used to assess your general state of health and to screen for certain conditions, such as anaemia.

During an FBC, a small sample of blood will be taken from a vein in your arm. The amount of different types of blood cells in the sample will be measured.

On its own, an FBC cannot usually provide a definitive diagnosis of a condition, but it can provide important 'clues' about possible problems with your health.

Low haemoglobin indicates anaemia, which has a number of possible causes, including internal bleeding or a poor diet.

High haemoglobin may be due to an underlying lung disease or problems with the bone marrow.

A low white blood cell count may be due to problems with your bone marrow, a viral infection or more rarely, cancer of the bone marrow. However, a low white blood count can also be genetic and of no significance.

A high white blood cell count usually suggests that you have an infection somewhere in your body. Rarely, this could be a sign of leukaemia.

A low platelet count may be due to a viral infection or an autoimmune condition (where the immune system attacks healthy tissue).

A high platelet count may be due to inflammatory conditions, infection or a problem with the bone marrow.

Electrolyte Test

An electrolyte test is used to measure the levels of electrolytes in blood. This is sometimes known as electrolyte balance. Electrolytes are minerals that are found in the body.

There are three main electrolytes that can be measured with an electrolyte test:

Sodium; potassium; chloride.

Raised or lowered levels of any of these electrolytes can have various possible causes.

A raised sodium level (hypernatremia) could be the result of dehydration, uncontrolled diabetes or persistent diarrhoea.

A low sodium level (hyponatremia) is usually due to certain types of medication, such as diuretics. Rarely, it could be due to a condition such as diabetes insipidus.

A raised potassium level (hyperkalaemia) could be the results of kidney failure. Certain medications can raise potassium, for example ACE inhibitors, which are used to treat heart failure and high blood pressure.

A low potassium level (hypokalaemia) could be the result of heavy sweating or persistent vomiting or diarrhoea. It can also be caused by certain medications.

Erythrocyte Sedimentation Rate (ESR)

An erythrocyte sedimentation rate (ESR) test is a blood test that is used to check whether there is inflammation in the body.

Blood Glucose (blood sugar) Test

A blood glucose test is used to help diagnose diabetes and to monitor the health of people who have been diagnosed with diabetes.

Diabetes develops either because the body cannot produce enough insulin or because the insulin doesn't work in the right way. Insulin is a hormone that the body uses to convert glucose (sugar) into energy.

People with diabetes often have high levels of glucose in their blood. Reducing the glucose levels is an important part of the treatment of diabetes. This is because if the blood sugar levels become too high, a range of serious complications, such as kidney disease or nerve damage, may occur.

Therefore, most people with diabetes will need regular blood glucose tests. Blood glucose test kits may be available to use at home. These only require a small 'pin prick' of blood for testing.

People with type 2 diabetes usually don't need to check their sugar at home, it will be tested every three-to-six months at your GP surgery or hospital. The test shows the average blood sugar level over the past three months.

Some types of blood glucose test require one not to eat anything for several hours before the test. The GP or diabetes care team can tell whether this is the case.

Blood Typing

A blood-typing test is used to identify your blood group. Your blood group is determined by two specialised proteins, known as antigens, which are found on the surface of your red blood cells.

Blood typing is used before a blood transfusion is given (or before you provide blood for donation). This is because it's important that anyone who receives blood is given blood that matches his or her blood group. If you were given blood that did not match your blood group, your immune system may attack the red blood cells, which could lead to potentially life-threatening complications.

Blood typing is also used during pregnancy as there is a small risk that the unborn child may have a different blood group from the mother. This could lead to the mother's immune system attacking the baby's red blood cells. This is known as rhesus disease.

If testing reveals that there is a risk of rhesus disease developing, extra precautions can be taken to safeguard the health of your baby. For example, a blood transfusion can be given to the baby when it is still in the womb to increase their number of red blood cells.

Blood Cholesterol Test

Cholesterol is a fatty substance known as a lipid. It is mostly created by the liver from the fatty foods in your diet and is vital for the normal functioning of the body.

Having too many lipids in your blood (hyperlipidaemia) can have a serious effect on your health because it increases your risk of having a heart attack or stroke.

Blood cholesterol testing is usually recommended if you are at an increased risk of developing cardiovascular disease (CVD). A cardiovascular disease, such as a stroke or heart attack, affects the normal flow of blood through the body.

Things that increase your risk of CVD include:

- Being over 40 years old
- Being obese
- Being a smoker
- Being male
- Having high blood pressure (hypertension)

Blood cholesterol levels are measured with a simple blood test. Before having the test, one may be asked not to eat for 12 hours (which usually includes when one's asleep). This will ensure that all food is completely digested and won't affect the outcome of the test.

The GP or practice nurse can carry out the blood test and will take a blood sample, either using a needle and a syringe or by pricking your finger.

Liver Function Test

A liver function test is a type of blood test that is used to help diagnose certain liver conditions, such as:

- Hepatitis (infection of the liver)
- Cirrhosis (scarring of the liver)
- Alcoholic liver disease (liver damage and related loss of function which is caused by excessive alcohol consumption)

When the liver is damaged, it releases enzymes into the blood and levels of proteins that the liver produces begin to drop. By measuring the levels of these enzymes and proteins, it's possible to build up a picture of how well the liver is functioning.

Tests that require fasting

Blood cholesterol, triglyceride and glucose levels are the most common tests that require fasting. Vitamin levels, such as vitamin E or A, also need to be drawn when the patient is fasting.

Time Frame

Typically at least a 12-hour fast is required for cholesterol and triglyceride screenings. Vitamin levels and glucose tests usually only require an eight-hour fast. Following the guidelines is important to make sure your blood sample is not influenced by food or drink.

What is allowed?

Water is allowed even when fasting. Usually your regular dose of medication can be taken, although some medicines do affect results, so check with your physician first. Black coffee or tea may be allowed, but again, check with the laboratory or your physician, because caffeine can alter some test results.

What is not allowed?

No food at all is allowed. Gum chewing, especially of gum with sugar in it, is forbidden. No liquid, other than water, should be consumed without the express permission of your physician.

Consequences

Results may be inaccurate if fasting was not done prior to the test. This might lead to treatment for a disease such as diabetes or a condition such as high cholesterol that you do not have. The specimen will need to be repeated because an accurate result is necessary.

If a GP informs of abnormal test results, ask if fasting was required. If one did not fast as needed, the GP must be told immediately.

Urine Tests

These tests are carried out to screen for metabolic and kidney disorders and for urinary tract infections. During a routine physical or when one has symptoms of a urinary tract infection, such as abdominal pain, back pain, frequent or painful urination; as part of a pregnancy check-up, a hospital admission, or a pre-surgical work-up, these tests are initiated.

A urinalysis is a group of chemical and microscopic tests. Urine is generally yellow and relatively clear, but each time someone urinates, the colour, quantity, concentration, and content of the urine will be slightly different because of varying constituents.

Many disorders can be diagnosed in their early stages by detecting abnormalities in the urine. Abnormalities include increased concentrations of constituents that are not usually found in significant quantities in the urine, such as: glucose, protein, bilirubin, red blood cells, white blood cells, crystals, and bacteria.

Urine for a urinalysis can be collected at any time. The first morning sample is considered the most valuable because it is more concentrated and more likely to yield abnormalities if present. As you start to urinate, let some urine fall into the toilet, then collect one to two ounces of urine in the container provided, then void the rest into the toilet. This type of collection is called a 'midstream collection' or a 'clean catch'. No sample preparation is needed.

A urine sample will only be useful for a urinalysis if taken to the doctor's office or laboratory for processing within a short period of time. If it is longer than an hour between collection and transport time, then the urine should be refrigerated or a preservative may be added.

Other Tests

Thyroid Blood Tests

Thyroid Symptoms

- Thyroid Disease
- Underactive Thyroid
- Underactive Thyroid Gland
- Thyroid Testing

Diagnosing thyroid disease is a process that can incorporate numerous factors, including clinical evaluation, blood tests, imaging tests, biopsies and other tests. In this article, you'll learn more about the blood tests that are used as part of thyroid disease diagnosis and management.

TSH Test

The most common thyroid test is the blood test that measures the amount of thyroid-stimulating hormone (TSH) in your bloodstream. The test is sometimes called the thyrotropin-stimulating hormone test.

TSH that is elevated, or above normal, is considered indicative of hypothyroidism. TSH that is 'suppressed' or below normal, is considered evidence of hyperthyroidism.

As of 2003, the normal range runs from 0.3 to 3.0, versus the older range of 0.5 to 5.5. So, according to the new standards, levels above 3.0 are evidence of possible hypothyroidism, and levels below 0.3 are evidence of possible hyperthyroidism. Keep in mind that there is disagreement among practitioners, and some follow the older range, others use the newer range.

Free T4/Free Thyroxin

Free T4 measures the free, unbound thyroxin levels in your bloodstream. Free T4 is typically elevated in hyperthyroidism, and lowered in hypothyroidism.

Total T4/Total Thyroxin/Serum Thyroxine

This test measures the total amount of circulating thyroxin in your blood. Thyroxine, a hormone produced by the thyroid, is also known as T4. A high value can indicate hyperthyroidism, a low value can indicate hypothyroidism.

Total T4 levels can be elevated due to pregnancy, and other high oestrogen states, including use of oestrogen replacement or birth control pills.

TSH = approx. reference range for this test is 0.4 to 4.5.

TT4 = approx. reference range for this test is 50 to 160.

FT4 = approx. reference range for this test is 10 to 24

The thyroid is a gland found in the neck. Its main function is to make hormones.

Hormones are chemicals, which are released into the bloodstream. They act as messengers, affecting cells and tissues in distant parts of your body. Thyroid hormones affect the body's metabolic rate and the levels of certain minerals in the blood.

The thyroid makes three hormones that it secretes into the bloodstream. Two of these hormones, called thyroxin (T4) and triiodothyronine (T3), increase your body's metabolic rate. The other hormone helps to control the amount of calcium in the blood.

In order to make T3 and T4, the thyroid gland needs iodine, a substance found in the food we eat. T4 is called this because it contains four atoms of iodine. T3 contains three atoms of iodine. In the cells and tissues of the body most T4 is converted to T3. T3 is the more active hormone; it influences the activity of all the cells and tissues of your body.

2.3.8 Job Rota

This has to be prepared for each week, about at least a week in advance. The receptionists should check and correct if they have any issues about the rota.

Ideally it should be laid out for the whole month or longer, with notes to include, who covers whom in case of holidays, sick leave, absences etc.

The PMgr should ensure that there is no favouritism in assignment of tasks or times while preparing the rota.

A typical rota with comments on tasks is attached for the receptionists (See 2.3.8a). The requirements have changed due to improvement in use of computers by the GPs and this format can be modified to suit present circumstances.

2.3.8a Receptionists' Job Rota

GENERAL PRACTICE MANAGEMENT

	Surgery 1	Surgery 2	Surgery 3	Surgery 4	Surgery 5	Surgery 6	Surgery 7	Surgery 8	Surgery 9	Surgery 10	Surgery 11
Morning		<-----	R1 ----->	Appoint.	<-----	R2 ----->	^	<-----	R3 ----->	<-----	R4 ----->
		9-11.15	Front	Letter	9.00-11.15	Prescrip.	Tel/Pres.	9.00-9.40	Registn. M,W,TH,F	9.00-9.30	File Prev. day's records Emer./Pres. Notes
"		11.15-1.00	Back	Filing only	11.15-1.00	Front	Tel	9.40-11.15	Emer./Pres. Notes	9.30-11.15	File prev. /today's records
"								11.15-12.00	Regn. In computer	11.15-1.00	
"								12.00-1.00	Pres Notes/ file records		
A/Noon							^	<-----	R5 ----->		
					1.00-3.00	Prescrip.	M,T,W,F	3.00-4.00	Clinic-W, F & altern. T		
"								4.00-5.00	File records - Wed only		
Evening					4.00-6.00	Prescrip.	Tel/Pres.	4.00-6.00	Front - Appoint.	4.00-6.00	Back - take 1 day's notes. 3 GPs in morning, Nurse, clinics and 2 GPs in evening and file records
						<-----	R2 ----->	<-----	R5 ----->	<-----	R4 ----->

Note:

1. Registration – Mainly 9.00-9.30 but anyone coming after 9.30 should not be asked to come later. Registration is open for the four days till 12.15 PM. If nurse is busy, do GMS1 in the morning and health check in the afternoon. Registration is also open 3.00-3.30 PM Mon & Fri.

2. Tel. calls to be between 11.30 to 1.00 PM as in Registration Manual. Once they call between the hours for appointment, they should not be asked to call at a later time. Appointments should be given at convenient times for the caller.

3. Appointments – Normal till 9.55 AM for the mornings and 4.45PM (M, T, F) and 5.45 PM (W) for the evenings. Emergencies max 8, preferably 6.

4. **Same person to file letters each day – specific role.** That day's letters to be filed first followed by backlog letters.

5. Receptionists answering tel. calls should be extremely polite even when provoked. Should never be rude or put the phone down.

6. Home visits – Receptionists should not agree to the visit without referring to the GP in the surgery, who should talk to the patient and decide.

7. Prescription – request patients to come after 48 hours, preferably in the evening, if possible. Instead of Thur, request them to come on Fri even.

8. Minimal referral to be made to IT supervisor or Practice Manager. Always ask Senior Receptionist.

9. Do not disturb the GPs during the surgery by asking for prescriptions to be signed. Avoid frequent calls to GPs – SR to sort out

10. Estimated workload and duration to complete tasks: Previous day's records for filing – Max 72 Nos. = 2 hours. Daily letters/hospital results etc. – Max 45 = 1.5 hours. Take 1 day's records – 3 GPs+Nurse+clinics+2 GPs = max 60 = 1 hour. Prescription notes = Max 40 = 1.5 hours. Removal of records/deductions etc. 12 = 30 mins.

11. Train receptionists for all types of tasks – rotate, say, every 2 weeks or so.

12. Letters/lab. Results to upstairs GP for signature by 10.00 AM each morning and bring it down for filing by 12.00 noon each day.

13. Each morning/each evening and each day's task to be completed in that period with no backlog.

2.4 Appointments

All surgeries use an appointment only system for the majority of cases. Appointments can be booked in advance, or if it is more urgent, booking on the day one wishes to be seen. If it is an urgent appointment it may not be with the doctor of one's choice. Walk-in appointments are also offered for emergency situations.

Surgeries try to make sure one sees the GP one is registered with, but if that GP is not available one may have to see another GP.

If one is too ill to come to the surgery and require a visit at home, one should call the surgery before the surgery stipulated time. Home visits take up much more of a doctor's time than a consultation in the surgery. So if the patient is mobile then the patient should try to come to the surgery to be seen by a GP.

2.4.1 General Requirements

If one is not sure about whether one is ill or not, then an appointment to the surgery may not be necessary; other local health services are available in such cases:

- **Pharmacist**

Patients can consult their local pharmacist on a range of problems, from colds, flu, infant teething and colic, to discussions regarding the medication prescribed and possible side effects. Some pharmacists can supply the Emergency Contraceptive pill. In some circumstances they are able to issue an emergency supply of repeat prescription drugs if a patient runs out of medication, allowing some time to request the prescription from the doctor.

- **NHS 111 (replaced NHS Direct)**

Patients can access NHS 111 or on the Internet at www.nhs.uk. They will offer advice and tell where the nearest help is to be found.

- **NHS Walk-in Centre/Minor Injuries**

These are often open longer than a GP surgery. Walk-in Centres do not usually treat children under the age of two years. The surgeries would usually display location details of these centres.

- **Accident and Emergency Departments**

Nearest ones to the surgery should also be displayed in the surgery reception area or entrance hall.

- **Out of Hours Service**

This service usually operates from 6.30pm until 8am Monday-Friday and all day Saturdays and Sundays and Bank Holidays. If a patient rings the surgery during these times the call will be redirected to this service. An alternative number to call may also be given.

- **Leaflets**

Leaflets for many conditions can be found at www.patient.co.uk. These leaflets give impartial advice and might answer a lot of questions.

Most requested leaflets include:

Irritable Bowel Syndrome
Haemorrhoids (Piles)
Vitamin D Deficiency
Chickenpox in Children under 12
Shingles
Hypothyroidism – Underactive Thyroid
Thrush – Vaginal
Slapped Cheek Disease
Threadworms
Acid Reflux and Esophagitis
Lymph Glands Swollen
Cramps in the Leg
Fungal Nail Infection
Back Pain (Non-specific)
Cancer
Depression

2.4.2 Surgery Hours

The surgery hours would normally be displayed on the surgery door and in the Reception area. The surgery websites would also give the details.

Monday to Friday – surgeries usually open for 3 hours in the morning and two hours in the evening. It may also be open for two hours in the afternoon – 4 days only – for clinics. One afternoon per week, the surgery would be closed. A typical time of opening would be:

Mondays to Fridays – mornings – 9am-12 noon (although some days, due to being busy and emergencies, they may remain open till 1PM or so)

Mondays and Tuesdays – 2.00 pm to 4.00 pm – clinics

Thursdays and Fridays – 2.00 pm to 4.00 pm – clinics

Wednesdays, it might be that the surgery would be closed in the afternoon. However, GP surgeries can opt for any other day as a half-day e.g. Mondays instead of Wednesdays.

Saturdays and Sundays – surgery would remain closed. Moves are afoot for surgeries to be open 24/7 – a government directive may come after consultations and cost evaluations.

In some surgeries patients are allowed to collect their prescriptions during the opening hours and are not limited to patients' visiting hours; with arrangements through the GP secretary, allowing her to do copies of results etc., they can collect the test results during the surgery open hours.

Even though the surgery may be open, say 9.30 to 5.30pm, the visits by patients are limited to the consultation hours only in most surgeries. The surgery staff may be busy with all associated work outside consultation hours.

2.4.3 Appointment Types

The appointment refers here not only to the surgery but also to Health Visitors, outside clinics, hospitals etc.

For surgery appointments to see GPs, nurses and Healthcare Assistant pre-booked appointments are the norm. However, it is possible to visit the surgery on the day to make same day appointment, if available.

Section 2.4.4 covers do's and don'ts for appointments but in the main appointment types include:

- Registered patients with the surgery needing medical attention.
- Pre-booked and sometimes as walk-in in some inner city surgeries.
- Emergencies

- Temporary patients (Section 2.4.8) which includes:
- Temporary residents between 2 weeks and less than 3 months
- Immediately Necessary Treatment – less than 48 hours
- Private patients.

2.4.4 Do's and Don'ts

Do's:

1. Always start with Appointments Screen.
2. Confirm reason for appointment (ensure it is for health reasons).
3. Always get the patient's first name, surname and date of birth for giving appointments (request them to spell names correctly or write it down and then use Appointments screen to give appointment). Date of birth is only for checking the name details once the patient records are open.
4. Enter 3 characters of surname only in space after Patients to get a list of patients. This is to ensure that the patient is only given appointment if his/her record is not closed. (First name and surname, date of birth, NHS number or CHI number may open the record without the receptionist knowing whether the record is closed or not.

Some systems may not always show 'Record Closed' screen.

5. Take an extra minute to check 'iv' to prevent mistakes occurring – do not rush or short cut entries lest wrong appointments are given.
6. Always give appointments to a patient:

Who is registered or is waiting for approval.

For health reasons only

Where small children are involved

For exceptional circumstances – e.g. bitten by a dog.

Don'ts:

Don't give appointments without checking whether the patient's record is closed or not.

Don't enter first name and surname, date of birth, NHS or CHI number to access the records (see 4 above).

Don't give appointments to patients:

Who are not registered, unless it is for temporary services;

Who have been removed at GP or at HA/PCT requests;

For services like form filling, medical records etc.;

For clinics, during normal surgery hours;

Without checking the appointments screen;

For mother and child or two patients in one time slot.

Don't give emergency appointments to patients for:

Non-emergency conditions;

Persistently seek emergency appointments;

Missing appointments – too many 'DNAs';

Coming after closing hours.

2.4.5 Priorities

In general, appointments are to be given on first come, first served basis. However, there are certain principles to adopt so that the patient conditions and situations are taken into account.

- People with disabilities are given appointments so that a GP or nurse usually sees them downstairs and they do not have to climb the stairs.
- Mothers with children are given same day appointments even as an emergency and they should not be sent back to come later.
- Patients bitten by a dog, having severe breathing problems, pregnant women having contractions or acute pain etc., are seen immediately by a nurse and hospital visits arranged ASAP.

2.4.6 Healthcare Specialists

Healthcare specialists in GP surgeries might include:

Healthcare assistant to do the health checking of patients and in some cases for registration purposes to approve the patients. They do continual monitoring of patients. They may be full-time or part-time employees of the practice.

Midwives may be employed part-time to do antenatal and postnatal work with a GP providing the lead.

PCTs may provide dieticians to visit GP surgeries for patients to be advised on their diets and health issues. Normally there is no charge for their visits to the surgeries.

Surgeries may also arrange visits by Community and District Nurses as required and usually there is no charge for such a visit.

GPs will usually refer patients to Consultants in the hospitals who may send the patients to healthcare specialists e.g. physiotherapists, audiology, mental health, foot care; and in special circumstances to practitioners of alternative medicines like ayurvedic, acupuncture, homeopathy etc. District Nurses, Health Visitors, midwives and counsellors.

The details of the District Nurses under PCT should be displayed on a notice board in the reception area or entrance hall.

If one of the doctors advises that patient's problem could be helped by psychological therapy and, if the patient agrees, referral will be made to the specialist. The patient will be sent all information and assessment forms to complete. Until the patient returns the completed form, the patient will not be given an appointment.

There are a number of treatment options including CBT, group therapy and individual counselling available for a GP to prescribe.

These members of staff may be attached to the surgery to care for our patients, but employed by other NHS agencies. Surgery staff work closely with these members and share patient information to provide good continuity of care.

District Nurse Team

The details of the District Nurse Team under the PCT should be displayed on a notice board in the reception area or entrance hall. The name of the Lead Sister and where they are based should be clearly indicated with contact details. The team provides care in the home for those patients not able to attend surgery.

Services include:
- Wound management and dressings
- Injections
- Blood tests
- Leg ulcer care
- Incontinence assessment
- Provision of appliances
- Post-operative care
- Catheter care
- Terminal care

They do not provide social care such as bathing and home care (see useful numbers page given by the PMgr).

Their location in the same building means they liaise with our Practice Nurses and the GPs over patient care and have access to the computer system and staff to facilitate excellent communication.

The District Nurses are available seven days a week from 0830 to 1700hrs, including Bank Holidays. There is an evening District Nursing Service available from 1800 to 2230hrs.

Referrals to the District Nurse can be made directly by patients Monday-Friday and at weekends.

To contact the District Nurses outside normal hours i.e. Evenings and Bank Holidays, a contact number should be provided.

Health Visitor

Baby Clinics and Child Health Surveillance

Baby Clinics

The baby clinic dates and times should be clearly stated and unfortunately these may not be a walk-in service.

PCT Health staff – Health Visitor and Nursery Nurse may run these clinics. No doctor is usually present in the clinic. The surgery should indicate the telephone number to make appointments.

Child Health Surveillance

8-week baby checks and other child development assessments are performed. These clinics run on certain dates, morning or afternoons and usually by appointment.

When a baby is registered with the Practice, the parent is advised to book the 8-week check and immunisation appointments.

Surgery coordinates the development checks with the Health Visitors who record the weight and length of babies in the red book.

Baby Immunisations

The surgery nurse normally does baby immunisations on given dates and times indicating morning or afternoon. Refer to any schedule displayed.

The surgery finds this a convenient time as it coincides with the walk-in baby clinic run by the Health Visitors and developmental checks. A parent is free to book at other times for maximum flexibility but please inform the receptionist that the appointment is for baby immunisation. See Section 2.5 for details of immunisations needed.

Midwife

GP involvement in the care of pregnant women has declined significantly over the past 30 years and midwives are now the main health care providers for 'low risk' pregnancies.

The role of GPs in maternity care could disappear completely, unless valid future responsibilities can be defined and clarified.

Midwives care for and support pregnant women, their partners and babies, before, during and after the birth. Some midwives give advice before a baby is conceived, but most will support the mother after pregnancy has been confirmed.

The work of a midwife includes:

- Monitoring the health of the mother and baby with physical examinations and ultrasound scans

- Counselling the expectant mother on issues such as healthy eating, giving up smoking, giving up drinking, domestic abuse, exercise

- Exploring the mother's options for the birth, for example natural childbirth, pain controlling drugs, hospital or home delivery

- Looking after the mother and baby during labour and birth, and for up to a month after the birth.

- Advice on method of feeding baby, in particular encouraging and supporting women to choose breastfeeding. Although at the same time supporting the mother if she chooses to bottle feed her baby.

- Midwives run antenatal and parenting classes which involves teaching.

In the current, cost-conscious climate, the most effective solution would be for a pregnant woman to book in with a midwife, for the midwife to have her medical records on her first visit, and the midwife then informing the GP of the pregnancy of one of their patients. Where there are pre-existing medical problems, the woman should be referred by the midwife to the appropriate service, which may be the GP or may be other services.

Women in England currently have a choice to receive their care from their GP or a midwife. The midwife will explain this choice to them when they book their first GP involvement.

The role of GPs in maternity care could disappear completely, unless valid future responsibilities can be defined and clarified for a visit.

GPs' knowledge of maternity issues has fallen behind current evidence and a considerable amount of retraining will be required to enable them to fulfil their role in pregnancy in relation to the health of the woman and the baby who have medical needs. Even more training would be required if GPs are expected to deal with the pregnancy and birth and the postpartum period, as a midwife would.

Antenatal Care

As soon as the patient finds out that she is pregnant she should make an appointment with a doctor. At this initial appointment the patient will be expected to provide the date of her last menstrual period. The doctor will take a history and examine the patient including her blood pressure (no internal examination is required), then help her choose where she would like to have her baby. She can calculate her due date and gestation using the pregnancy dates calculator available with the GP in the surgery.

It is possible these days using the Choose and BOOK system to book directly with the hospital using their online booking.

The patient will be informed about booking appointments and ultrasound scans.

A midwife from the hospital (http://www.kingstonmaternity.org.uk/), runs antenatal clinics every week at set times and dates. Antenatal care is shared between the doctors and the midwife. Surgery GPs do not perform home deliveries. The midwife would be happy to discuss home delivery and other preferences.

Postnatal Checks

Postnatal – Following the birth of your baby, all mothers should have a check-up at 6 weeks. All GPs can undertake postnatal checks. This is a good opportunity to ask the doctor any questions the patient may have about her progress. The GP will discuss many aspects about the postnatal period, take blood pressure, perform any necessary examinations and discuss contraception.

GPs like to allow more time (20 minutes) for these appointments. Please ensure that receptionists are advised about the nature of appointment when booking.

The baby development checks are not part of the postnatal check. These are performed at the developmental clinic by appointment.

2.4.7 Emergencies

Life-threatening Emergencies:

In case of a life-threatening emergency, such as sudden severe chest pain, loss of consciousness or severe bleeding – please dial 999 before ringing the surgery.

In the event of sudden onset of your illness, you can be treated as an emergency patient by making an appointment to see the Duty Doctor up to 48 hours in advance or

Nurse Practitioner up to 24 hours in advance.

They have a rota of duty doctors during surgery times where a doctor is appointed specifically to deal with emergency patients by appointment. A patient may not be able to see a doctor of the patient's choice.

There are guidances about:

Non-urgent conditions:

Ongoing, stable conditions; repeat prescription requests; sickness certificate requests; routine test requests. These do not require an emergency appointment.

Urgent Conditions:

Chest pains; breathlessness; wheezing; earache; bleeding; painful eyes; blackouts; stomach pains; any severe pain. Request an immediate appointment.

Attending A&E:

For life-threatening conditions such as choking, chest pain, blood loss or blacking out, do not hesitate to call 999. Tell the operator that there is a medical emergency; a response vehicle will be sent to your location.

A&E departments assess and treat patients with serious injuries or illnesses. Generally, you should visit A&E or call 999 for life-threatening emergencies, such as: loss of consciousness, acute confused state and fits that are not stopping, persistent, severe chest pain, breathing difficulties, severe bleeding that cannot be stopped. If an ambulance is needed, call 999, the emergency phone number in the UK. You can also dial 112, which is the ambulance number throughout the European Union.

Major A&E departments offer access 24 hours a day, 365 days a year, although not all hospitals have an A&E department. At A&E a doctor or nurse will assess your condition and decide on further action.

If it is not an immediate emergency, call NHS 111. The service is available 24 hours a day, seven days a week, and can provide medical advice and advise you on the best local service to offer the care you need.

2.4.8 Temporary

Temporary Residents

To register as a temporary resident with a GP please search the web to find GP surgeries in the area – you'll need a surgery that covers the area where you're staying.

- Contact the surgery and ask to register as a temporary resident.

The surgery will ask you to complete a GMS3 form.

You could register as a temporary resident with a GP in England, if you are in the area for longer than 24 hours but less than three months.

Temporary Residents up to 2 weeks – complete a temporary registration form (Blue)

Temporary Residents 2 weeks to 3 months – complete a temporary registration form (Blue).

You can register temporarily with a GP near where you're staying if you're ill or need medical advice while you're away from home, for example, working, studying or on holiday.

One can still remain registered with your permanent GP but you can see your temporary GP for up to three months.

One's temporary GP will pass details of any treatment you have to your permanent GP, who will add the information to your medical records.

One should have the following information when seeing a temporary GP for the first time:

- Details of any medical conditions one has
- Details of medical conditions one has had in the past
- The name of any medicines one is currently taking
- Details of anything one is allergic to
- Contact details for one's permanent or previous GP

For residents of the EU and some other countries, reciprocal agreements apply. On production of a valid E111 (EU) they can be seen for treatment in an acute illness or emergency. Most of the cost of treatment can then be claimed back from their 'home' health department. The E111 does not cover ongoing care of medical conditions. A

British passport does not entitle a person normally resident outside the UK to healthcare under the NHS (being resident in the UK for more than 6 months does).

Surgeries will provide their services on a private basis to those without proof of NHS entitlement. A list of fees should be available at reception.

Immediately Necessary Patients

If one is visiting the area for 24 hours or less and is suffering from a condition that needs immediate attention, the surgery will see it as an 'Immediately Necessary Patient'. One will need to complete a 'Blue' registration form and have details of one's doctor's name and address. The registration then follows the same path as a temporary resident of less than two weeks, as above. This registration covers only for the day on which one receives the 'Immediately Necessary Treatment'. One will be asked to provide some form of identification.

Private Patients

The surgery would provide services on a private basis to those without proof of NHS entitlement. A list of fees should be available at reception. Acute medical conditions will be seen by the 'Doctor of the day'. Please contact the receptionist for guidance if one is in doubt about one's entitlement to NHS registration. Application to the doctor's list could be refused. One's current home, work and/or mobile telephone number need to be given in case the surgery needs to contact.

2.4.9 NHS Number

Everyone registered with a GP in England and Wales has his or her own unique ten-digit number.

It helps healthcare staff find the health records. It will help healthcare staff share your records safely with other healthcare providers involved in your care.

It is important that once you obtain your NHS number you are able to provide it whenever you come into contact with healthcare providers.

If you are registered with a GP practice you will already have an NHS number. It is printed on your medical card, prescription paperwork and referral letter. If you do not have any of these documents, next time you visit your GP you can ask them for your NHS number. They might ask you for proof of identification such as a photo driving licence or passport.

If you are not registered with a GP, you need to register with one to get an NHS number. You can ring 0800 78 333 96 to find out your nearest GP practice.

If you are not registered with a GP but think you have an NHS number, ring 0800

78 333 96 and inform them that you would like to know your NHS number.

You will be asked for some personal details. Your NHS number will then be sent to you.

If you have an old medical card you will have an old-style NHS number with both digits and letters, a ten-digit only number has replaced this.

Babies

Babies born in English and Welsh hospitals have an NHS number allocated to them at birth.

If the baby was born at home, an NHS number will be allocated when the baby's birth is registered.

NHS Card and number must be kept in a safe place.

2.4.10 Choose and Book

When the patient and a GP agree that the patient needs to see a specialist, Choose and Book is a service that allows them to choose the hospital or clinic and book an appointment with a specialist 'online'. They will be able to choose, with the help of the GP, from at least four hospitals or clinics.

The GP will discuss the reasons for referral and will offer a choice of hospitals that meet the patient's need. Once they decide which hospital they wish to go to, an administrator within the practice will contact the patient. He/she will ask the patient to collect some paperwork from reception. This is the referral confirmation detail. Please keep these in a safe place.

An administrator within the practice has completed the request for the patient's referral.

The patient **now** needs to call – 084560 88 88 8 to arrange a convenient outpatient appointment. **(Check telephone number)**.

PLEASE HAVE THE ORIGINAL PAPERWORK TO HAND WHEN MAKING THIS PHONE CALL, AS SOME OF THE DETAILS NEED TO BE REFERRED TO.

The appointment request issued should be taken to the outpatient appointment.

No further action needs to be taken.

HOWEVER, IF THE PATIENT HAS **NOT** CONTACTED 084560 88 88 8 WITHIN 9 DAYS, AUTOMATICALLY A REMINDER LETTER WILL BE SENT. A SECOND REMINDER LETTER WILL BE ISSUED AFTER 18 DAYS.

PLEASE NOTE: IF NO CONTACT HAS BEEN MADE WITHIN THE 18 DAY TIME LIMIT, THEN THE REFERRAL WILL BE CANCELLED.

2.5 Immunisations

Some basic details about vaccines, which a receptionist and other staff should know about are given below. However, non-clinical staff should direct patients to nurses for advice and any leaflets on display in the surgery.

2.5.1 Children

There are primary, secondary and tertiary immunisations

Child immunisation will only be carried out if the following two items are brought to the surgery:

- The Red Book
- A written and signed consent letter from a parent, if the child is going to be accompanied by a guardian/friend of the family.

2.5.1.1 Immunisation Schedule

At birth:

Hepatitis B vaccine for babies born to hepatitis B positive mothers (often detected as part of the routine Hepatitis B screening programme).

BCG mainly for babies of some immigrant families and for those in household contact with TB.

Here's a checklist of the vaccines that are routinely offered to everyone in the UK for free on the NHS, and the age at which the baby should ideally have them.

Primary Immunisation

Primary Immunisations	
At Birth	• Hepatitis B vaccine for babies born to hepatitis B positive mothers (often detected as part of the routine Hepatitis B screening programme) • BCG for babies of some immigrant families and those in

	household contact with TB
2 Months	• Polio • Diphtheria/Tetanus/Pertussis + Hib • Men C
3 Months	• Polio • Diphtheria/Tetanus/Pertussis + Hib • Men C
4 Months	• Polio • Diphtheria/Tetanus/Pertussis + Hib • Men C
12-15 Months	• Measles/Mumps/Rubella
Secondary Immunisations	
4-5 Years	• Boosters of Polio + Diphtheria/Tetanus + MMR
Tertiary Immunisations	
10-14 Years	• BCG
13-18 Years	• Polio + Td (i.e. adult low-dose diphtheria)

Notes:

- All children should be offered immunisation even if they present outside the recommended ages.
- No opportunity to offer immunisation should be missed.
- There is no upper age limit for immunisation, including pertussis.
- MMR can be given regardless of age.
- Children attending for their school leaving immunisations should have their immunisation histories checked and offered MMR if appropriate.

2 months:

- 5-in-1 (DTaP/IPV/Hib). This single jab contains vaccines to protect against five separate diseases – diphtheria, tetanus, pertussis (whooping cough), polio and Haemophilus influenza type b (Hib, a bacterial infection that can cause severe pneumonia or meningitis in young children).
- Pneumococcal infection.

3 months:

5-in-1, second dose (DTaP/IPV/Hib)
Meningitis C.

5 months:

- 5-in-1, third dose (DTaP/IPV/Hib)
- Pneumococcal infection, second dose
- Meningitis C, second dose.

Between 12 and 13 months:

Hib/Men C booster. Given as a single jab containing meningitis C, third dose and Hib, fourth dose.
MMR (measles, mumps and rubella), given as a single jab
Pneumococcal infection, third dose.

3 years and 4 months, or soon after:

- MMR second jab
- 4-in-1 pre-school booster (DtaP/IPV). Given as a single jab containing vaccines against diphtheria, tetanus, pertussis and polio.

Around 12-13 years:

HPV vaccine, which protects against cervical cancer (girls only): three jabs given within six months.

Around 13-18 years:

- 3-in-1 teenage booster (Td/IPV). Given as a single jab, which contains vaccines against diphtheria, tetanus and polio.

65 and over:

- Flu (every year)
- Pneumococcal

Vaccines for risk groups

People who fall into certain risk groups may be offered extra vaccines. These include vaccinations against diseases such as hepatitis B, tuberculosis (TB), flu and chickenpox. See our sections on vaccines for adults to find out whether you should have one.

Notes:

All children should be offered immunisation even if they outside the recommended ages.

No opportunity to offer immunisation should be missed.

There is no upper age limit for immunisation, including pertussis.

MMR can be given regardless of age.

Children attending for their school leaving immunisations should have their immunisation histories checked and offered MMR if appropriate.

Most childhood vaccines, except the 15-year-olds, are given in the Baby Clinic. When this is not possible, children are seen in Treatment Room. Nurses must be familiar with the recommendations for the giving of vaccinations together with a knowledge of individual vaccines as detailed in 'Immunisation against Infectious Diseases'.

Injection Site – Nurses are aware of this.

Immunisations to be recorded, including site, in notes on yellow vaccination card and computer records.

Parents are asked to remain with the child on the premises for 15 minutes following any vaccination.

Doctor to be in surgery or two nurses on duty whilst vaccines being given.

Nurses to have annual update of anaphylaxis procedure and CPR.

Nurse to be familiar with the vaccine cold chain process and storage of vaccines.

Complete unscheduled immunisation form and leave for Isobel.

Prescription for Diftavax.

DTP-Hib Vaccine

The DTP-Hib vaccine protects against three different diseases: Diphtheria, Tetanus and Pertussis (whooping cough) and against infection by the bacteria called Haemophilus influenza type b (Hib).

Diphtheria:

This disease begins with a sore throat and can progress rapidly to cause problems with breathing. It can damage the heart and the nervous system and in severe cases it can kill. Diphtheria has almost been wiped out in the UK, but it still exists in other parts of the world and it is on the increase in parts of Eastern Europe.

Tetanus:

Tetanus germs are found in soil. They enter the body through a cut or burn. Tetanus is a painful disease that affects the muscles and can cause breathing problems. If it is not treated, it can kill.

Whooping Cough (pertussis):

Whooping cough can be very distressing. In young children it can last for several weeks. Children become exhausted by long bouts of coughing, which often cause vomiting and choking. In severe cases pertussis can kill.

The actual whooping cough disease, but not the vaccine, can cause brain damage.

Hib:

Hib is an infection that can cause a number of serious illnesses including blood poisoning, pneumonia and meningitis. All of these diseases can be dangerous if not treated quickly. The Hib vaccine protects the child against one specific type of meningitis. The Hib vaccine does not protect against any other type of meningitis.

Side Effects of the DTP-Hib Vaccine:

It is quite normal for the baby to be miserable within 48 hours of the injection.

Some babies develop a fever.

Sometimes a small lump develops where the injection was given. This lump can last for several weeks. If the child has a worse reaction to the DTP-Hib vaccine – for example, some form of fit – your doctor may not give your child any more doses of the vaccine. If this happens, talk to the doctor, nurse or health visitor.

If a baby has a fit in the first 48 hours after being given the DTP-Hib vaccine at 2, 3 and 4 months, it is no more common than at any other time for young babies. But if you delay the immunisation, it increases the chances of fits after DTP-Hib.

So, it's important to make sure the child gets vaccinated on time.

Polio Vaccine

Polio vaccine protects against the disease poliomyelitis.

Polio is a virus that attacks the nervous system and can cause permanent muscle paralysis. If it affects the chest muscles it can kill. The virus is passed in the faeces (poo) of infected people or those who have just been immunised against polio. Routine immunisation has meant that the natural virus no longer causes cases of polio in the UK. But polio is still around in other parts of the world, especially in India.

Unlike other immunisations, you take the polio vaccine by swallowing it. The doctor or nurse drops the liquid into child's mouth.

The polio vaccine is passed into the child's nappies for up to six weeks after the vaccine is given. If someone who has not been immunised against polio changes your child's nappy, it is possible for him or her to be affected by the virus. There is about one case each year. This works out at about one case for every 1.5 million doses used. You must wash your hands thoroughly to prevent this happening.

If you think you have not had the polio immunisation, contact your doctor. You can arrange to have it at the same time as your child. This also goes for anyone else in the family who looks after your child.

MMR Vaccine

The MMR vaccine protects your child against Measles, Mumps and Rubella (German measles).

The measles virus is very infectious. It causes a high fever and a rash. About one in 15 children who gets measles is at risk of complications, which may include chest infections, fits and brain damage. In severe cases measles can kill.

The mumps virus causes swollen glands in the face. Before immunisation was introduced, mumps was the commonest cause of viral meningitis in children under 15. It can also cause deafness, and swelling of the testicles in boys and ovaries in girls.

Rubella, German measles, is usually very mild and isn't likely to cause the child any problems. However, if a pregnant woman catches it in her early pregnancy, it can harm the unborn baby.

In some children the illness may pass almost unnoticed, but others can be very ill. The most dangerous thing about these illnesses is that they can cause complications. Before the vaccine was introduced, about 90 children a year in the UK died from measles. Because of immunisation, children no longer die of measles.

The child will receive two doses because measles, mumps and rubella; vaccines don't always work well enough on the first go. The second MMR immunisation makes sure that your child gets the best protection against these three diseases. This also gives a second chance for those children who missed out the first time around. So, you can be sure your child is well protected before they start school.

The MMR vaccine is prepared in egg but it can be given to children who are allergic to eggs. If your child has had a serious reaction to eating eggs, or food containing egg, then talk to your doctor. The usual signs of a serious allergic reaction are a rash that covers the face and body, a swollen mouth and throat, breathing difficulties and shock. In these cases your doctor can make special arrangements for the immunisation to be given safely.

About a week to 10 days after the MMR immunisation some children become feverish, develop a measles-like rash and go off their food for two or three days. Very rarely, a child will get a mild form of mumps about three weeks after the injection. Your child will not be infectious at this time, so they can mix with other people as normal. Occasionally, children do have a bad reaction to the MMR vaccine. About one child in a thousand will have a fit. A child who actually has measles is 10 times more likely to have a fit as a result of the illness.

BCG Vaccine

This is given when a child is between 10 and 14 years old. It is sometimes given to babies shortly after they are born. The BCG vaccine gives protection against TB (tuberculosis).

TB is an infection that usually affects the lungs. It can also affect other parts of the body such as the brain and bones.

Although TB is no longer common in this country, there are between 5,000 and 6,000 cases a year. TB is on the increase in Asia, Africa and some Eastern European countries.

Most children have the BCG injection when they are between 10 and 14. The child will have a skin test to see if they already have immunity to TB. If not, the immunisation is given. Babies under three months who are having the immunisation don't need to have the skin test.

A small blister or sore appears where the injection is given. This is quite normal. It gradually heals, leaving a small scar.

Hepatitis B Vaccine

This vaccine gives protection against hepatitis B.

There are several different types of hepatitis and they all cause inflammation of the liver. The hepatitis B virus is passed through infected blood and may also be sexually transmitted. Some people carry the virus in their blood without actually having the disease itself. If a pregnant woman is a hepatitis B carrier, or gets the disease during pregnancy, she can pass it on to her child. The child may not be ill but has a high chance of becoming a carrier and developing liver disease later in life.

Pregnant women are offered a test for hepatitis B during their antenatal care. Babies born to infected mothers should receive a course of vaccine to prevent them getting hepatitis B and becoming a carrier. The first dose should be given within two days of birth, and two more doses should be given before the child is six months.

Side effects of the vaccine tend to be quite mild. The injection site is often red and can be sore for a few days afterwards.

A mother having hepatitis B can still safely breastfeed.

2.5.2 Adults

Flu Vaccine – Protects Against: Flu Including Swine Flu

All people aged 65 years and over

All those with a long-term health condition

People of all ages who are in the following Clinical risk groups:

- Chronic respiratory disease and asthma that requires continuous or repeated use of inhaled or systemic steroids or with previous exacerbations requiring hospital admission
- Chronic heart disease
- Chronic renal disease
- Chronic liver disease
- Chronic neurological disease
- Diabetes
- Immunosuppression
- Healthcare workers
- All pregnant women at any stage of pregnancy

Given: every year starting in October/November.

Patients who want to have a flu vaccine but do not qualify under the criteria above, can obtain vaccination from their chemist or other outside agencies.

2.5.3 Pneumococcal

The pneumococcal vaccination (the pneumo jab) protects against pneumococcal infections.

Pneumococcal infections are caused by the bacterium Streptococcus pneumonia, which is sometimes referred to as the pneumococcus bacterium.

The bacterium can cause several conditions including:

- Pneumonia: inflammation (infection) of the lungs
- Septicaemia: a form of blood poisoning from an infection in the blood
- Meningitis: an infection of the membranes that surround the brain and spinal cord

At-Risk Groups

A pneumococcal infection can affect anyone. However, some groups of people need the vaccination because they have a higher risk of an infection developing into a serious health condition.

These include:

- Children under the age of two (as part of the childhood vaccination programme)
- Adults aged 65 or over
- Children and adults with certain chronic (long-term) health conditions, such as a serious heart or kidney condition.

Types of Pneumococcal Vaccine

There are two different types of pneumococcal vaccine:

- Pneumococcal conjugate vaccine (PCV): this is given to all children under two years old as part of the childhood vaccination programme.
- Pneumococcal polysaccharide vaccine (PPV): this is given to people aged 65 or over, and to people at high risk due to chronic health conditions.

Things to consider before vaccination

In rare cases the vaccination may need to be delayed, or may not be safe to have. The reasons are listed below:

Allergic reactions. Tell your GP if you've had a bad reaction to any vaccination in the past. If you have had a confirmed anaphylactic reaction (a severe allergic reaction) to the vaccine, or any ingredient in the vaccine, you should not have it. However, if it was only a mild reaction, such as a rash, it is probably safe for you to have the vaccine.

Being unwell. If you're mildly unwell at the time of the vaccination, it is still safe to have the vaccine. However, if you are 'actively unwell', for example, if you have a high temperature (fever), it is likely that the vaccination will be delayed. This is because it will be difficult to tell the difference between the symptoms of your condition and a bad reaction to the vaccine.

Pregnancy and breastfeeding. The pneumococcal vaccine is thought to be safe to receive during pregnancy and breastfeeding. As a precaution, if you are pregnant, you may be advised to wait until you have had your baby (unless the benefits of having the vaccine outweigh the risks to your child).

Suppressed immune system. If you have a suppressed immune system, for example, because you have HIV or AIDS, you may need to have extra doses of the pneumococcal vaccination. This is because you may not produce enough antibodies (proteins that destroy disease-carrying organisms) to provide immunity after the standard dose of the vaccine. Ask your GP for more information.

Side Effects

Although the pneumococcal vaccinations are considered safe and rarely cause problems, both the PCV and PPV vaccines can cause mild side effects including:

- A slightly raised temperature (mild fever)
- Redness at the site of the injection
- Hardness or swelling at the site of the injection

In rare cases, some people react badly to the vaccine and develop serious side effects. If you develop any unusual symptoms after having the vaccination, call your GP or NHS Direct on 0845 46 47 (**check current number**).

2.5.4 Travel

Children may need extra immunisations depending on their age, which country you are visiting, and how long you plan to stay. You should contact your doctor or a travel clinic for up-to-date information on the immunisations your child may need. If you are travelling to an area where there is malaria, your child will need protection. This is one of the most serious health problems in tropical countries. There isn't an immunisation against malaria, but some anti-malarial drugs can be given to children. It is essential to do all you can to avoid getting bitten by mosquitoes. Insect repellent, mosquito nets soaked in repellent and making sure arms and legs are covered between dusk and dawn will all help. Be careful not to use too much repellent on your child's skin.

Travel and Other Vaccines

There are also optional vaccines that you may be able to have free on the NHS from your local surgery, including travel vaccinations, such as hepatitis A, typhoid and cholera.

If you're not sure whether you or your child have had all your vaccinations, ask your GP or practice nurse.

For information on vaccination for travelling abroad refer to:

Health advice for travellers (T5), an information leaflet produced by the Department of Health, from the post office.

Stay Healthy Abroad, a Health Education Authority publication, gives advice and information for each country.

Health Information for Overseas Travel, produced by the Department of Health and published by HMSO, contains advice and information for each country.

"The Guide to Childhood Immunisations" (HEA).

2.5.5 Charges

The National Health Service provides most health care to most people free of charge, but there are exceptions: prescription charges have existed since 1951 and there are a number of other services for which fees are charged.

Sometimes the charge is made to cover some of the cost of treatment, for example, dental fees; in other cases, it is because the service is not covered by the NHS, for example, providing copies of health records or producing medical reports for insurance companies.

Certificates and extracts from records

Suggested fees for services provided only by patient's own GP or other attending doctor can be found at:

http://bma.org.uk/practical-support-at-work/pay-fees-allowances/fees/~/link.aspx?_id=71744817586349BBB95BCE7400467E4F&_z=z

Certificates without examination

Straight forward certificates of fact £16.50

Patient or company requesting more complex certificates £28.00 to £58.50

Work in surgery:
a)   Extract from records 62.50
b)   Report on a pro forma, no examination (e.g. 20 minutes) £83.50
c)   Written report without exam, with detailed opinion and statement on condition of patient (e.g. 30 minutes) £124.50

Some services provided do not come within the treatment available under the NHS. These services are subject to a charge dependent on the time required. Examples include:

Private medical examinations.

Health Reports.

Doctor's certificates for less than 7 days.

Please note: As a matter of policy, the practice should not provide signatures on shotgun certificate and passport applications.

Health checks for patients over 75: Annual health checks for patients of 75 and over. These are carried out by a practice nurse or by a doctor. A district nurse can also perform these health checks for those who are unable to attend surgery.

2.6 Telephones

2.6.1 Service Providers

Some of the major providers are listed below:

- **BT**
- **Virgin Media**
- **TalkTalk**
- **Sky**
- **Others**

All provide good service at competitive rates and offer 0845 or other numbers at or slightly above national call charges (not premium) for patients dialling the surgery. The practice of free calls by dialling 0800 has been long discontinued.

Also, these providers prevented the surgeries from direct dialling the landline numbers using the argument that patients may get busy tones and not be able to access the surgery quickly. Nowadays most have packages for calling these numbers free 24/7; of course they pay a small upfront charges to the provider. Some providers do offer unlimited calls to 0845 and other numbers for a small monthly charge.

2.6.2 Telephone Answering and Etiquette

The way a receptionist talks on the phone, the tone, expressions etc., are of paramount importance and should be checked by the senior receptionists and the Practice Manager before the person is allowed to take calls from the patients. It is crucial that during induction training this aspect is focused first, as the person is the first contact, and the wrong tone or comments may infuriate the patient with consequential complaints. The table below lists some of the telephone responses and this can be expanded to suit individual surgery needs. This list should also be in the reception area for easy reference.

The receptionists should practice the responses for each question, as prepared by the Practice Manager, so that it comes out very fluently and they sound quite confident. This simple exercise would educate the receptionists about the rules, procedures and telephone etiquette and make them deal with the patients and public much better.

2.6.3 Surgery Telephone Numbers

The service providers do give a number of options for patients to select the service they need from the surgery by selection of 1-9 and 0 for the operator. It is prudent to restrict the calls during busy surgery hours to those seeking appointments only or from hospitals.

2.6.4 Training Module

This gives an outline of a system used in earlier years for an extremely busy inner city surgery. This format was used for in-house training purposes and should be modified to suit present day situations. (See 2.6.4a)

2.6.4a Training Modules for Receptionists – No. 3

Telephone – General:

a. during the surgery hours 9.00 to 11.15 AM or 4.00-5.00 PM or 5.00-6.00 PM Wed. only

Query	Details	Action Points
1. Who answers the two telephones?	The receptionist, who is responsible for taking requests for prescriptions and giving prescriptions ready for collection, will have to answer the telephones during surgery hours (to be decided by the Senior Receptionist).	This way the receptionists in the front can focus during surgery hours on dealing with the incoming patients for normal and emergency appointments, and deal with the telephone calls from the GPs which are a priority.
2. What to say to enquirers on the phones?	If the call is during surgery hours – 9.00 AM to 11.15 AM or 4.00 – 5.00 PM or 5.00 – 6 PM Wed. only.	Request the callers to phone between 11.30 AM to 1.00 PM
	a. appointments;	Ensure that the appointment is given when they phone between 11.30 AM to 1.00 PM. Do not ask them to call again etc. Appointment must be given.
	b. insurance queries;	Request them to call after 11.30 AM if possible. This call to be put through to the medical secretary.
	c. any type of form filling;	Request them to leave the form in the surgery with the medical secretary and the person should call back the next day to find out when it would be ready and whether the person needs to see a GP.
	d. Healthcall, hospitals, consultants, police etc.	Put the call through to the relevant person or deal with it immediately. Always ascertain the nature of the call before disturbing the GP in surgery.
	e. Health Authority, PCT, Transport services from hosp.	Request whether they can call back between 11.30 and 1.00

		PM; if they cannot then, put the call through to the relevant person.
	f. Medical representatives	Ask them to see speak to a manager or the GP between 12.00 and 1.00 PM.
	g. Sales persons.	Ask them to see speak to the manager between 12.00 and 1.00 PM.
	h. Pharmacists	Request them to call after 11.30 AM, if possible.
	i. Job applicants etc.	Request them to call after 11.30 AM, if possible.
	j. medical certificate (for immediate appointment only, make an appointment as an emergency patient).	If the certificate is needed for the first week of ailment, then explain that statutory rules allow then to self-certify for the 1st week. If they still need it, then explain about £10 charge and if acceptable, give appointment same day as emergency. **Certificates cannot be issued 'back dated' as it is illegal.** They should see the GP 'as emergency patient' before the day it expires.

Telephone – General: (contd.,)

a. during the surgery hours 9.00 to 11.15 AM or 4.00-5.00 PM or 5.00-6.00 PM Wed. only

Query	Details	Action Points
3. What about wanting prescriptions over the phone?	Always request them to leave the white copy of the previous prescription and find out how many days the medication will last.	To get the details of the person's, medication name, dosage and frequency correctly established. Request them to collect in the evenings 5-5.50 PM and for Thursday evenings – request to collect on Friday evenings.

	Exceptions:	
	a. Persons who are disabled and unable to move out of the house and has no one to bring details to the surgery	If the pharmacist delivers the drugs, ask them to contact the pharmacists to send and leave the requests in writing to get the details correct
	b. Carers/district nurses phoning on behalf of patients	Get the details correctly (request whether we can keep the white copy in the surgery for easier repeat prescription request).
	c. Hospital staff making request for repeat medication	Get the details correctly and note the date and time.
	d. Pharmacists making request on behalf of patients	If the pharmacist delivers the drugs, ask them to contact the pharmacists to send and leave the requests in writing to get details correct
4. Callers who want to make a complaint.	Request them to phone between 11.30 and 100 PM or see the manager in person, if they so wish. They can also send a complaint by post.	Be polite and say you are busy with patients during surgery times. If persistent, be apologetic and say you will have to put her on hold for a while.

2.6.5 Others

Swine Flu Incident Room in PCT.

When a large incidence of swine flu occurs then patients are likely to call the incident room for advice regarding swine flu. Surgeries should give the contact telephone numbers of PCT to patients as this is solely for doctors and staff to call.

PCT would normally issue procedures for all surgeries to follow when such an outbreak occurs.

2.7 Registrations

Choosing a GP

GMC

The General Medical Council (GMC) is the body which holds the official register of all medical doctors working in the UK. One can contact them to see if a particular doctor is on the UK Medical Register, or one can link to the List of Registered Medical Practitioners on the GMC's website and then search for a doctor by name. The GMC does not, however, usually provide contact details for individual doctors.

Directories

There is a publication called *The Medical Directory*, www.crcpress.com, which contains entries for most, but not all, doctors practising in the UK. Doctors submit their contact details for inclusion in this publication on a voluntary basis. Most large public libraries hold a reference copy of the Medical Directory.

Websites

If one is searching for an NHS GP and know the postcode/place/organisation where the GP is working, you can search the NHS choices website. Many GP surgeries also have their own website.

Registering with a new GP practice

Choose the GP surgery that you want to register with and check it covers the area where you live.

When you move to a new practice, take along your NHS medical card. This has details of your current practice and your NHS number on it, which will make it easier for you to register. Your NHS number ensures that your new practice will be sent your medical records quickly.

If you don't have an NHS card, you can get your NHS number from your current practice. It's a good idea to write this down along with their name and address. Keep this sort of information safe because you'll need it whenever you move practices.

When you have found a practice you like, you'll have to formally register with it as an NHS patient by submitting a registration form to them. The GMS1 form is available in the practice or can be downloaded from the Internet.

The form may request details such as:

- Your name and address
- Your date of birth
- Your NHS number (if you know it)
- Other information, such as the name and address of your previous GP

Some GP surgeries will also ask to see proof of identity, for example:

Photo identity, such as passport or driving licence.

Proof of current address, such as a recent utility bill (gas, electricity, water or phone bill, but not a mobile phone bill) or Council Tax bill.

The GP surgery may ask you for your NHS medical card or your NHS number. However, you don't need either of these to register with a GP or to get NHS treatment.

When you register with a GP, some PCTs would send you a new NHS medical card. However, not all PCTs issue medical cards and some will only do so on request.

Forms may vary slightly. Usually, PCTs order them for their practices centrally, but some practices use their own version.

When completed and returned the form, your local PCT will transfer your medical records to your new practice and write to you to confirm your registration as a patient with that practice.

Parents or guardians can register a baby at a practice by completing and presenting form FP58, which is issued at the same time as a birth certificate.

Once you've registered with your new practice, you should be invited to the surgery for an initial consultation. At this consultation, you will be asked questions about your health and lifestyle.

Ensure that the nurse has done a health check and approved the patient to be taken on GP list for Registration.

Should the nurse be absent for any reason, no registration will be done that day. Please confirm with Receptionists for any change in the above schedule.

Registration may be done during stipulated times each morning or only for a few days a week, depending on the number of patients wanting to register. Some surgeries, like inner cities, have a large floating population and they cater differently compared to rural surgeries.

One could also make appointments to see a doctor or nurse at the practice when one needs treatment for illnesses and other medical conditions. Until PCT approves the registration, only minor illnesses and medication would be given by the surgery.

One would be registered with the GP surgery, rather than an individual GP.

If one prefers to see a specific GP, the surgery can note this in one's records. However, one may have to wait longer to see your preferred GP; see someone else if your preferred GP is unavailable.

2.7.1 Do's

Register the patients if within the catchment area, as evidenced by proof of current address, and the surgery has an 'open' list i.e. accepting new patients.

Current GP catchment areas are determined by population density rather than geographical area.

The average list size is about 6,000 patients for a three-doctor practice.

Do register patients allocated by PCT from time to time, even if they are difficult patients. 'NHS practices are contractually obliged to accept patients in their catchment area'. PCT in some instances may rotate the registration to other surgeries within its area after 3 months.

2.7.2 Don'ts

Don't register the patient if outside the catchment area. The reason is home visits, which a GP is contracted to make with PCT. Such visits take time, are quite expensive and not practicable.

Don't register the patient if the list is 'Closed'. PCT allows refusal to take more patients when the list is 'Closed'.

Don't refuse registration unless there is a reasonable ground for doing so. These must not relate to race, gender, social class, age, religion, sexual orientation, appearance, disability, or a medical condition. If refused, the surgery must give reasons for its decision in writing. This could be a long, drawn-out process, pitching the surgery against the PCT.

2.7.3 Training Guides

The table 2.7.3a lists various issues and these can be modified to suit present-day circumstances.

2.7.3a Training Modules for Receptionists

Registration – General:

Query	Details	Action Points
1. Who to register	Residents in the catchment area for over 3 months:	
	Already resident in the UK/living in our catchment area	} GMS1 Male(Red)/Female(Blue continuation card
	Going to be resident in our catchment area	} Male(red)/Female(Blue Health Promotion Band 3 card
	Even staying temporarily for over 3 months	} and Male(Red)/Female(Blue) record envelope
	Patients allocated by Health Authority	}
	Exception: GP authorised patients outside area	
	Check: previous GP's address for already resident in UK NHS number – **crucial**	
2. Who not to register?	Temporary Services only for:	
	Foreigners on short stay – e.g. holidays, visits etc.	Temporary Services GMS form 'tick' – Immediate Necessary Treatment only
	Persons staying temporarily	GMS 3 form 'tick' <15 days

	for less than 15 days	(computer default as 'short stay')
	Persons staying temporarily for less than 3 months	GMS 3 form 'tick' over 15 days (computer default as 'long stay')
	Foreigners seeking pregnancy treatments etc.	As a private patient only – otherwise send them to walk-in clinic in NMH
	Records 'closed' due to removal to new FHSA	GMS 3 only; if they are going to be resident in the catchment area then GMS 1
	Internal transfer	GMS 3 only; if they are going to be resident in the catchment area then GMS 1
	Removal requested by GP	GMS 3 Immediately Necessary Treatment only – **do not register**
	Any other reasons	GMS 3 only
	Under 16s, if parents are registered with another practice	GMS 3 only (family to be with same GP)
3. Who decides registration?	Only GPs and Practice Nurses decide about suitability for registration based solely on the health checks and on responses to the questions regarding the applicant's life styles etc. Receptionists should have no input and should not influence GP/nurse's decision. Only GPs and Practice Nurses decide about refusing to register the applicant Receptionists, in this instance, can give an opinion to GPs/Practice	Receptionist should not discuss with the applicant about whether they will be registered or not – say, "Once GP/Nurse decide we will notify in writing within 48 hours (Sat, Sun not counted)." Send standard letter. Receptionists to send standard letter within 48 hours, as above, without giving reasons for refusal. They should not also tell the applicant the reasons if he/she comes to the surgery to discuss in person. Do not be intimidated and give HA telephone number – **020 8272 5500** – Registration Department

GENERAL PRACTICE MANAGEMENT

	Nurses about the applicant's abusive, violent behaviour or any other justifiable reasons.	
4. Where to register?	In the surgery at all times for most patients above 16 yrs.	Receptionists should insist on the applicant being present at the time of filling the forms for registration unless for exceptional circumstances.
	Exceptions:	
	Patients allocated by HA who are housebound	GPs/District Nurse may complete the GMS 1 form in patients home
5. When to register?	High Road: (6 sessions)	Receptionists to note that the main timings for registration. However, due to the need to increase the patient list size, the timings has to be increased to:

mornings – till 12.15 PM;

evenings – health checks in the main but new registration, if applicants come.

Check: the nurses are not overbooked or double-booked. Consult the nurse.

Health checks in the afternoon if possible

Do not turn away applicant lest they register elsewhere |
	M, W, Th, F – morning 9.00-9.30 AM	
	M, T (no clinic days), F – afternoon 3.00-3.30 PM	
	Lordship Lane: (7 sessions)	
	M, T, W, F – morning 9.00-9.30 AM	
	M, T (no clinic days), F – afternoon 3.00-3.30 PM	
6. Why to register?	The surgery is losing about 100 patients per month in deductions, mostly due to – new FHSA, internal transfer, and others. About 600 were removed due to 'Returned undelivered' –	Register to improve the list size.

Aim to register a total of 250 per month:

HR – 120 per month = 30 per week = 6 per morning and 3 per |

	however, none since April 2002.	a/noon session LL – 100 per month = 25 per week = 5 per morning and ~3 per a/noon session
	Loss in capitation fees and related 'items of service' claims. Significant reduction in surgery income.	This means a net gain of 150 patients per month – initial target for – 2002-2003
7. What is needed for registration?	All applicants should have documents as proof of identity: Passport – check name, surname(family name), DoB Utility bill with address – check proof of address Letter from Home Office, DSS, Asylum Centre, Care Centres, Police, HA, Hospitals etc. NHS card – from previous GP practice Red Book/Form – for children under 5	We do not have Home Office role to check on status of applicant – legal or illegal immigrant, valid for a short period only etc. We also do not have DSS role – just medical condition assessment only. In case of short term visitors seeking expensive medical treatment – then we have the right to tell them to go as private patients as stated in '2' above.
	Letter from a Solicitor is not acceptable, if any of the other documents are not available However, for students, a letter from the university along with a passport is adequate for identity.	Request the applicant to get any other evidence for proof of name, DoB and adress.

Registration – Procedures

Query	Details	Action Points
1. GMS 1	a. Surname (family name); b. Forename(s); c. Title; d. Date of Birth(DoB); e. **NHS**	Normal format – to be filled in by the patient/agent only – not

	Number (if available); f. Sex; g. Town and country of birth; h. Home full address and full post code; i. telephone numbers; **j. previous address in UK; k. previous GP**; l. date first came to UK. m. child under 5 years; n. signature of patient/ representative; o. date; p. GP's name; *q. HA code; r. practice stamp; s. person registering – initials/date*	by receptionists. **Bold format – optional.** *Italics – to be filled in by the receptionist registering the patient* To be filled in the surgery – applicant (representative if person less than 16) Note: writing must be clear, block capitals Family name is used in some countries instead of surname Date came to UK as **'ddmmyyyy'** – without date/month, no claim can be made. **Try to get an approximate date and month – CRUCIAL.**	
2. Checks	a. All details are filled in clearly by the applicant b. Patient list in the system – 1st letter of forename and 2 or 3 letters of surname. c. Patient name in the removal folder d. Patient previously denied approval – check in folder	Receptionist to insist proper completion for registration examination Receptionist to get the list (not the record) to ensure that the applicant has not previously registered and record closed and, if so, check for reasons. } Receptionist to inform nurse – not the applicant.	
3. Continuation Card	Surname; ii. Forename(s); iii. Full address; iv. NHS number; v. DoB; vi. Date	To be filled by Receptionist – **all BLOCK CAPITALS.** Male (red) and Female (blue) colour cards.	
4. Health Promot. Band 3 card	i. Surname; ii. Forename(s); iii. Full address; iv. NHS number; v. DoB; vi. Date	To be filled by Receptionist – **all BLOCK CAPITALS.** Male (red) and Female (blue)	

			colour cards.
5. Health Check	**All applicants over 5 years**		**Registration/claim not complete, if health check is not done by GP/nurse** *Receptionist to give the above forms to nurse/GP for health check*
6. GPs/Nurse	Health check of applicant and other details		Give health check appointments, preferably same day afternoon if applicant is not able to wait in the morning.
7. Registration approval	Receptionists may inform applicant when they call about approval in our list. Alternatively, send letter.		*Receptionist to collect by 11.30 AM on reg., days the records from GP/nurses* **Receptionist – register patient in the computer and return notes to nurse**
8. Registration declined	Send letter to the applicant within 48 hours confirming refusal – no reasons to be given		Receptionist **should not give reasons** when asked by the applicant over the telephone or requests in person – **give only HA tel. no. 020 8272 5500**
9. Record envelope	For applicant accepted as patient only		Receptionist to fill details in the envelope and place the continuation card and health promotion band 3 card in the envelope and give to nurse within 24 hrs. Receptionist to file GMS1 form in folder for future reference
	For applicant refused as patient		Receptionist to file GMS1 form in folder for future reference
10. Health check data	Nurse to input data in the computer system within 36 hours of receipt of record envelope from the receptionist		Without the health check data the payment for claim by HA will not be made Give the record back to receptionist for making claim
11. For making claim for registration	Receptionist should then make IoS (item of service) claim via computer		Fill in GMS 4 (green) form and tick 'registration' – only registration details for 10 patients to be filled and then given to IT supervisor. No other services to be mixed. Do not fill

		GMS 4 form, if health check is not done.
12. For making claim for contraceptive	Nurse should fill in GMS 4 form and tick 'Contraceptive Services' max 10 in the form – advice to 16-60 yr females	Nurse to give to IT supervisor when form is complete with 10 patients' details – all for contraceptive services. Also, to record advice given in notes/computer

Payment from HA only if advice given is not recorded in notes or comp. |
| 13. GMS 4 forms | For registration and contraceptive services to be given to IT supervisor by the receptionist and nurse respectively | These forms should be sent as soon as the 10 patients' details are completed. Delay will mean late payment by HA. **No backlog of work to be kept.** |
| 14. Data entry in computer | Check all spellings, forenames, middle names and surnames, date of birth, street number and name, post code etc.

Receptionist should be extra cautious – check and correct errors in typing/transcription before transmitting data to HA. | Receptionists should exercise greater care in 1st time data entry as any error would mean registering the patient with wrong details; also, correction of data would result in two or three entries for the same patient.

Check all details before data transmission to HA.

For errors spotted after transmission, correct it only after getting approval from IT Supervisor. |
| 15. Approval by HA | Usually within 3-4 working days. | For any delays, IT supervisor to contact HA and retransmit, if necessary. |
| 16. **Temporary Services** | GMS 3 form – fill in the details with two addresses

INT, <15 days or >15 days as appropriate. | Claim cannot be made without two addresses. If the person cannot give two addresses then ask him/her to go walk-in centre in NMH. **Do not compromise** |
| 17. Data input | Enter the details in the computer prior to sending the person to the GP indicating nature of Temporary Services | Crucial so that GP can enter details in the system and any prescription he may prescribe to the person. The data input should not be delayed by |

	treatment – INT, <15 days or more than 15 days	receptionist – after the GP sees the patient – as examination records will not be in the system.

Registration – Telephone/Direct Communication

Query	Details	Action Points
1	We have been waiting since 8 AM and want to register this morning	Register them, if possible. If nurse is too busy, then request them to come in the afternoon for Health checks so that GMS 1 is filled in.
2	We cannot come for health check this afternoon	Then say politely that we like to do the form filling and health check on the day and when they come next, we will register them. Inform about our registration dates and times.
3	I want my child to be registered here but I am with another GP	Tell them politely that it is our policy and in the long-term interest of the family both mother and children should be registered in the same practice. Decline.
4	I am registered in LL or HR but my child to be registered at HR or LL respectively	Politely decline and should go to the other surgery for registration.
5	I do not have any papers except solicitor's letter	Say politely that we will register only when we have the proof of identity and once they bring those we will proceed.
6	The applicant is abusive, uses 'expletives' and is violent	Say politely that as he/she has a right to choose GPs, GPs have a right to decide on registration of applicant. His approach will prevent such registration.
7	I will complain to HA about this surgery	Say politely that the HA number is 020 8272 5500

8	If a person is abusive etc. and wants another one to be registered (not himself)	Politely ask him whether he is a patient of this surgery. If not, ask him politely the age of person he wants registered and if they are related.
		If under 16 and not related, then request letter of consent form the parents so that he can act as the person's representative.
		If the applicant is over 16 then politely tell him that you would like to talk to the applicant directly.
		If the applicant is not able to speak English, then go through the GMS 1 and inform the nurse about the problems of communications etc.
9	If a person's record is closed for reasons other than 'Return undelivered' and he is causing problems	Go through GMS 1 and inform nurse of the problems.
		Avoid arguments and minimise problem situations.
10	if a person's record is closed for 'return undelivered'	Fill in GMS 1 and health check etc.
11	A person wants GP appointment and registration on the same day.	Tell him/her that appointment can only be given after acceptance of registration Ask him/her to proceed to walk-in centre in NMH

Registration – Crisis Situations

Query	Details	Action Points
1	Applicant violent	Inform senior receptionist and manager; if not IT supervisor; if not GP. Call 999 and seek police help. Deal with calmness and firmness. Do not or show panic.
2	Too many to register and	Deal calmly. Give afternoon or next day appointments. Split

	applicants impatient	morning GMS 1 and afternoon health check appointments. Confirm with nurse on actions.
3	Nurse not available but applicants turned up!	Speak to nurse in the other surgery and confirm time for visit to this surgery. Explain with politeness the problems and alternative arrangement being made. If they are not willing to come, request GPs whether they can do the health checks. If the applicants are willing, give appointments when nurse is due back.
4	Person abusive about application being rejected.	Inform him/her politely that just as he/she has the right to choose any GP, GP has the right to decline an application without the need to give specific reason. Advise him/her to contact HA 020 8272 5500 for any complaints.
5	I do not have any papers except solicitor's letter	Say politely that we will register only when we have the proof of identity and once they bring those we will proceed
6	Person wants to complain to the manager	Inform senior receptionist to deal with the patient. As he is not our patient, complaints procedures do not apply. He has to be politely told to register with another GP and manager will tell the same. Contact HA 020 8373 5500.
Receptionists	– See Computer Manual for Registration	Re-Registration and Temporary Services data input and IoS claims

Receptionists – see Computer Manual for Registration, Re-Registration and Temporary Services data input and IoS claims.

Receptionist should deal with above procedures confidently; deal with patients/applicants calmly even when provoked; complete registration details each when provoked; complete registration details each morning and give GMS 4 forms duly completed to IT supervisor; should not keep any back-log of registration. Make minimum reference to Senior Receptionist or the IT Supervisor or the Practice Manager. Refer to them only in exceptional circumstances. If this manual has to be improved, give details to the Practice Manager 'ASAP'.

2.7.4 Complaints

If one disagrees with the way the GP wants to treat one's health problem, or is unhappy about the service provided by the GP practice, tell them openly. However, if one is unable to do so or is unhappy with the response received, then one may wish to make a complaint. All GP practices have a written complaints procedure. This can be found at the reception or on the practice website. As a first step, speak to the PMgr. One can also complain to the practice in writing or by email. If this doesn't resolve the problem, or one would rather not raise the issue directly with the practice, one can complain to the local primary care trust (PCT).

2.7.5 Miscellaneous

A GP may be able to remove you from the patient register in some situations, for example, because you move out of the practice area or are physically or verbally abusive to people at the practice. In most cases, the GP must have given you a warning, and provided you with the reasons for your removal from the register.

The GP will inform the Primary Care Trust (PCT) who then notifies you. The removal from the register takes effect from the eighth day after the PCT receives the GP's notice, or from the date that you are included on another register if this is sooner.

You are entitled to emergency treatment, or the continuation of treatment, which is occurring more than once a week, until you are accepted by another GP.

If you have been violent, or have threatened to be violent, towards your GP or practice staff, and the police have been informed, you can be removed immediately from the GP's list. You will only be accepted for emergency treatment by the GP who has removed you, if the GP is satisfied that it is clinically necessary. It is prudent of the PMgr to produce a weekly report on status of registrations.

The report used as weekly report to the GPs on various areas are attached (See 2.7.5a):

This is self-explanatory and the computer system may generate these now. If not, it is useful to have such a control document for the surgery.

2.7.5a Weekly Status of Registration, Prescriptions, letter/report/results filing etc.

Month:

DETAILS	NOTE	MONDAY	TUESDAY	WEDNESDAY	THURSDAY	FRIDAY	TOTAL
DATE:							
REGISTRATION: (NUMBERS)							
- APPLICATIONS MADE	1						
- HEALTH CHECKS GIVEN	2						
- HEALTH CHECKS DUE	3						
- APPROVED BY GP/PN	4						
- ENTERED IN COMPUTER	5						
- NOT ENTERED IN COMPUTER	6						
- REFUSED /REJECTED	7						
- REFUSAL LETTER SENT	8						
PRESCRIPTIONS : (NUMBERS)							
- REQUESTED FROM PHARM.	9						
- PRESCRIPTIO	10						

NS TO PHARM.								
DEDUCTIONS: (NUMBERS)								
- PATIENTS REMOVED BY HA	11							
- NOTES SENT BACK TO BANDELE	12							
PATIENT LIST: (NUMBERS)								
- NUMBER GAINED/LOSS								
DAILY FILING OF LETTERS (YES OR NO)	13							
BACK LOG OF LETTERS IN DAYS	14							

Note:

1. No. seeking registration – no limit per day
2. Health check same day by PN – GPs 2 per session, if PN not available
3. Do not delay health check as it affects payment and may also be forgotten.
4. Get verbal clearance from PN/GP before giving appointment, entering in computer etc.
5. Always enter in computer by 12.15 PM each day for approved applicants.
6. Reasons for not entering in computer along with the number.
7. File application forms GMS1 in folder for future reference.
8. Send letters same day for such applicants without stating reason.
9. Requested by receptionists to Pharmacists – should be 'nil'. Always issue prescriptions first.
10. Do not delay more than 72 hours, if prescription has to be issued after supply of medicine.

'9' and '10' – not recommended to have any value. Preferred '0' for both.

11. Take out the notes and close the record after talking to Mr. Omotesho (except Ret. Under.)
12. Send the notes promptly to Mr. Omotesho

13. Daily filing of letters – letters, results, hospital reports received on the day to be files same day.
14. Back log of filing of letters in days to be indicated – expected value '0'.

2.8 Prescriptions

2.8.1 Procedures

Prescriptions are issued in three ways:

In a GP surgery by GPs only and no one else for:
- Acute – one-off drugs – first time prescribed or for antibiotics.
- Repeats – of previously prescribed by the GP and can be issued without the need to see the GP; however, some surgeries may stipulate 4-6 as maximum repeats, after which the patient has to see the GP. Repeats are prepared by the receptionists and signed by the GP; sometimes a GP may give repeats on seeing the patient in the surgery during a routine appointment.
- In a hospital by a consultant to the patient – this has to be included in the list of items to prescribe from them to the patient in the GP surgery.

Acute Prescriptions by the GPs and prescriptions in the hospital by the consultants are issued by very capable clinical persons and are not covered here.

The basic procedures for repeats are as below:

48 hours' notice is usually required for a repeat prescription to be issued. The prescription will normally be ready within 2 working days after requesting it; however, it is not uncommon to see these issued earlier than 48 hours, depending on the medication and urgency.

All requests for repeat prescriptions should be made using the right-hand portion of the slip issued with your last prescriptions.

All other written requests include:
- Name and address
- Name of medicines, dosage and frequency
- Date last supplied
- Contact phone number
- Name of GP

Telephone requests not to be accepted.

Fax requests to surgery fax number would be allowed.

Online requests could be made on the surgery website.

Postal requests, with a stamped addressed envelope; please allow for extra time for prescription to be returned.

Requesting a pharmacy from the surgery would be advised as these can be collected on late evenings and Saturdays when the surgery would be closed.

Only request items that are needed. This avoids waste of medicines and unnecessary medicines lying around the house. However, one should not intentionally stop taking a prescribed medication without a GP's approval.

All prescriptions are reviewed on a regular basis, with or without the patient's presence. There may be a review date at the bottom of the prescriptions.

For going away on a holiday, or for ordering more medication than normal, specific reasons need to be given for such a request. A GP is not obliged to give more than 3 months' supply at any one time and this too only in exceptional circumstances.

Apart from the patients, carer, District Nurse, pharmacist and care home staff may request repeats and in those cases it is crucial to maintain confidentiality, accuracy of medication information and guarantee probity.

Collection of repeats as well as acute prescriptions:

The procedures to follow after the GPs have signed and sent to reception, are:

- Keep the signed prescriptions in a secure place not visible to the public.
- Check the name, address and date of birth with the person collecting the prescription to ensure the correct identity of the patient.
- Signed consent from patient for collection by a pharmacy would mean handing over these to the pharmacist's representative
- Collection by underage or unauthorised persons without a written request should be refused.
- Prescriptions not collected for over 2-3 weeks should be highlighted and even destroyed and issue deleted from patient records.

2.8.2 Training for Doing Prescriptions

It is crucial for surgeries to give the utmost importance to the issue of prescriptions. The person doing the repeat prescriptions should be very well trained, supervised, checked and re-checked before the person is allowed to prepare repeats. There are certain procedures and training time needs to be followed sanctimoniously.

The dedicated receptionist should be working in the surgery for a period of 3 months before initial training is contemplated for repeats.

- The preparation of repeats must always be using the computer system and set up to generate counterfoils.
- The significance of checking the name, middle name and surname of the person before starting to prepare the repeats must be stressed. This is especially so if requests are made in writing, fax or online. Use of counterfoil would simplify this enormously and avoid errors.
- The significance of sticking only to the previously prescribed medicines, dosage and frequency should also to be stressed. If the request contains a new medicine, branded version instead of generic prescribed hitherto, new dosage or any variant, then the receptionist should not prepare the repeats and refer the issue to the Senior Receptionist for clarification and action.
- The receptionists should always have BNF book while preparing the repeats (MIMS should not to be used except to refer to it for pricing information).
- Never to take instructions over the telephone from the patient or his family or representative about repeats. The procedure stated above – 'Telephone requests not accepted' – should be rigidly followed.
- The trained receptionists should be taught how to prepare repeats; once the Senior Receptionist or PMgr is satisfied in the first instance about the accuracy and the skill of the receptionist then they should allow her a trial of 10 repeats to prepare, with BNF for reference.
- Once the trail batch is correctly prepared, accuracy is more important than speed, and checked, the receptionist could be asked to do repeats but SR or PMgr should check for the first 8-10 days, and only then forward to the GPs to sign.
- Prescription is an important aspect of a GP surgery and any errors can result in tragic results affecting a GP's career. Hence, receptionist training is very important.
- Use of BNF is recommended because it would explain the details of the medication. Initially they may not seem very relevant; however, repeat is not a copying exercise alone from the counterfoil medications. For the long term, this knowledge gained by BNF referral would be of great advantage to the receptionist, the surgery and GPs.
- Items not suitable for generic prescribing.
- Some drugs should be prescribed by BRAND name – not by GENERIC name due to differences in product formulations.
- Items not suitable as repeat medication – acute.
- Controlled Drug Prescriptions.

A prescription for Schedule 2 and 3 CDs (with the exception of temazepam and preparations containing it) must contain certain details and receptionist must follow surgery procedures.

2.8.3 Do's and Don'ts

Dos – always ensure:

1. That the prescription required to be given has already been prescribed to the patient by checking the records/hospital notes.
2. The dosage, quantity and frequency are similar to those previously prescribed.
3. That the patient has to wait 48 hours (2 working days) before the prescription can be issued.
4. That the patient is also made aware that if the medicine has not been prescribed during the previous three months then the patient has to be seen by the doctor before medication can be given.

Don'ts – issue prescriptions – (seek GP's advice)

- If the drug(s) has not been prescribed previously.
- If the dosage or quantity or frequency is not clear.
- If the drug has not been prescribed in the previous three months.
- If it is 'branded' drug (opt for 'generic' variety).
- If it is not available in NHS.
- If the drug is prohibitively expensive.
- If it is an 'Acute' drug – one off treatment which is not a repeat e.g. antibiotics.

i) New:

GPs to give prescriptions for any new drug not prescribed before.

If it is recommended by the hospital following a referral – then receptionist can issue prescriptions.

If the hospital recommends a drug, for example 30 mg for 30 days and then reduce to 20 mg for 30 days, do not, repeat do not, issue two prescriptions, one with 30 mg and one with 20 mg at the same time.

The patient might take 50 mg each day, leading to disastrous results.

Issue 30 mg prescription for 30 days and then ask the patient to come and collect 20 mg prescription after 30 days.

ii) Acute:

These are one-off drugs (not repeats) and should be given only by a GP – never by receptionists.

2.8.4 Branded and Generics

The following is a list of some common drugs and their well-known brand names – usually the original patent-holder's name (See 2.8.4a).

Note that generic names are normally written with a lower case initial letter. Brand names are capitalised.

There are various publications giving extensive lists of branded and generic drugs. Many branded drugs are also available 'generically'. These are chemically identical drugs produced by manufacturers who specialise in unbranded products.

Doctors have been encouraged to prescribe generic versions where these exist in an attempt to control costs. Unbranded versions of non-prescription products – such as common painkillers – can also be bought, often at much lower prices than the equivalent brands. Although the packaging and tablet size, shape and colour may differ, the active ingredient is identical.

2.8.4a Generics and Branded Drugs Prescribing

The following is a list of some common drugs and their well-known brand names – usually the original patent-holder's name. Note that generic names are normally written with a lower case initial letter. Brand names are capitalised.

Generic name:	Well-known brand name:	Used for:
salbutamol	Ventolin	(asthma inhaler)
fluoxetine	Prozac	(antidepressant)
sildenafil	Viagra	(impotence)
diclofenac	Voltarol	(non-steroidal anti-inflammatory drug)
enalapril	Innovace	(ACE inhibitor for heart failure and high blood pressure)
loratadine	Claritin	(antihistamine for allergy)
propranolol	Inderal	(beta-blocker for blood pressure)
paracetamol	Panadol	(painkiller)
ibuprofen	Nurofen	(painkiller)

Many branded drugs are also available 'generically'. These are chemically identical drugs produced by manufacturers who specialise in unbranded products. Doctors have been encouraged to prescribe generic versions where these exist in an attempt to control costs. Unbranded versions of non-prescription products – such as common painkillers – can also be bought, often at much lower prices than the equivalent brands. Although the packaging and tablet size, shape and colour may differ, the active ingredient is identical.

2.8.5 Pharmacists

A number of very large practices have employed a practice pharmacist, although the majority of practices will rely on the expertise of PCT medicines management pharmacists or those employed by practice based commissioning (PBC) groups. The practice pharmacist may also have a prescribing qualification, which adds significant scope and flexibility to their role.

The practice pharmacist would undertake many duties including:

- Preparing practice formulary
- NICE guidance interpretation and implementation within the practice
- Repeat prescription review
- Clinical audits and associated recommendations
- Clinical switching programmes
- Patient medication review
- Clinics for long-term conditions.

2.8.6 Complaints

The majority of complaints would be about not giving the repeats within 48 hours and in some instances sooner than 48 hours as the patient has run out of medication.

However, it is the few complaints, which usually are very serious. These would invariably pertain to wrong dosage and wrong medication due to misreading the name of the patient. These can lead to serious side effects and even end with the GP facing 'Fitness to Practice' investigations.

If the surgery has a healthy rapport with the local pharmacies, generally the pharmacists will be able to stop issuing the medicine and get these corrected without the patient knowing. If the pharmacist is away, then the error would be precipitated and lead to serious consequences.

The practice has to be very vigilant when it comes to issue of repeat prescriptions.

2.8.7 Miscellaneous

i. There are several procedures involved in prescribing and these are too detailed to include; generally each surgery would have methodology for each; if not, the PMgr should make it a point to have instruction for each of these to assist the GP, nurses and staff:

- Management Control
- Authorisation
- Compliance check
- Flagging of problems
- Hospital Discharge Medication/Outpatient attendance/Home Visits
- Hospital communications
- Patient information
- Quality assurance
- Clinical controls – Review of medication
- Specific patient groups
- Domiciliary visits
- Electronic Prescription Service (EPS) is a new service that will make it easier for GPs to issue prescriptions and more convenient for patients to collect their medicines. Using EPS means that prescriptions by GPs and other prescribers will be transferred electronically to the pharmacist nominated by the patient. The prescriptions will also be sent automatically to the Prescription Pricing Authority.

ii. All practices must have good control of prescription costs and on the amount of acute prescriptions to repeats. Both clinical and management controls should be in place to control costs:

- Conduct an audit to prescriptions issued – acute and repeats
- Recall patients over 6/12 monthly intervals for determining over and under use of medicines
- Find out any medication they no longer require
- GPs have to ensure the repeat prescription is appropriate and the drug is effective
- Have procedures for recently discharged patients from hospitals using their hospital care plan
- Have procedures for medications for newly registered patients
- Review procedures for certain long-standing medications.
- Procedures for changes to medication when a hospital letter is received.

2.9 Practice Manager

Practice Manager (PMgr) duties and responsibilities are quite substantial and their attitude, rather than their aptitude, dictates the effective performance of the surgery.

The blogs list varied aspects of surgery management and it is implied that the PMgr duties and responsibilities can be culled from the various sections. The PMgr is the administrative 'supremo' and should make sure even inadvertently, areas into clinical fields are not encroached, leaving this to GPs, nurses and Healthcare Professionals.

In some larger practices this role may be split across the two roles of a business manager and an administrative manager:

- The business manager is often responsible for providing financial and business advice to the partners for the development and implementation of the practice corporate strategy.
- The practice (administration) manager's role in such surgeries can include a wide variety of functions depending on the staffing structure of the practice. This role will be responsible for the management of practice staff, patient liaison and daily operations within the practice. They are usually the first point of contact for anything relating to the management of the GP contract and QOF, prescription management and IT functionality for the practice.

2.9.1 Daily Tasks

The PMgr role is one of planning, problem solving, decision making, coordinating, organising, controlling, measuring, researching (of information on all aspects of surgery operation), patient records, training notes, statutory information e.g. health and safety, personnel records, clinical, prescribing, equipment, PCT financing, GP contracts, patient literature and advice, disciplinary and complaints procedures, statistical information on patients etc.

It is better to break this down into components as laid out in sections below:

2.9.2 Training

List of areas to cover for Practice Manager Training:

These are the entire details in the eBook but for initial exposure only the headings are given:

Reception	Registration	Prescriptions	Telephone/ Communications
Appointments	Staff Rota	GP Rota	Computer system/ IMT
Immunisations	Protocols	Medical Secretary	QOF/Claims
Discipline	Complaints	Medicines	Fax/Scanner
Payroll	PBC	Healthcare Specialists	Reports
Referrals	Audits	Practice Booklets	Data storage/ Security
Job Appraisals	Accounts	Recruitment	Copyright laws
GPs	Nurses	PCT/Others	Forms

All the above areas have been covered in the eBook.

Usually a surgery would expect a trained person, nowadays a suitably qualified person in surgery management, to become a PMgr. However, people from other industries have entered the profession due to their skills in man-management, HR, finance, etc.

In most cases, the actual training of a PMgr in the surgery is non-existent as GPs are too busy to do any structured training. There are courses offered by PCT from time to time but the surgery would expect the PMgr to perform 'from the date of joining'. Hence, a PMgr should be a self-motivated person and able to grasp things by observation, previous notes, talking to the nurses, HCA, SR and others in the PCT about various issues. He must also search the web for information on various issues and become aware of the various aspects of surgery management. He should aim to be the right-hand person for the partners within 2-3 months of joining the surgery.

2.9.3 Care Quality Commission (CQC) (see Section 20.2)

From July this year the race begins for practices to register with the Care Quality Commission (CQC), the independent regulator of all health and adult social care in England.

This registration should have been completed by 1 April 2013, when new legislation will come into force requiring providers, whose sole or main purpose is, for NHS primary medical services to register with the CQC.

This includes those providers of General Medical Services (GMS), Personal Medical

Services (PMS) and Alternative Provider Medical Services (APMS). Regulations require practices to register as an individual, a partnership or an organisation.

As part of the process practices will also be required to adhere to a set of essential quality standards, which will be continuously monitored.

It seems very likely that the CQC will consider a well-documented programme of mandatory training to be a basic requirement for practices. To demonstrate compliance with CQC Outcome 14, Regulation 23, practices would need to demonstrate that staff is competent to carry out their work and are properly trained, supervised and appraised.

Practices may wish to keep a simple spreadsheet record of staff training – where the cells in the spreadsheet contain the date on which each named employee last had training in a particular mandatory topic.

2.9.4 Rota – GPs, Receptionists

The PMgr should aim to give a monthly rota, of GPs, nurses, HCA, clinics and receptionists, at least one week prior to the beginning of the following month. The PMgr should have in the Annual Planner the holidays and special days booked by GPs, nurses and other staff.

The rota should indicate all the morning and evening surgeries, clinics and any late evening meetings for the patients, e.g. Patient Participation Group was formed to discuss issues with the patients.

This advance notification is for GPs, nurses and staff to check their availability and suggest any changes. Once agreed upon, the rota is final for the month and the surgery should operate like clockwork.

In the event of any sudden illness or absenteeism, the Senior Receptionist (SR) should make quick adjustments to the rota, so that the surgery operation and effectiveness is not compromised.

When a GP is unfortunately absent, then the patients booked should be shared with the other GPs in the practice. All patients should be given the option to have a late appointment or make new ones, if they want to see that particular GP.

2.9.5 Healthcare Professionals

The role of the HCA can vary depending on the number of services provided by practice nurses. They often provide assistance to nurses, as well as undertaking routine tasks such as phlebotomy, chaperoning and taking patient blood pressure and weight measurements for long-term conditions clinics. See Section 21 for further details.

2.9.6 Practice

The whole write-up for the eBook is about the surgery practice and this is laid out in several sections. One key issue that will be dealt here is the creation and maintenance of a website for the surgery. A good IMT specialist should be able to design a web page for the surgery, otherwise the designs are available from external specialists at a modest cost. (www.mysurgerywebsite.co.uk/).

The IMT specialist has to maintain it and the site should be most useful for patients and others in the area.

The site should layout the following:

Opening hours, appointments, prescriptions (including repeats), clinics & services, policies, practice staff, new patients, feedback and contact details for the surgery, NHS111, walk-in centres, PCT/CCGs, hospitals, etc.

The website should be regularly updated so that people accessing it will have confidence in the information provided by the site.

2.9.7 Complaints

If you disagree with the way your GP wants to treat you, or you're unhappy about the service provided by your GP surgery, tell them openly. However, if you feel unable to do so or you're unhappy with the response you receive, you may wish to make a complaint.

All GP surgeries should have a written complaints procedure, and you will find this at reception or on the practice website.

As a first step, speak to the practice manager. You can also complain to the practice in writing, or by email.

If this doesn't resolve the problem, or you'd rather not raise the issue directly with the practice, you can complain to the local primary care trust (PCT).

Find out more about how to complain in the NHS.

The Practice Manager should have, in the surgery folders, one folder for Complaints Procedures – a lengthy documents running to several pages with several forms to be completed in terms of a complaint. A similar copy should also be in the reception area for senior receptionist to refer and advise receptionists.

The practice manager should record the complaint in paper (not the form) and assure the person that his/her comments would be discussed with the GP partners in the next few hours and would try to seek an amicable solution.

If the complaint is of a serious nature involving a nurse, HCA or GP, then attempts could be made to fix a meeting with them for discussion. Should the person not be satisfied and want to fill in a complaint form, then the form should be given to the person to fill it. Trying to help in filling the form might go a long way towards toning down the person's strong wordings in the form. Generally strong wordings would be magnified when PCT Complaints Manager gets a copy.

It is prudent of the PMgr to sound the PCT complaints manager.

2.9.8 Meetings

The Practice Manager has to organise monthly meetings with all GPs, nurses, HCAs and staff. Usually it should be on the day when surgery has afternoon off e.g. Wednesday or Thursday afternoon when the surgery is closed. If there are two surgeries under on practice, then staff from both surgeries should attend.

Meetings should be reasonably formal and everyone should be allowed to express their opinion. This is a forum for the staff, especially the junior staff, to speak and make their views heard. GPs and Practice Manager (PMgr) should not take over the proceedings and turn it into a **'tell'** and not a **'listening'** meeting. The concept is 'all points expressed are useful' and 'none to be dismissed'. Only then would the staff participate fully and effectively. They must be made to realise that they are also part of the team and their contribution counts, as they might know more about the 'pulse of the patients' and what makes them do certain things.

Understanding these and being sensitive would make the meetings very productive. This should be a forum where the staff can see the GPs close by, talk to them, and listen to GPs' views expressed openly to the staff directly.

Everyone should treat the meeting as an important event and they should desist from lengthy explanations and anecdotes. Points should be crisp and succinct. It is better to write down what one wants to say so that errors will be less. All staff should come with a pad and pen and not expect the PMgr to dish out these. It is an in-house meeting and everyone has to do his or her part. It is better to be a bit formal and aim to finish the meeting quickly and effectively than prolong it and waste half a day of earned holiday in the week.

The PMgr should circulate an agenda for the meeting well in advance to all and place a notice in the Reception Hall. The agenda should be specific and list areas to be covered. The start time and date are to be given. Any patient(s) invited to the meeting should also be mentioned. This invitation would be a strong PR exercise for the surgery in the **'eyes'** of the PCT about involvement of patients. It does have to be the same representatives coming for all meetings. The PMgr should vary the representation for each meeting.

The format of a succinct report for the monthly meeting is attached (see 2.9.8a).

2.9.8a Continuous Practice Development

Practice Stamp	Purpose of Meeting; Monthly	Date:		
Subject	Relevant Details	Decision	Target Date	Comments
			Action by? Initials	
1. CHD	Visit by PCT –	use templates provided monthly monitoring	from date	
2. Appointment system	Normal surgery + Emergency	5 + all patients before 11 AM surgeries 5 + all patients before 5.30/6.30PM surgery as at present – surgery (NO change)	from date Receptionists	
3. PPA expenses	Overspending years	Monitor drug prescription and expenses	all GPs – from date	
4. R/U mail and records closed	over 500 records closed/R/U	Fill in form provided as record for surgery	from date	Imm. Neces. Claims and re-registration
5/6. Computer Training + Clinic Templates	Computer use not made by some GPs	GPs to have individual training with IT specialist; record all surgery visits by patients	from date all GPs; BO	
7. Post-Natal/CHS clinics	balanced use of P/N times in both surgeries	alternate week clinics in 2 surgeries	from date	surgery patients circular to inform patients

8. Registrations	HA deducted about … patients	extra sessions for registrations in HR/LL	from date	circular to inform patients
9. Clinic Appointments	single ailments of diabetes, CHD or Asthma	Respective clinics only	from date all GPs to follow the new clinic appointments	priority and hierarchy of ailments and appropriate clinic appointments
	Diabetes + Multiple ailments including CHD and Asthma	Diabetes clinic only		
	CHD + multiple ailments – NO diabetes	CHD clinic only		
	Asthma + multiple ailments – NO CHD or Diabetes	Asthma Clinic only		

Previously there used to be Patient Participation Group one evening in 2-3 months but as this involved a willing volunteer from the patient group and active work to arrange the meetings etc., these groups no longer exist. It would be always preferable to resurrect such groups, if possible.

These sorts of group lift the profile of the surgery and would significantly reduce complaints against the surgery. It is also recommended that one person chairs the meeting for that time and even junior can be given opportunity to be the 'Chair'. Rotation of people to chair the meeting would be good for staff morale and make them think laterally about their jobs and commitments.

A typical agenda to be circulated may be like this, depending on the issues to be important at that time –

Meeting to be held on date, month, year, day and time from and to.

The topics to be covered:

Actions arising from previous meeting.

Asthma

Appointment System

Computer training and clinical templates

Post and Antenatal clinics

Registrations

R/U (returned undelivered) mail and records closed

ANother (any other)

These meetings form the basis for Continuous Practice Development. The purpose of the meeting has to be clearly defined. Meetings should start on time. Introduce patient representatives, who have been requested to attend the meeting. Deal with each topic effectively. It is preferable for staff to organise and collect their views beforehand and they can nominate within themselves, who would address a particular issue. This prevents lot of people saying the same thing. Also, such organising means it is no longer an individual issue but a collective one. GPs should not 'bulldoze' ideas or opinions but give a patient an encouraging hearing. They have to exhibit the 'listening' side of them when they are normally perceived as having a 'telling' side to them.

Patient representatives should be given a chance to express their opinions and if required actions. Then when those actions are completed later, these representatives should be informed of the results of the actions via mobile phone calls and recorded in the next month's meeting minutes.

When the meeting is duly finished, the PMgr should do the minutes of the meeting by next day and circulate it. It should be a one-page format, printed laterally, split into sections, for example:

Horizontal axis:

Date; Chairman Name; PCT Visitor's name (if applicable).

Subject; Relevant details; Decision; Target Date; Comments; Action by; Initials.

Vertical axis: (list key issues discussed)

CHD; Use PCT Template (if applicable).

Monitoring issues; Registration shortfall; R/U patients list; any backlog of work.

2.9.9 Backlog

With all the best intentions in the world, a PMgr will periodically find a considerable backlog of issues that need to be dealt with in the practice and at the same time would need to keep abreast of new developments and the increased paperwork generated. A good PMgr should identify the priorities for the practice.

A typical list is attached with suggested backlog work (See 2.9.9a).

One of the suggested ways to tackle is to ask 4 questions (applies to all aspects in life – education, career, job change, place change, etc.):

Where am I now? Identify backlogs, shortage of staff and skill levels, finance etc.

Where do I want to be? Set a date, say, a month ahead; target reduce backlog by 80%; GPs seeing all patients in clinical list; aim 95%QOF

What are the ways of getting there? Various but getting funding for increased staff would be difficult in the short term.

What is the best way for me right now? Delegate and also involve yourself to motivate and speed up the work and set a good example for staff.

2.9.9a List of Things To Do

Re:	Details	By whom	Action by (date)	Comments
A	**Present Status:**			
A1	Surgery is working well except for 1 GP F/T vacancy			
A2	Contact HMRC…			
A3	Pension DD update when forms are sent			
B	**Locum GP:**			
B1	GP – as locum			
B2	Confirm split of F/T between Dr Curran and locum Evening C/Morning L or L doing F/T			
B3	Confirm with PCT on payments for 3 months and amounts			
B4	Locum GP to give details to complete form along with CV			
B5	Locum GP Training Schedule – M/Training 1st month			
B6	Form for Training assessment – form draft by M			
B7	Assessment of Locum GP data entry,			

	diagnosis etc.			
B8	GP-Job Specification, Description, Advert, Journals to advertise – M			
B9	GP Contract – short format – Temporary & Permanent			
B10	Locum GP Temporary contract for 1 month – draft by M			
C	**Partnership/GP Contracts:**			
C1	Contracts for GPs			
C2	Partnership application forms for GPs			
C3	Sessions, Hours, Clinics, Admin., on-call, home visits details along with Rates, NI, Pensions etc. – format by M			
C4	Contract format for F/T GP – Format by M			
C5	Correspondences with PCT/Partners			
C6	New Partnership Details			
C7	New Name for Surgery			
C8	Notification of New name to PCT by letter and start date			
D	**Salaries for GP, Nurse and Staff:**			
D1	Sessions & Rates for GP/Nurses; Hours & Rates – Reception			
D2	Salary Budget with hours and personnel			
E	**Payroll:**			
E1	Monthly payroll to ensure Net Pay always equals Autopay			
E2	P14 and P60 for all staff – by July 19th – late submission?			
E3	If late, inform HMRC reasons for delay to avoid penalty			
E4	Prepare Payroll Folder			

E5	Run Yearly data for P35 from Ferguson Payroll System			
E6	Give to staff and send forms to HMRC			
E7	P11D for staff earning more than £8500 p.a.			
E8	Electronic filing of Tax Return – Activation code etc. from HMRC			
F	**Reception Staff –**			
F1	Staff Job Descriptions – Reception, Sr. receptionists, PM			
F2	Time sheets, payroll NI, Tax code data from staff			
F3	Demonstration of filling Time sheets for one staff			
F4	Assessment and allocation of new roles			
F5	Decide Need for extra staff – PM/Receptionist			
G	**Recruitment of Staff – Receptionists, Sr. Rec. Nurses,:**			
G1	Job Description and Job Specification			
G2	Contract of Employment – existing and New recruits in future			
G3	Advertisement Format			
G4	Advertisement Agencies/Job Centre/Costs			
G5	Training Schedule for New reception staff			
G6	Monitoring of Progress of Reception Staff			
G7	Do's and Don'ts for Reception Staff			
J	**Job Appraisals:**			
J1	Appraisal Format			

J2	Appraisal of one Receptionist – model interview				
J3	Appraisal form for completion by all other receptionists				
J4	Appraisal of Sr. Receptionist – end of each year after appointment				
J5	Appraisal of Practice Manager				
J6	Appraisal of Nurse – end of each year after appointment				
J7	Appraisal of GPs – end of each year after appointment				
J8	Appraisal of GPs – by PCT as required				
K	**Accounts:**				
K1	Completion of year				
K2	Preparation of Folder for above accounts for Accountant				
K3	Completion of 4 months account – Apr-Jul year				
K4	Check List – details needed for completion of accounts				
L	**QOF Status monthly:**				
L1	Run Programme 3rd or 5th of month to have previous month's values				
L2	List size and capitation figures				
L3	Domain values and adjustments details				
L4	Check List of monthly forecast of performance figures				
L5	Child Immunisation Data vs actual performance				
L6	New Registration completion within 6 weeks				
L7	Comprehensive list for predictions & checking performance monthly				

M	Complaints:			
M1	Complaints procedures			
M2	Receptionists aware of procedures			
M3	Receptionists following procedures			
M4	Record of Complaints, response in time, folder for status			
M5	Record of verbal complaints and action points			
M6	Liaising with Complaints Manager in PCT			
N	Protocols:			
N1	List of Admin. Protocols and documentation access for each			
N2	List of Clinical Protocols and documentation access for each			
N3	Protocols for highly sensitive issues			

2.9.10 Miscellaneous

Most of the surgeries pay scant attention to Copyright Laws. It is common to see in some surgeries either playing music or have TV turned on for waiting patients. These contravene Copyright Laws. The Copyright and Patents Act 1988 outlines the principal legislation covering intellectual property rights in UK and the work to which it applies.

The Law gives the creators of literary, musical, artistic works, sound recordings, broadcasts, films and typographical arrangement of published editions, rights to control the ways in which their material may be used. The details are very clearly stated in the Law and it can be accessed in the website given. Copyright lasts between 70 to 125 years.

It is recommended that the Practice Manager contact the Copyright Licensing Agency for Music, PRS for Music. It is strongly recommended that the annual fee of around £ 100 – 150 be paid to conform to the laws and the Certificates displayed in Reception area.

2.9.11 Documents in Practice

There are several documents which should be readily available in the surgery for

GPs and everyone to refer to. These become more important if, due to any inadvertent reasons, the GPs have to follow remedial procedures, when PCT would make a big and pertinent issue of this omission in the surgery practice.

It is the Practice Manager's sole and key responsibility to ensure such omissions never occur.

The surgery should have for all staff including GPs, nurses, HCP, and receptionists etc. up-to-date:

- Job Specifications
- Job Descriptions
- Appointment Orders and Contracts of Employment
- Personal folders with job evaluations, salary increases, disciplinary details etc.
- Induction Programmes and training details for all staff
- Employment Rules, and Regulations and key Laws
- Pension plans under NHS schemes
- HMRC Tax/NI details
- Complaints Procedures
- Grievance Procedures
- Clinical Supervision
- Clinical Protocol List and individual folders for ready reference
- All other day-to-day operational contact details

2.9.12 Checklist of Policies

The policies for performance assessment – appraisal or otherwise – are in practice files. The Practice Manager helps the practitioners in getting any relevant information for such assessment and also does a checklist on areas to cover for the practitioner. All documents in forms of reports and results are given to the practitioner well in advance to prepare for such an assessment. Relevant staff know about the policies. Policies are reviewed yearly.

Policies regarding confidentiality are in place and are of utmost importance for the practitioner and for the practice. All are made aware of the policy at the time of joining the practice and issued raised periodically at the monthly meetings.

2.9.13 Pandemic Situations

An audit regarding surgical masks should be done at the outset of the crisis.

- In a pandemic situation, do you have sufficient surgical masks at your disposal at reception? Note down the quantities and order more if needed.
- Secondly, ensure there are facilities for patients to decontaminate their hands at reception/surgery.

2.9.14 Suggestions

There must be a suggestions box for all staff to input their ideas and there must be a monthly review of those suggestions by the PMgr, IMT specialist, Senior Receptionist, one receptionist, a nurse and a GP, all selected on rota basis to review the suggestions.

The staff must be encouraged to suggest around all aspects of surgery operations, within and outside the premises, dealing with persons within and outside the premises, any others they think would improve the performance, effectiveness morale, patient satisfaction, reduce complaints, reduce costs etc. No suggestion should be ridiculed and any not followed up must have a valid reason for doing so. The PMgr should thank the staff individually after the review meeting for their input and explain the committee decision in either following their suggestion or not doing so with reasons. Such interactions are a positive way to improve staff morale and should keep the staff feeling involved as they perceive that GPs and the PMgr care.

2.9.15 Psychological Issues for the PMgr to Know

Eye contact is a strong indicator of mood. More eye contact – positive mood; looking down or away from person – bad mood.

Familiarity breeds contempt is not true; it breeds fondness – just the opposite is true. The greater the exposure the more positive the response.

Maybe in magnetism 'opposites attract' – in the business world similarities seem to attract more.

Rapport creates trust, allowing one to build a psychological bridge.

Smile often – it encourages confidence, happiness, enthusiasm and most notably, acceptance.

First impressions are no doubt very important; equally with staff that are quite young working in a GP surgery, the PMgr should be aware that 'a book should not be judged by the cover'.

The PMgr should instil in staff that when an error is made, saying 'I am embarrassed' achieves three things – self-realisation that an error was made which was unacceptable, that the person is human and takes responsibility for it, and finally the person is honest.

One should be aware of manipulations by seniors or even peer groups – these include guilt, intimidation, appeal to ego, fear, curiosity, and one's desire to be liked and loved.

Use the Law of Inertia – people in motion tend to stay in motion; people at rest tend to stay at rest! The PMgr should also be aware that if he gives the staff a small task to complete easily, they are more likely to accept a big task. The PMgr should avoid asking staff to do a big job lest personality issues clash and work gets undone.

3. IMT

Information, Management and Technology (IMT)

Many practices now employ a dedicated IT manager to oversee the daily management of the IT infrastructure and functionality within practices. Some of the IT development programmes, within the practice, will be part of the wider NHS National Programme for IT (NPfIT), which includes:

- Choose and Book (C&B)
- GP to GP transfer of patients' records (GP2GP)
- Electronic Prescription Service (EPS)
- Summary Care Record (SCR).

The GP IMT systems offer a range of functions in addition to traditional appointment scheduling, clinical records and prescribing. GPs can use their systems to review QOF data, provide patient recall functions, run audits and reports, manage referrals and test requests, incorporate pathology test reports and in some cases, analyse referral and prescribing costs and trends within the practice.

The computer specialist dealing with Information and Management Systems (IMT) has a crucial role in a modern surgery. Since 2005, all data has been requested to be input onto computers, making the old system of paper records obsolete. These paper records have to be kept for reference to diagnosis and treatment in previous years and must **NEVER** be destroyed.

In earlier years, 2003, the computer system Torex Premier was Windows based. However, EMIS did not have a Windows-based system (using Function keys only), and still relied on manual computation for data for various reports. Since 2006 or so Torex Synergy, Vision and EMIS (now Windows based) have made significant strides in computations of data. Various reports were self-generated, highlighting areas to act on to reach the required targets and increase income for the surgery. Still, the amount of data generated was so much, that the IMT specialist's task was multiplied into other areas. He had to be very alert and methodical so that his tasks were completed on time and he could avoid a backlog.

With a lot of older GPs, who are used to paper records rather than computers, the change to use the latter is very difficult. The IMT specialist and the PMgr have to ascertain the basic issues involved in their reluctance to use the computers – technical, lack of training or time (10 min. appointments too short for data input or search for these GPs), delays etc., and try to address those issues initially. The new generation of younger GPs is well adept in the use of computers and the above issues do not exist.

3.1 Tasks

3.1 Tasks to Perform

There are several key tasks to be performed each day and these are as given below:

- Computers – check all systems are functioning well. If not, contact network assistance so that GPs and nurses are not affected during surgery hours.
- Pathlinks – results from the pathology laboratory are sent to the surgery via link and these are usually processed first thing in the morning, either by a trained receptionist or IMT specialist. Normal patient results are allocated to their records; highlighted ones – let the respective GP know so that they can check and take action during morning surgery when they switch on their computers. In severe cases, low levels set by the GPs, like cholesterol, if below 5, then a personal written note should be sent to the respective GP in addition to highlighting it on the computer.
- In a very small surgery – 2-3 GPs and about 4,000 patients – IMT specialist may be a previously experienced receptionist and he/she may do the following jobs. Also, she may also do some of the medical secretary's job. For a larger practice usually a trained receptionist would do these tasks and not an IMT specialist due to other work priorities: opening mail – sorting out insurance letters, DSS forms, solicitor letters etc.
- Ask other receptionists to get patients' records to GP, nurses and healthcare specialists' rooms before surgery starts.
- Ensure the solicitors, private patients pay the fees before work is commenced. Correspond with them for payment of fees ASAP. Also, keep record of all cash and cheque payments.
- Keep logbook entry of dates received, dates processed, dates paid, dates collected by patients etc.

A typical list of tasks is given with estimated duration for completion. These can be modified to suit current needs.

See Table 3.1a for tasks.

3.1a Details of IMT Tasks

Re	Task	Details	Duration (h;m)	Comments
1	Computers	Check all systems are okay; otherwise contact network assistance	2m	Longer, if problem.
2	Pathlinks	1st job of the day; allocate normal result patients' details to their records; highlighted ones – let GP know so that they can check during morning surgery	30m	
3	Information & management	Includes areas covered below		
4a	Open mail	Sort out insurance letters, DSS forms, solicitors' letters…	25m	
4b	For GP actions	Ask receptionists to get records for above for GPs		
4c	Ensure fees paid	Send letters to solicitors, private patients for fees before work is commenced; keep record of cash payments		
4d	log book entry	for dates recd; dates processed; dates collected etc.		
5a	Patient registrations	Only when problem pertaining to computer arises on patients registered by receptionists	5a-5e ~ 30m/wk	
5b	Patient transfers	To other surgeries		

5c	Patient deductions	When requested by PCT via link		
5d	Patient amendments	To original data given at the time of registration		
5e	Change of details	To existing patients – names, date of birth due to incorrect entries, address change etc.		
6	Referrals	Varies but typically 2h/day max	2h/day	
7	Training	of Receptionists, Nurses, HCA and GPs of the system		
8	Summarising	of new registered patients ~ 7/week; within 3 weeks.	~ 20m/day	
9	Scanning	~ 20 documents/day; Mondays more, other days – less	~ 1 h	
10	Receptionist Rota	Prepare monthly; prepare a week before the next month	30m/mo	
11	Healthcall	Check monthly report and highlight any issues to GP	15m/mo	
12	Complaints	Deal with complaints and involve GPs as appropriate	30m/wk	
13	QMAS audits:			
13a	Monthly	New Disease Register data – QMAS uploads – 8th of month	30m/mo	
13b	Monthly	Check patients seen from list of patients; invite patients …	30m/mo	
13c	Quarterly	Enhanced Services Report	60m/mo	
13d	Quarterly	PBC report	60m/mo	
14	Liaise – PCT/EMIS	PCT – registrations, list sizes, deductions, counts, waiting for approvals, acknowledgements etc. EMIS – As required on		As need arises.

		software problems or use of PCS		
15	Data storage & security	Ensure that each week's data storage tape is stored outside the surgery in case of fire, theft etc. Check with EMIS		
16	Report Searches	as required	1h/mo	
17	Ordering of supplies for communication equipment	Includes, telephones, faxes, printers, scanners – toners, papers etc.	30m/mo	
18	Any other		2h/mo	

Patient details:

• Patient registrations when problems arise due to computer entry faults on patients registered by the receptionists.
• Patient transfers – to other surgeries
• Patient deductions – when requested by PCT via link. However, if the patient is known to have not come to the surgery for a while but is still a surgery patient, then notify PCT without deductions.
• Patient amendments – to original data given at the time of registration e.g. change of surname, change of name by Deed Poll, change of address etc.
• Change details – due to incorrect spelling of first and surnames, date of birth, address and postcode changes.
• Referrals of patients to hospital consultant appointments etc.

General

• Training – of receptionists, nurses, healthcare specialists and GPs in computer system operation.
• Summarising – of new registered patients within 3 weeks of registering the patients; about 7 a week should be a working target.

- Scanning – about 20-25 documents a day.
- Receptionists' rota – prepare monthly; prepare a week before the end of the month.
- Healthcall – check monthly report issued by them and highlight any issues to GPs regarding correct entries for patients they have contacted.
- Complaints – deal with complaints when received by mail and involve practice manager and GPs as appropriate.

QOF

Quality Management and Analysis subsystem (QMAS) audits:

- Monthly – new disease register data – QMAS upload – 8th of the month – check date with IT department in PCT.
- Monthly – check payments seen from list of patients and invite patients to the surgery to increase targets and thereby income to the surgery.
- Quarterly – enhanced services report and check for accuracy and inform GPs, as it would affect income received.
- Quarterly – Practice Based Commissioning (PBC) reports and check for accuracy and inform GPs, as it would affect income received.
- Liaise PCT/Torex or Vision or EMIS system specialists

a. PCT on issues relating to registrations, list sizes, deductions, counts, waiting for approval of newly registered patients (usually within 5 days for approval), acknowledgements etc.

b. Torex/Vision or EMIS – for software problems or in use of PCs in the surgery.

Security

- Data storage and security – ensure that each week's data storage tape is stored outside the surgery in case of fire, theft etc. Check with the system provider. In recent years this procedure may not be necessary as it is automatically stored in the system providers' computers. Please check.
- Report searches – as required.

Miscellaneous

1. Ordering of supplies for communication equipment only – telephones, faxes, printers, scanners, toners, papers etc.
2. Recording all patient records received from Health Authority (HA) in the system.

3. Green card checking and return to HA.

4. Ensure all telephones printers, scanners, faxes are all in working order and if not, contact appropriate companies for help.

3.2 Procedures

Procedures for all the tasks (in Section 3.1) to perform including the most important QOF monitoring – monthly, quarterly and yearly; reports, targets and shortfalls with action points should be all clearly laid out by the computer system providers, and, hence, are not dealt with here in detail at all.

3.3 READ Codes

Only very basic information is given, as there are voluminous articles on Read Codes, their applications, uses, etc.

The reader is advised to go through references to gain further knowledge, if required. Read Codes are in the realm of clinical personnel.

Read Codes are a hierarchical classification system of clinical and administrative terms used on most GP computer systems as a means of recording information.

Read Codes allow practices to:

- Record data more consistently
- Retrieve data with greater ease
- Analyse/audit data more thoroughly, aiding health needs assessment
- Communicate data to hospitals and other agencies by the browser; available on CD-ROM and utilises a graphical user interface to display Clinical Terms and Codes. Each browser has a range of functions, including key word searching, code based searching, hierarchical navigation and details of synonyms. Browsers are not designed to be used as working clinical systems and therefore should not be considered as a formal release of the Read Codes.

There are two clinical coding systems; READ and Snomed–CT. READ codes are the most well known in primary care and are used in general practice. Snomed-CT coding is an international coding standard and is expected to replace or subsume the READ coding system in general practice in the future.

The codes cover a wide range of topics in different categories such as illness signs and symptoms, treatments and therapies, investigations, occupations, diagnoses, and drugs and appliances. This enables the recording of episodes of care as part of a full electronic patient record.

http://www.nhsemployers.org/SiteCollectionDocuments/Guide_to_general_practice_

One of the biggest developments in the medical field is in the use of Read Codes by GPs in the computer systems to maximise data quality and understand clinical data.

These were highlighted by the article written succinctly by Dr. M T Gerald in May 2001, which is a must-read for all.

The Read Codes are a lexicon of terms commonly used in general practice. They were originally developed by GPs for GPs.

Most terms GPs need are in there, in particular:

- Symptoms
- Diagnoses
- Common administrative tasks (e.g. '1st cervical smear recall letter sent')
- Lab results
- Imaging results
- Preventative procedures
- Operative procedures
- Employment etc.

Hard data vs. soft data

Hard data is simple factual information. For example, "The ECG showed left bundle branch block."

Soft data is somewhat more uncertain. For example, "This patient might have had **'flu'**".

Note: If a diagnosis is not certain, DO NOT CODE IT! Wrong coded diagnoses left in the system will foul future audits and reports.

The Read Codes Drug and Appliance Dictionary is part of the Clinical Terms (The Read Codes) and covers medicinal products, appliances, special foods, reagents and dressings.

The dictionary may be used in a number of different types of computer healthcare software, such as:

- Computerised patient clinical records to record drug history, treatment, adverse reactions;

- Electronic, knowledge databases as the underlying set of core concepts and terms to identify medicinal and appliance products;
- Systems to generate electronic prescriptions;
- Computerised dispensing and administration systems;
- Stock control computer systems;
- Analysis of drug usage.

A clinical knowledge base, providing information on drug use, doses, side effects, contra-indications and interactions, is not provided within the Read Codes Drug and Appliance Dictionary.

3.4 Claims

IMT specialists' key task is to ensure that all claims are duly received on time; if not, the specialist should liaise with the PCT finance section for payment and find out reasons for the delay i.e. whether any claim has been made incorrectly or made after due date for the current month's payments. Unless the specialist is involved in the accounts, which in most cases, they would not be, then the PMgr, GP Partners and the accountant should deal it.

IOS claims are dealt with in Section 5.

Considerable details can be found at the website given in the Reference section and is a must-read for all. PCT might also send notifications of these in their bulletins to GP practices.

3.5 Other Tasks

The IMT specialist has to generate reports (readily available in all computer systems now) for:

- Each of the areas for payments
- Each GP
- Patient contacted
- Appointments to be given

To maximise the income for each quarter.

This has to be done a few weeks before closing of the period for next payment by the PCT so that more patients could be called and seen to maximise targets.

One example is given below:

3.5.1 Immunisation

It is highly recommended that the Child Immunisations for each quarter should be checked before the end of the quarter to ensure that each GP meets the target – 90-100% to ensure the surgery gets the maximum income possible for that quarter.

By highlighting the shortfall, the patients' parents or guardians will be invited, by mobile or text or telephone using landlines, to come to surgery before the cut-off date for payment.

The report should identify:

- Total number of children in the GP's list, GP, Clinic, Unknown, Total and % for target;
- Classified for 1-5 year olds and over 5-year-olds;
- 2-5 years – diphtheria 3rd, pertussis 3rd, MMR single, HIB;

Over 5 years – Preschool DIP, booster.

4. Medical Secretaries

The job of a medical secretary is one of the key tasks, and it has to be performed by a qualified and trained member with several years' experience in the field. Knowledge of medical terms is crucial.

She not only has to read the unclear and wavy writings of the GPs, but translate a few remarks dictated into a meaningful memo for the hospital consultant, in case of referrals.

She should be computer literate in that she should be able to access various data about the patients from the many screens available to make notes for the referral letter.

She must know shorthand and audio typing. She must have a good command of English, particularly in writing as well as speaking.

Medical secretaries need a good qualification and are members of the Association of Medical Secretaries, Practice Managers, Administrators and Receptionists (AMSPAR).

AMSPAR run a variety of courses including:

- The Level 2 Diploma in Medical Administration
- The Level 3 Diploma for Medical Secretaries
- The Level 3 Certificate in Medical Administration
- The Level 3 Certificate in Medical Terminology
- Most employers will look for at least four GCSEs (A-C grades, including English).
- They would also be expected to be confident with technology and good at typing.

Taking a general secretarial course, such as the City & Guilds, OCR and London Chamber of Commerce and Industry would help one get noticed. These courses are available (full, part-time and distance learning) at many colleges and private colleges across the UK.

In recent years some of the skills of the medial secretary are absent. This is because the younger GPs formulate the referral letters from their computers and they are also not adept in dictating letters, as older generation GPs were.

Consequently, only the big surgeries have a dedicated medical secretary and smaller ones use a good receptionist to type the letters with the GP providing support in terms of corrections to the letter. Very rarely would a good medical secretary's letter need correction.

4.1 Tasks

Tasks to perform

- Sorting of letters and posting.
- Clinical correspondences scanned first and details entered in patients' records.
- Letters received electronically and during mid-morning should also be acted upon.
- GPs request for all dictations and action points, particularly referral letters.
- Transmit correspondence and medical records by mail, e-mail, or fax.
- Operate office equipment such as voicemail messaging systems, and use word processing, spreadsheet and other software applications to prepare reports, invoices, financial statements, letters, case histories and medical records.
- Communicating with people outside the organisation, representing the organisation to customers, the public, government, and other external sources. This information could be exchanged in person, in writing, or by telephone or e-mail. Always obtain GP Partners' approval before writing to external organisations.
- Insurance company letters should be logged according to date and passed on to the GP for action. Any insurance correspondence acted upon by the GP, should be posted to the company ONLY after ensuring the company has paid for the work.
- In this field of work, regarding payment to the surgery, follow the principle **'it is prudent to catch a bull by its horn and very difficult to catch it by the tail'**. There are exemptions to certain correspondences and please ensure these are rigidly applied.
- Patients might come to get an update about their applications, test results etc. Please make sure they are informed about these. Reception staff should send to the medical secretary only those patients whose results and other information are ready for collection. Any others should not be sent to the medical secretary. Also, they should see her at stipulated times, so that she can get on with her other pressing work.
- Contact hospital consultants and any specialists to chase results or to make appointments. Please record these appointments in the computer, as appropriate.

Many skills are needed for being a good medical secretary:

* Good at multi-tasking
* Good and clear communication, written and verbal
* Quite sympathetic
* Strong IMT and organisational management
* Extremely discreet, with an ability to deal with very sensitive patient medical information.

The job specifications and job descriptions for a medical secretary are given in Section 9.1.4.

5. Claims

The various claims a surgery has to process to derive its income are given below:

- Registrations
- Immunisation
- PPA – Prescription prescribing authority
- Pneumococcal
- Flu-Influenza
- Medicines – prescription issued
- Others – services provided for the patients include:

Incoming:

CH — Child Health Surveillance
CS — Contraceptive Services
IN — Immediately Necessary Treatment
MA — Maternity Services
MS — Minor Surgery
NV — Night Visits
RF — Registration Fee
TR — Temporary Residents
VI — Vaccinations and Immunisations.

The following claims types would be received at the surgeries HA from fringe HAs:
MX — Fringe Maternity Services
RX — Fringe Registration Fee

Outgoing:

* Child Health Cancellations – notification to the GP Practice that their CH claim has been cancelled. These transactions are generated automatically for the relevant GP Practice when the relevant claim is either manually cancelled or superseded by a newer claim.
* Contraceptive Services Cancellations – notification to the GP Practice that their CS claim has been cancelled. These transactions are generated automatically for the relevant GP Practice when the relevant claim is either manually cancelled or superseded by a newer claim.
* Fringe Maternity Services (MX) – submitted for authorisation to the HA with whom the claiming GP is responsible. These transactions are automatically generated for claims, which have been entered manually, received from IOS, linked GP Practices, or for adjustments made on the GM screen to paid maternity claims for non-responsible GPs.
* Fringe Registration Fee (RX) – submitted for authorisation to the HA with whom the claiming GP is responsible. These transactions are automatically generated for claims that have either been entered manually or received from IOS linked GP Practices.
* Quarterly Cut-Off Dates – these transactions are generated automatically for IOS linked GP Practices (only for GP Practices who are responsible to your HA) either initially using the Link Code Cross Reference (PT) screen when upgrading the GP Practice to IOS, or by closing the finance quarter on the GMS General Data (GG) screen. The cut-off dates are generated from the information set up on the Links Cut-Off Dates (QD) screen.
* Payment Notifications – notification to the GP Practice that the relevant claim has been authorised for payment
* Reject Notifications – notification to the GP Practice that the relevant claim has not been authorised for payment (along with any reasons for justifying the rejection).
* Maternity Adjustments – notification to the GP Practice (only for GP Practices who are responsible to your HA) when an adjustment has been made to the eligible fee for a Maternity Service claim.
* GP Payment Statements – GMSQP payment statements can be sent in electronic form to linked GP Practices. The GP Practice can receive electronic payments statements (generated by closing the finance quarter on the GG screen) even if they are only linked for Registration.

5.1 Background

5.1.1 Background to HA-PCT/GP Links

The HA/GP Links Project is a national initiative to provide Electronic Data Interchange (EDI) between HAs and GP Practices operating throughout England and Wales.

The objective of the project was to move towards a paperless transaction base between GP Practices and HAs/PCTs by replacing Registration and Items of Service (IOS) forms with electronic transactions transmitted via a communications network (NHSNET).

This was achieved by:

- Receiving registration details from GP Practices and providing the means for automatic update of the HA patient database.

- Transmitting to GP Practices the details of registration changes made on the HA patient database to allow the same patient details to be updated onto the Practice's patient database.

- Receiving IOS claims from GP Practices and providing the facility to both automatically validate and update the HA General Medical Services Quarterly Payment (GMSQP) system with those claims which are eligible for payment.

- Transmitting electronic GP statements to GP Practices.

5.1.2 Benefits

The major benefits of the project would be:

- Speedier exchange of information between GP Practices and HAs/PCTs.

- Improved accuracy of information between GP Practices and HAs/PCTs.

- Data will be captured once at the GP Practice, thereby eliminating duplication of effort.

- Reduced administration costs for GP Practices and HAs/PCTs.

- Reduced costs for GP Practices and HAs/PCTs in support of existing communication methods (e.g. telephone, postage).

- Standard national approach to data collection and thus complete compatibility between GP Practices and HAs/PCTs.

- Audit trail of data exchanged between GP Practices and HAs/PCTs, thus reducing the possibility of discrepancies.

5.1.3 Items of Service (IOS) Link

The success and reliability of the computerised link depends upon both the accuracy of the data being exchanged and on the number of GP Practices using the link.

The reconciliation process is fundamental to the smooth running of the Items of Service (IOS) Link because much of the data used for patient identification with regard to claims relies on both the GP Practice and HA/PCT systems holding the same patient information. If time does not allow a full reconciliation to be performed then the minimum patient information should be reconciled, i.e. Surname, Forename(s), Date of Birth, NHS Number, GP Code, and Sex.

A GP Practice can only become linked for IOS once its link for Registration is running successfully.

Registration Links

Achieved via the following transactions:

Incoming:

- Acceptances – new patient registrations onto a GP's list.
- Amendments – changes to patient registration details.
- Removals (Out of Area)
- Reconciliation Downloads

Outgoing:

1 Amendments – changes to patient registration details.
2 Deductions – removes patient from GP's list.
3 Rejections – rejection of a GP Acceptance transaction.
4 Approvals – notification of a patient being accepted onto GP's list.
5 Medical Record Flag Removals
6 Medical Records Sent Reconciliation Uploads

Phase 2 Registration Links

The Phase 2 functionality includes the following additional transactions:

Incoming:

1 Deduction Requests – allows a GP Practice to request the deduction of a patient for reasons of Death, Embarkation or Other Reason.

Outgoing:

1 Close Quarter Notifications – notification to the GP Practice to close the registration quarter on their system.

2 FP69 Prior Notifications.

3 FP69 Flag Removals – notification to the GP Practice that a patient's FP69 status has been cancelled.

4 Deduction Request Rejections – notification to the GP Practice that the request to deduct a patient from the list had been refused.

Acknowledgement Transactions

Pay/Reject acknowledgements will advise whether Maternity Services claims and adjustments and Registration Fee claims sent have been authorised for payment or rejected.

Cut-off Dates

Cut-off dates currently enable identification of claims which will be included in a particular financial period.

A cut-off date must be set for each type of claim and these must be transmitted to each GP Practice using the Health Link Network. Until this has been done no transmission of claims information can occur.

Once the Link's cut-off dates have been received by a GP Practice, they can start submitting their first claim transactions over the Health link Network.

This tightening of controls has the benefit that the Practice can more easily reconcile their payment, and thus significantly reduces the number of queries a Practice will have regarding the claims they have transmitted.

http://www.connectingforhealth.nhs.uk/systemsandservices/ssd/downloads/ioslinks/contents/2-overvw#CutoffDates

6. Patients

Patients – A Different Approach

It is time to review the Practice work and the three aspects which play key parts in the goodwill of the surgery, are:

- Practice treating Patients as Customers
- Motivation of Practice Staff
- Human Psychology.

The PMgr and in fact all GPs, nurses and staff should treat patients as **Customers** – all patients, current and new as well as all employees. This concept is sacrosanct for the prestige and growth of the surgery.

Customers:

The term Customers might have different connotations when applied to surgery practices:

* GPs have captive 'patients/customers' within the NHS defined catchment areas;
* GPs' incomes are related to the patient lists and for extra services provided as well.
* GPs income is paid monthly irrespective of type of service provided.
* Only when complaints reach above a certain level are the GPs investigated.
* The GPs may be struck off in severe cases of malpractice but customer numbers stay nearly the same and new GPs take over.
* No other business enjoys the privileges of guaranteed income with rent, rates and grants offered for expansion or improvements to the business a surgery enjoys.
* However, in Practices, the time allocated to the patients/customers is strictly rationed – normal appointments only 10 min and appointment for clinics 20 min.

It is common for GPs:

- To take the high plane and look down on the patients, and even feel that the patients should be more grateful and not moan and complain. Several GPs and Nurses still have not learnt how to **'communicate'** at all and they rarely **'listen'**. They are more used to **'tell'** where patients are concerned.

- To write the prescription even before asking the patient the reason for the appointment!

For years GPs have been perceived as **'semi-gods'** and held in high esteem without patients questioning them of the service they have provided. Things have changed since the New Contract in 2003 and GPs and the practice are accountable, and their services are measured and investigated when complaints arise.

Surgery management has to shift their thinking and treat patients as customers. This is a big ask because the saying **'customer is king'** does not apply to patients who view the GPs as **'semi-gods'**. Statements like **'How may I help you?'** feel more like **'cheque is in the post'**. Customer service is not just dealing with complaints and problem solving. Good customer service is not an option; in today's environment it is crucial to outperform other surgeries.

A number of surgeries were much too complacent and they didn't even know or wouldn't even admit it.

The change in thinking has to start with a sense of awareness. Complacency leads to a false sense of awareness. Increasing this awareness can be dealt with in four ways: bring the outside in, behave with awareness every day, find opportunity in crisis, and deal robustly with all **'No-no's'**. Awareness should be kept focused each day and behave as if the future begins today.

Motivation and Psychology:

These are very complex subjects and innumerable books deal with these areas exhaustively. An attempt is made to highlight certain areas, leaving the rest to be sourced by the reader. The PMgr needs to have honed these skills to improve his/her performance.

Motivation:

Overinvest in people – attract, motivate, train and reward; overinvest with emotional currency – trust, independence, praise, freedom, and encouragement

People will accept many flaws in their leaders but would never respect and trust an 'anti-people' character.

Hire people according to three 'I's' – **integrity; I** could do it attitude, which is very critical; **I** to **treat all people as special – make people feel that they are:**

Paid a fair day's wages.

Measure staff performance and not be behind their backs; trust them.

Train yourself not to 'tell' staff; allow dialogue and ideas from them.

Good contributors to the practice and not just costs.

The PMgr should not hesitate to say 'please and thank you' to the staff often.

The PMgr should compliment people and not be frugal about it

- Credit them when they do a good job.
- Appreciate their efforts.
- Appreciate their being in your team.
- 'I need your help' is better than **'you do this'**.

The PMgr should also ensure that he/she:

- Give staff due credit when due.
- Give informal surprise bonuses.
- Is polite with everyone.
- Stays out of office politics
- Does not go over the budget – tight budget promotes creativity, ingenuity and inventiveness – consider it as a challenge.
- Never underestimates an opponent.

Psychology

1 Never write a nasty memo that criticises, belittles, degrades, is hurtful, cynical, condescending, and unkind, in anger or in frustration.

2 Keep **'idea notebook'** and also 'to do' lists.

3 Be friendly with their peers' subordinates.

4 Know everybody by his or her first names – pronounce it correctly.

5 Organise 'one-line, good-job' tours.

6   Keep and use special idea book – prepare 'to do' lists.

7   Keep a people profile – people linkage and invest in people by devoting time.

8   Occasional personal hand written memos would improve staff attitudes.

9   Don't try to cover up – sort it out quickly.

10 Talk is cheap, so put it in action. Creativity without implementation is irresponsibility; Ideas are nothing without execution.

11 Stop, look, and listen – good listeners are considered great conversationalists; listening is equated with wisdom and intelligence. **Listen, listen, and listen.**

12 Never panic or lose your temper – 'Nothing gives one person so much advantage over another as to remain cool and unruffled under all circumstances' – Thomas Jefferson.

13 Learn to speak and write in plain English – communications must be precise, complete and totally comprehensible.

6.1 Customer Service

To perceive Patients as Customers is a '**big ask**' but unless the change occurs the surgery would fall into bad reputation, with serious consequences.

It is, therefore, crucial that GPs, nurses and healthcare staff must change to treat patients as Customers. They all should do their own internal review of their attitudes and change to meet the new requirements for the welfare of the patients/customers and thereby the surgery. Good quality customer service gives the edge over competitors – surgeries within the catchment area. Regardless of industry, the following key principals of good customer service always make business sense.

6.1.1 Giving good service to existing customers (patients)

Satisfied patients stay with a surgery longer and spread the word to friends and contacts in the community, which will attract new patients.

6.1.2 Customer service costs real money

Real costs are associated with providing good customer service. Surgeries in 'leafy suburbs' with better facilities and decor generally benefit from more customer satisfaction.

Answering machines with long, extended messages are more impersonal and may alienate the patients. So aim for short messages followed by a receptionist's response to the call would satisfy the patients, as they feel happy that they are talking to someone.

6.1.3 Understanding customers' needs and aim to meet them

To meet customers' needs, the surgery must know what those needs were. To understand the customer's needs, surgery should listen to the 'voice of the customer' and take action accordingly.

Customer listening can be done in many ways, for example, feedback forms and satisfaction surveys.

6.1.4 Good process and product design is important

Good quality customer service is only one factor in meeting customer needs. The overall processes should meet customers' needs more often. Adherence to good clinical governance is crucial in this aspect.

6.1.5 Customer service must be consistent

Customers expect consistent quality of customer service. Not only is clinical excellence important, but also the behaviour of the receptionists, nurses and staff, in general, play a key part of the service.

6.1.6 Employees are also Customers

The quality management movement should highlight the concept of internal and external customers. Traditionally, the focus is usually on external customers with little thought given to how internal department interact. Improving relationships with internal customers and suppliers assists delivery of better customer service to external customers, through reduced lead-times, increased quality, and better communication.

The circular relationship between employees, customers and Partners need to be understood. Under-staffed, under-trained employees will not deliver good quality customer service, driving customers away. Equal effort must be made in attracting, motivating and retaining employees as is made for customers, ultimately delivering improved returns to the partners. Better returns to partners mean more money is available to invest in employees and so the circle continues.

6.1.7 Open all communications channels

The customer wants to contact you in many ways – face to face, by mail, phone, fax, and email – and will expect all of these communication channels to be open and easily inter-mingled.

This presents a technical challenge, as it requires an integrated, streamlined solution providing the employee with the information they need to effectively service the customer.

6.1.8 Every customer contact is a chance to shine

If a customer has a reason for a complaint, then the SR and PMgr should be able to resolve the complaint swiftly, possibly enhancing the customer's perception of the surgery. Feeding back this information allows corrective action to be made, stopping further occurrences of the error.

6.1.9 People expect good customer service everywhere

Patients become frustrated when their expectations are not met, and increasingly demand higher service quality in more areas of their lives.

Providing outstanding customer service at the right price is the focus of most surgeries. It is worth remembering that we all experience customer service every day. We can learn from these and apply them in our own line of work, whatever it may be. The quality of good customer service will make the surgery stand out from other surgeries and for the right reasons!

6.2 Quality & Customer Service

The **Quality and Customer Service** should focus on the monitoring and development of systems that monitor and promote patient safety. This is **Risk Management** and is the process for determining what, where, when, why and how something could happen that might adversely affect a patient or system outcome and the surgery should work to ensure it does not happen again. The surgery should use a variety of tools and tests, both from within the surgery set-up and from external sources, to gauge how surgery is performing. The surgery should respond to the information by extending what works well and finding new and better ways to manage activities that are not as efficient or successful as the surgery and Partners would like.

6.2.1 Clinical Governance

This is the way surgery ensures it has in place the right people and right systems so that it continues to provide patients/customers with the highest standards of care. Clinical Governance is implemented through a framework, which promotes consumer participation, clinical effectiveness, as an effective workforce and risk management.

- **Infection Prevention and Control** is an important unit that is responsible for monitoring infection prevention and risks to patients and staff, to ensure a safe hospital environment. The surgery should implement measures to reduce infections and the impact of those infections on patients. Surgery staff are encouraged to develop guidelines and policies that guide clinical practice, educate, support and monitor staff in infection control practices including hand hygiene and staff immunisation.

- The **Mortality, Morbidity and Major Review** to be carried out on patient safety issues. The Committee should review sentinel events, serious adverse events and deaths with the assistance of independent audit undertaken by an external medical expert.

- **Patient Safety** is everyone's responsibility and fully investigates types of events to improve practice.

- The surgery is responsible for responding to complaints and concerns. These should be viewed as providing an opportunity to better understand how best to improve its services.

6.2.2 Service Quality

This is to be treated as a comparison of expectations with performance.

1 A surgery with high service quality will meet customer needs whilst remaining economically competitive. This aim may be achieved by understanding and improving operational processes; identifying problems quickly and systematically; establishing valid and reliable service performance measures and measuring customer satisfaction and other performance outcomes.

2 Service quality can be related to service potential (for example, staff qualifications), service process (for example, the quickness of service), and service result (customer satisfaction).

3 A customer's expectation of a particular service is determined by factors such as recommendations, personal needs and past experiences. The expected service and the perceived service sometimes may not be equal, thus leaving a gap.

6.2.3 Dimensions of Service Quality Competence

This is the possession of the required skills and knowledge to perform the service.

Courtesy is the consideration for the customer's property and a clean and neat appearance of contact personnel, manifesting as politeness, respect, and friendliness.

Credibility is the factors such as trustworthiness, belief and honesty.

Security is the customer feeling free from danger, risk or doubt including physical safety, financial security and confidentiality.

Access is approachability and ease of contact.

Communication means both informing customers in a language they are able to understand and also listening to customers.

Knowing the customer means making an effort to understand the customer's individual needs, providing individualised attention, recognising the customer when they arrive, and so on.

Tangibles are the physical evidence of the service, for instance, the appearance of the physical facilities, tools and equipment used to provide the service. Also, the appearance of personnel, communication materials and the presence of other customers in the service facility are important too.

Reliability is the ability to perform the promised service in a dependable and accurate manner.

Responsiveness is to the readiness and willingness of surgery staff to help customers in providing prompt timely services.

Empathy: The caring, individualised attention the firm provides to its customers.

6.2.4 Service Quality – GAPs

Customers generally have a tendency to compare the service they '**experience**' with the service they '**expect**'. If the **experience does not match the expectation**, there arises a gap.

- **Gap between consumer expectation and management perception:** This gap arises when the management does not correctly perceive what the customers want.

- **Gap between management perception and service quality specification:** Here, the management might correctly perceive what the customer wants, but may not set a performance standard.

- **Gap between service quality specification and service delivery:** This gap may arise owing to the service personnel. The reasons being poor training, incapability or unwillingness to meet the set service standard.

- **Gap between service delivery and external communication:** Consumer expectations are highly influenced by statements made by company representatives and advertisements. The gap arises when these assumed expectations are not fulfilled at the time of delivery of the service.

- **Gap between expected service and experienced service:** This gap arises when the consumer misinterprets the service quality.

6.2.5 Measuring Service Quality

Measuring service quality may involve both subjective and objective processes. In both cases, it is often some aspect of customer satisfaction, which is being assessed. However, customer satisfaction is an indirect measure of service quality.

- **Subjective elements** – e.g. critical incident assessments.

Objective elements – e.g. customer complaints.

7. Premises

The various details are:

7.1. Rent
7.2. Rates
7.3. Heat and Light
7.4. Communications
7.5. Out of Hours Services
7.6. Maintenance
7.7. Modifications
7.8. Security
7.9. Disabled Services
7.10. Insurances
7.11. Mortgage

7.1 Rent

The usual way of funding GP owned surgeries is by either Notional Rent or Cost Rent. Cost Rent is divided into fixed and variable, the former being by far the more common.

In the days of GMS, Cost Rents were funded from the Cash limited GMS fund and Notional Rents from the Non-Cash limited GMS Fund. The Cash-limited Fund was essentially fixed and it also had to fund practice staff budgets, practice computers and improvement grants. So, when, as was usual, after a few years of receiving cost rent, practices changed over to notional rent this was to PCTs' advantage and released funds to be used elsewhere.

Under the new regime, since 2004, all practice rents – Notional, Cost, Current Market, Local Authority and Health Centre, come from the same allocation, adjusted appropriately for approved growth caused by new schemes or extensions and increased each year for inflation. In this situation, it is, generally speaking, to a PCTs advantage for Cost Rent-funded practices to remain on Cost Rent as Variable Cost Rents only move in accordance with movements in interest rates – which have tended not to be significant over the last few years – and Fixed Cost Rents do not move at all. As the whole of the rent payment made by a PCT is inflated, this releases funds to pay for unusual increases in other rents or even some small developments.

There remains, however, one circumstance in which a practice moving from Cost to Notional rent can still be to the host PCT's advantage.

A common way of setting up a Cost Rent-funded surgery was to agree a fixed-rate Cost Rent and to take out a fixed-rate mortgage, usually with GPFC. Then, no matter what happened to interest rates, the Cost Rent would pay the mortgage, giving the practice some long-term security.

Some of these Cost Rents were agreed at, and are still at, very high rates – 15% or even more than 20% with mortgages to match. However, there may be practices which are still in receipt of a high fixed Cost Rent but who have re-mortgaged to a more reasonable rate.

PCA is responsible for making Rent and Rates payments including Notional Rents, Actual Rents and Cost Rents to practices on a monthly basis with the Global Sum and PMS payments.

In addition, PCA is responsible for ensuring that GP premises are reviewed on a three yearly basis and when a new rent has been assessed by the District Valuer and approved by the PCT, PCA pay the new rent to the practice and pay any rent arrears that may be due.

PCA also make direct payments for Non-Domestic Rates and water charges to Council and water companies on behalf of the practices. These payments are made on the Integra payments system.

7.2 Rates

The Council levies non-domestic rates, and these have to be paid by the surgery and it becomes part of its expenses. PCA makes the payment to the surgery via the Integra system.

7.3 Heat and Light

Also paid by PCA. The service provider has to be arranged by the surgery like any other business, but they can make a claim for reimbursement.

7.4 Communication Systems

Sections 8.1 and 8.2 deal with all the relevant aspects.

7.5 Out of Hours Services

If one is ill or is injured outside normal working hours there are a number of different ways one can be treated.

The following information gives advice on where you can get help for health problems outside of normal working hours depending on the nature and severity of your illness or injury's.

* Call or visit NHS Direct. This service is available 24 hours a day, seven days a week. It gives advice on what to do if you're feeling ill and you're not sure what to do. They can also give you details of local services, from late night pharmacists to emergency dentists. Visit www.nhsdirect.nhs.uk or call 0845 46 47.

* Visit your local community pharmacist. Community pharmacies are open longer than your GP. They are often open at weekends, and can be open late at night or on a bank holiday. Pharmacists are qualified medical professionals and can give you advice about common symptoms, medicines and healthy living. NHS Direct 0845 46 47 can tell you where to find your nearest community pharmacy.

* Pharmacies with early and late opening times. Some pharmacies are open 100 hours a week, when many other pharmacies are closed. The names, address, hours of opening with dates and telephone numbers would be displayed in the surgery at the entrance.

If one urgently needs a prescription at a time when no pharmacy is open please call NHS Direct on 0845 46 47 who will be able to advise you on the best course of action.

Out of hours GP services:

GP practices are generally open between 8am-6.30pm, Monday to Friday. The services provided, when your GP is closed, are called 'out of hours' GP services. If your GP surgery is closed and you need to see a doctor or nurse urgently, please phone the out of hours GP service for the area where you live. The telephone number to contact should be displayed in the surgery. When you ring the out of hours GP service, you will be asked to give your details and to describe how you are feeling. The out of hours service advisor will tell you what care you need based on this information. A doctor or nurse may need to talk to you over the phone, you may be asked to go to an out-of-hours centre or a doctor may come to see you at home.

A doctor would visit patients who are seriously ill or who cannot leave the house because of their health or other issues. The out of hours service advisor would tell you about home visits and what time you could expect the doctor or nurse at your home.

The out of hours GP service will not issue repeat prescriptions. These need to be ordered from your own GP and pharmacy and collected during normal working hours.

If you do run out of medication your local community pharmacist will provide an emergency supply. Please take empty prescription medicines with you to show the pharmacist what you had been prescribed along with some identification.

NHS walk-in centres and primary care access centres.

At walk-in centres and access centres you can be seen for minor issues such as coughs, cold, flu, cuts, sprains, minor burns and broken bones. At most walk-in centres you do not need to make an appointment but it is worth telephoning in advance to check that you can be treated – particularly for young children. At nurse-led clinics you can be treated for minor conditions, have dressings changed and wounds checked. Call ahead for a full list of the services available. There are walk-in centres and drop in services at locations near the surgery should also be displayed. The minor injuries units near the surgery should also be indicated clearly.

Accident & Emergency and 999 services:

Please only dial 999 or go to your nearest Accident & Emergency if the illness or injury is life threatening or can't wait. Unless you need urgent medical attention it is best to avoid A&E as it keeps the service free for those with critical injuries and illnesses. You should dial 999 immediately if you or someone else is seriously ill, for example, if someone:

- Has had a major accident
- Has problems with breathing
- Has severe chest pains
- Is unconscious
- Has lost a lot of blood

The local Accident and Emergency departments based in the area have to be mentioned and details to be given with telephone numbers to contact.

7.6 Maintenance

The PMgr must make sure that routine maintenance is carried out on all appliances and utilities. For these he must set up service contracts with most of them, like electricity, gas, building insurance etc. The PMgr should also ensure there is an indemnity insurance and cover for fire, theft, etc. The cover should also include accidents and injuries to patients and all visitors to the surgery. Water leaks and all plumbing work should be given top priority due to H&S hazards.

The surgery has lots of communication equipment and the suppliers of the equipment provide advice on how to maintain the units, cleaning, solutions to be used and general upkeep of the units. These websites are a source of information and the procedures to follow are not dealt with here. For example, people should not eat food or have drinks in the vicinity of the computers due to spillage and damage to electrical components. The kitchen is the right place to go for food and drinks.

The surgery may be required to be painted inside and outside, say, once in 3-4 years, and the costs may be covered by the PCT. The PMgr should be aware of making claims for such work by contacting contractors, getting the 3 best quotes and submitting to the PCT for approval. There should also be a guarantee that the patient's interests would not be compromised when the work is finally approved for carrying it out.

The PMgr should have all the contact numbers of contractors, architects, designers, plumbers, electricians, odd-jobs men, etc. The surgery on a day-to-day basis must be kept immaculately clean; ensure the cleaners do a proper job. This includes the standard of WCs – they should be clinically clean. It is better to have disposable paper towels than cloth towels due to infection.

Fire Safety for first day arrival of new staff is detailed in Section 2. It is now compulsory by law for all businesses that operate using business premises to conduct a fire risk assessment, as outlined by the Regulatory Reform (Fire Safety) Order 2005. The UK Fire Risk Advisory Service (UKFRAS) undertakes comprehensive fire safety risk assessment to provide you with information and written documentation to make your business fire risk and fire safety compliant. Under the Regulatory Reform (Fire Safety) Order 2005, surgeries are legally obliged to comply with a number of national fire safety regulations if you are responsible for the whole or any part of your GP premises.

The responsible person must carry out a Fire Safety Risk Assessment and implement and maintain a fire management plan. If required, all businesses must be able to provide proof that they have done this, and many insurers will ask to see documented proof that businesses are compliant with UK regulations.

Surveyors:

- Provide surgeries with a thorough Fire Safety Risk Assessment tailored to specific GP surgery and individual requirements.
- Point out areas of strength and areas of non-compliance.
- Provide with a realistic and cost effective action plan, which, once implemented, will mean surgery, is compliant with fire safety law – protecting the premises, staff and patient.

All medical equipment including BP monitors should be routinely checked and calibrated.

7.7 Modifications

All changes and modifications to the surgery buildings should be dealt through PCT planning section and approval obtained for compliance with their codes and also for any funding they might give. A good PMgr would have prioritised the surgery needs for modifications with budget costs and would keep in constant touch with the planning section personnel for any funds available immediately or due to be released soon, and if so, make the earliest application so that the 'early bird catches the worm'.

7.8 Security

Surgery security is of paramount importance; a suitable alarm system should be installed and annual contracts should be in place for its routine maintenance. The local company should be able to provide good service when any trouble with the system is experienced. The surgery has details of patients in the computer systems and any break-in would mean valuable personal data not only lost but liable to be misused. However, there is one major issue regarding false alarms. Should 3 false alarms occur then the police would not provide cover for a period of 6 months, and restart only after proof of no false alarm during the last 6 months. A tough call, and generally the systems might not be connected to the police at all. There should be enough video cameras provided in the surgery – near the entrances and in reception room – and the tapes should be stored for at least a period of 6 months before reuse.

In case of violent patients attacking GPs, nurses, HCA or PMgr, panic buttons should be provided in all the tables for easy and discreet access for outside help.

Also, a panic button in the form of a long pulling cord should be provided in disabled toilets should they experience any problems and seek help.

7.9 Disabled Services

All surgeries must provide sloping disabled access (in addition to steps for other able patients) to enter the surgery, and the doors and pathways wide enough to allow wheelchairs to pass through easily. There should be at least one toilet for disabled people and a panic pull up cord in case of emergencies. The WC facilities should be checked and kept immaculately clean.

7.10 Insurances

There are a number of insurances a PMgr should make sure the surgery has:

- Liability Insurance and displayed in the reception area
- Building insurance
- Fire and theft cover insurance
- Copyright cover insurance for playing music in the reception area.

7.11 Mortgage

For the premises owned by the GP Partners, they may seek a mortgage from lenders, and the PMgr should be able to handle this requirement. Having good contacts with banks and building societies would be a great help. Generally GPs would not have any problems in getting loans as they are viewed as very secure customers due to their income being derived through the government i.e. NHS. Still, practice accounts for last three years would be sought and if the Partners have good income then it is mere formality.

8. Administration

The PMgr is responsible for all aspects of administration in the surgery and here only certain areas are dealt with and reference to other sections are indicated.

The IMT specialist should take care of all issues regarding communications and the PMgr is responsible for the rest.

These sections are dealt with below:

8.1 – Communications – Telephones

8.2 – Computer, Printer, Scanner and Accessories

8.3 – Post, Printing and Stationery

8.4 – Travel

8.5 – Motor and Mileage

8.5.1 – Motor

8.5.2 – Mileage

8.5.3 – VAT

8.6 – Subscriptions

8.6.1 – BMA

8.6.2 – MDU-MPS

8.6.3 – GMC

8.6.4 – RCGP

8.6.5 – Courses

8.7 – Accounts

8.8 – Bank Charges

8.9 – Sundries

8.10 – Petty Cash

8.1 Communications – Telephones

Details dealt with in Section 2.6.

8.2 Computers

Computer, Printer, Scanner, Accessories:

Sections under 2 deal with the basics for the systems used – computers, printers, fax, scanners and computer systems. The PMgr would be the principle person for choosing the computer system provider along with GPs and the IMT specialist. Once the system is in place, the IMT specialist has to take over the running of the 'show' as detailed earlier in Section 3.0.

Modern surgeries have much better facilities:

- All staff have their own computers, apart from all GPs, nurses and HCA.

- Only in Reception they may share computers but at least two would be provided, sometimes three depending on the way the reception is set up. If they have 3 receptionists dealing with appointments, registration and telephones then each must have one computer for access and quick response.

- There should be a separate computer for doing prescriptions and at least two other rooms for HCP visits.

- Each room will have its own printer, as the costs for these have spiralled down.

- The main heavy-duty printer-copier along with a scanner may be in the main Administration room where usually the medical secretary is seated.

- All consumables and accessories – which are the expensive items like cartridges – have to be ordered on time, stored in a secure place, and attempts continually made to look for cheaper but good quality alternatives to reduce costs.

Computer system security units and disks need to be carefully kept away from anyone misusing it – only the IMT specialist or PMgr should have access to it as the whole surgery operation depends on the main unit, which is usually monitored by the system provider, to fix any faults from their offices.

8.3 Post

Post, Printing and Stationery

Traditionally, letters, duly addressed and stamped ready for the day are posted in the letterbox. The medical secretary usually does these as she leaves for home or sometimes it is done by any of the receptionists. The PMgr or senior receptionists usually deal with Post Office work relating to purchases of stamps, small items of stationery, etc. For regular supplies of stationery items, like copying paper, inks, cartridges etc., it is better to have accounts with three major suppliers like Staples, Office World and Vikings, to get maximum discounts from time to time. Newsagents usually sell stamps, saving a lot of time waiting in a queue at the Post Office.

8.4 Travel

Travel Expenses

All staff working in the surgery have to make their own arrangements for travel – bus, underground, trains or cars and daily expenses for these will not be reimbursed. This applies even to GPs. Expenses for surgery related travel, which is mostly local, can't be claimed as per HMRC rules.

Only when taxis have to be arranged in special cases for the patients to take them to hospitals, when it may not be a serious ambulance case, then the expenses have to be properly recorded, receipts filed and claimed as allowable expenses in the surgery accounts.

GP partners and other GPs, nurses, HCA, PMgr and other staff going for conferences and courses outside the area can claim reasonable travel and related expenses, ensuring the proper receipts are kept and handed over to the accountant or the PMgr when claiming.

8.5 Motor

8.5.1 Motor and Mileage

The above expenses can only be claimed by the GP partners and for mileage, as per

HMRC formula applicable.

This is a complex issue, particularly for a GP surgery, and the accountant should be able to deal with it while doing final accounts.

Motor expenses allowed using the HMRC approved mileage rates (45p for up to 1,000 miles and 25p for over 10,000 miles). These rates are designed to cover the routine running, maintenance and depreciation of that vehicle.

HMRC guidance states that costs not covered by the mileage rate are those specific to that journey; tolls, parking and congestion charges are allowable.

8.6 Subscriptions

8.6.1 BMA

The BMA is a voluntary membership organisation for doctors and, as such, under the Data Protection Act, their records are strictly confidential. They are, therefore, unable to provide members of the public with contact details for any of their members – or to pass on correspondence from third parties to their members.

8.6.2 MDU-MPS

See respective websites given in References on details of memberships and benefits.

Benefits for individual and a GP group scheme:

Advice service

Legal representation

MPS provides first-class specialist legal advice and representation in a range of circumstances, such as clinical negligence claims, disciplinary hearings, and GMC fitness to practise proceedings.

MPS Publications

MPS produces a range of serial publications to cover the main medico-legal issues GPs may face in their everyday practice.

Casebook – The flagship journal of MPS. Published three times a year, each issue is full of news, features, and case reports.

Your Practice – Looks at real problems and concerns that practices have, giving practical tips for use in your own practice.

GP Registrar – A magazine specifically for GP specialty trainees covering the medico-legal subjects that are important once they start working in general practice

Sessional GP – Features case studies and practical examples for locum and salaried GPs to help them avoid running into problems.

MPS also produces a wide range of factsheets and booklets, which provide practical advice on a variety of important medico-legal topics such as, consent, medical records, confidentiality, parental responsibility, and complaints.

8.6.3 GMC (General Medical Council)

The GP Register was established on 31 March 2006. From 1 April 2006, all doctors working in general practice in the health service in the UK, other than doctors in training such as GP Registrars, have been required to be included on the GP Register. This requirement extends to locums.

Eligibility for inclusion on the GP Register

Doctors are entitled to have their names included on the GP Register if, in addition to being a registered medical practitioner, they:

- Hold a Certificate of Completion of Training (CCT) in general practice.

- Are a national of a relevant European State, or have EC rights and hold qualifications in general practice listed in Annex 5.1.4. Of Directive 2005/36/EC.

- Have an acquired right to practise as a general practitioner in the UK

- Fall within such other categories provided for in the General Medical Council (Applications for General Practice and Specialist Registration) Regulations 2010

One can view these regulations in the GMC Legislation section, and can find out more about CCTs in background information on specialist and GP certification.

Accessing the GP Register

One can access the GP Register via our online register, the List of Registered Medical Practitioners.

Primary Care Organisations and performers' lists

Primary Care Organisations (PCOs) are primary care trusts in England, Health and Social Services Boards in Northern Ireland, Local Health Boards in Wales, and Primary Care Divisions within area health boards in Scotland.

PCOs are responsible for maintaining primary medical performers' lists.

GP registration (i.e. being included on the GP Register) is one requirement for entry to a medical performers' list for GPs, although this does not apply to doctors in training, such as GP Registrars. When a doctor applies to join a performers list, the PCO should check the List of Registered Medical Practitioners to see whether that doctor is on the GP Register, and make other pre-employment checks.

The criteria for entry to a medical performers list are set out in Department of Health guidance. See GMC guidance on employing a doctor for further information.

PCOs undertake a series of checks, in addition to registration checks, before admitting a doctor to their performers' lists. See the NHS Employers' guidance.

GP Registrar

If one is a GP Registrar, one needs to be included in a medical performers' list if one wishes to work in the UK health service. However, one does not need to be on the GP Register to complete training.

Before one completes training one will need to apply for a Certificate of Completion of Training (CCT).

Read more about CCTs in the background information about specialist and GP certification section.

8.6.4 RCGP

Practice teams, nurses and managers

If one is a practice manager, nurse or physician assistant, one can join RCGP through our General Practice Foundation (GPF). As well as access to the range of learning and development resources, membership allows all team members to get involved in shaping the future of general practice.

Through the General Practice Foundation (GPF), RCGP ensures that practice managers, nurses and physician assistants have a voice in the development of general practice. By joining, team members get access to the range of CPD and practice management resources.

To join the General Practice Foundation, you can either register online or download the form and see the website in References to get more detail on fees and term and conditions.

8.6.5 RCN

RCN Member Support Services

Member Support Services consists of five constituent services:

- Careers Service
- Counselling Service
- Immigration Advice Service
- Welfare Rights and Guidance Service
- Peer Support @ MSS (formerly the Work Injured Nurses Group and Disabled Nurses Network)

Pay rates for each year for RCNs, Agenda for Change pay bands etc. can be accessed using the website.

RCN and other outside organisations do provide courses – the former with no fees but the rest may charge a fee for participation. The free PCT courses should be attended, as these focus more on the work needed to be done for GP surgeries.

With cash-strapped surgeries, the opportunity to attend these courses would be severely limited and not all nurses might be able to attend. A lot of times these courses are not really practical – viewed from the surgery point of view.

For example, they may run a course on Job Specification and Job Description and it is not unusual to mention all the aspects of qualification, skills and experience, which would merit a very senior nurse on a pay of £30-40k, whereas the surgery may be seeking a nurse with a pay of £18-20k.

The courses, therefore, need not focus on what is needed as much as what they can impart – leaving the person to scale down expectations to meet surgery needs.

Courses pertaining to procedures are extremely relevant and useful and such courses are rare. It is often a better practice to follow self-help and use the Internet to gain knowledge followed by discussions with peers. GPs are rarely of help as they are quite busy and their tolerance level is extremely low.

Asking too many questions or clarifying doubts would eventually result in GPs thinking that the nurse needs a lot of support, and might go against the nurse when pay rise and staff evaluations are made.

8.7 Accounts

Section 18.0 deals with all aspects of surgery accounts.

The practice, depending on its size, may have an accountant working one day a week or even part-time. He will still be deemed as a staff member from HMRC's perspective and not as an independent contractor, unless the person comes for a few months on an ad hoc basis but not on fixed days to escape HMRC ruling.

In some practices, a PMgr with a good knowledge of the accounts, might deal with all day-to-day issues and act as a **'side kick'** to the accountant. The PMgr is expected to have tighter controls on all expenses and manage the petty cash expenses and income from all insurance work, HA, etc. More importantly, the PMgr should have a good handle on all claims and ensure due amounts were collected on time from the PCT appropriately.

All staff salaries to be paid by standing orders to their respective banks and the mandate should be set up within 2 weeks of the employee joining the surgery. GP partners may take cash advances each month for their expenses and the PMgr has to withdraw cash from the bank on the payment date. The PMgr should ensure that there is enough money in the current account and, if short, then a transfer should be made from a savings account.

Only GP partners would be signatory to the accounts. It is recommended that two partners sign each cheque issued for effective control. For withdrawing large sums of money from the bank, the PMgr should go with another person to the bank, even if it is close by. Crime in inner cities has increased and the surgery should not take chances with any attack on the PMgr, thereby losing cash and causing injury to the PMgr.

8.8 Bank Charges

These would generally relate to charges levied by the banks for the accounts operated by the surgery – current and savings. The surgery should have a separate account for capital expenses like building extensions and modifications etc., and income claimed from the PCT or other sources. The accountant usually deals with these. All fittings and furniture expenses should be charged to this account.

All bank accounts should be checked regularly for correctness and ensure unexplained payments or debits do not occur. If they do appear, then investigate thoroughly and obtain the correct transactions.

The PMgr should have a good rapport with the banks and be able to deal with them successfully in getting better loans and mortgages for the surgery premises and for any extensions to the premises envisaged. The PMgr should also ensure high bank charges are not incurred and bank accounts are in credit to meet all expenses.

8.9 Sundries

Sundries are for unbudgeted expenses and, as a rule, should not exceed 3% of the total surgery expenses. Also, any one item of expenditure should be less than £100, and preferably, most of the others less than £50.

It is important that the PMgr budgets expenses with all thoroughness and keeps sundries to a minimum. Food and hotel expenses for the GP partners, which are not allowed by HMRC, should not be claimed under sundries.

However, certain expenses on special occasions, like Christmas e.g. cards and presents to a select deserving few in the practice population, might be included. Christmas lunch for staff in a modest standard restaurant might also be included as a 'one-off'.

A common sense approach should prevail when claiming expenses under sundries.

8.10 Petty Cash

The Practice Manager (PMgr) should record all the income and expenses on a daily basis on a computer, and at the end of the month should prepare a statement as below for income and expenses for the year.

The PMgr should be taking some money each month as cash for expenses for the following month (See 8.10a for Petty Cash annual income expenses; 8.10.b for Petty Cash Typical Layout).

Usually the surgery would also be getting cash payments for some services e.g. travel vaccinations etc., from the nurses. In addition, the PMgr may make cash withdrawals for postage of various documents, and some income would accrue from some patients for insurance related work.

The major income would also be from cheques issued for insurance, mortgage work, passports, etc.

On the expenses front, wages would be paid in cash for cleaners. Also, small contractors would do maintenance or other work on payment of cash only. Other expenses would include: Salary for temporary staff and any salary advances, tea/coffee/biscuits/milk etc. for all surgery staff, postage and sundries.

GP Partners always perceive petty cash as a high expense area and think that the PMgr might not generally manage it properly. This paranoia is endemic in all GP surgeries and the PMgr should not be sensitive to these feelings or some brash comments dished out by the GP Partners.

If there were two partners, then one would be very sympathetic and seen to put up an argument for the PMgr. A wise PMgr would soon realise that it would be a **'Laurel Hardy'** act and both GPs feel the same, but one lets the other say the harsh comments.

Petty cash usually is such a small amount in comparison to the surgery income and expenses but GP Partners give undue heavy weighting! The good work of the PMgr would only be appreciated when he is able to make IOS claims on time and the GP Partners' income increases.

Date	Petty cash	Insurance Cash	Vacc./Travel cash	Insur. Bank Cr cheques	cleaners	Post	electrical	building	lunch	furnishing	sundries	cleaning	LL P/C	Locum	Total
year	746.54				386.00	22.37					25.84	50.00			484.21
April	697.50			903.13	400.00	25.11			18.13		45.05		39.00		527.29
May	500.00		350.00	737.84	400.00	21.82	25.54		25.00	75.00	60.11	44.00	56.00	90.00	896.47
June	697.50			0.00	500.00	29.27			36.60		7.98		100.00		573.85
July	600.00		691.00	944.16	400.00	88.85	164.50	250.35	42.20	60.00	68.62	21.60	48.00		1154.12
Aug	400.00		294.00	1099.41	410.00	74.02					42.66		115.00		886.68
Sept	1550.00		204.00	524.56	555.00	95.48	2.25	1372.74			115.89		9.44		2005.80
"				71.00	410.00										
Oct	1100.00	40.00	162.00	319.75		84.94	3.55	580.00	10.00	50.00	102.24	4.55	100.00	50.00	1496.28
Nov	800.00		651.00	0.00	511.00	129.62	17.25	210.00			57.13	15.96	15.00		944.96
Dec	1200.00	10.00	240.00	947.15	500.00	100.76					93.42			50.00	694.18
"				631.09	450.00						192.00				192.00
"				439.50							70.00				70.00
year											1050.00				1050.00
Jan	500.00		72.00	633.75	500.00	100.01					94.04				694.05
"	453.00			75.00											622.89
Feb	400.00	20.10	225.00	559.49	400.00	93.66	31.25				47.98		50.00		692.42
Mar	400.00			1090.51	500.00	5.44			63.40		23.58		100.00		
"	407.00			44.10	200.00	17.25					11.22		61.50		
Total	10451.54	70.10	2889.00	9020.44	6122.00	888.60	243.34	2413.09	195.33	185.00	2107.76	136.11	593.94	390.00	13275.17

8.10a Petty Cash Expenses (4.1.01-31.3.02_year-year)

GENERAL PRACTICE MANAGEMENT

Month	P/cash	Nurse 1	Nurse 2	Insurance	Stamps	Total	wages	sal adv	food	post	maint	sundries	total	month	to date	Income Insur. Chq
				←— Income —→					←———— Expenses ————→					←—Balance—→		
April	743.00	250.00	73.00	0.00	0.00	1066.00	400.00	300.00	67.96	23.18	194.52	69.39	1055.05	10.95	10.95	0.00
May	600.00	0.00	0.00	0.00	0.00	600.00	500.00	0.00	0.00	63.63	0.00	66.60	630.23	-30.23	-19.28	1067.28
June	600.00	195.00	203.00	31.50	0.00	1029.50	400.00	50.00	45.00	103.75	200.00	170.59	969.34	60.16	40.88	637.99
July	400.00	553.00	100.00	92.97	200.00	1345.97	600.00	25.00	0.00	264.11	840.60	123.11	1096.82	249.15	290.03	273.44
"																785.41
"																550.70
Aug	600.00	110.00	250.00	20.00	0.00	980.00	490.00	718.54	0.00	82.29	0.00	43.37	1354.20	-374.20	-84.17	843.50
"																1151.23
Sept	900.00	86.00	100.00	0.00	400.00	1486.00	610.00	50.00	90.00	309.56	90.00	190.48	1269.04	216.96	132.79	965.10
Oct	600.00	206.00	55.00	65.00	0.00	926.00	400.00	0.00	0.00	187.18	0.00	109.75	696.93	229.07	361.86	293.00
Nov	600.00	0.00	0.00	34.00	0.00	634.00	580.00	10.00	49.00	52.63	49.00	36.56	728.19	-94.19	267.67	575.00
Dec						0.00							0.00	0.00		
Jan						0.00							0.00	0.00		
Feb						0.00							0.00	0.00		
Mar						0.00							0.00	0.00		
Total	5043.00	1400.00	781.00	243.47	600.00	8067.47	3980.00	1153.54	151.96	618.12	809.85	7799.80				7142.65

8.10b Typical Layout – Petty Cash – Details of Income & Expenses

9. HR

This is a crucial aspect of work in any organisation and GP surgeries are no exception. In fact, certain demands are much greater than others, due to surgeries being a **'people industry'**. Apart from GPs, nurses and HCA and HCPs, most of the staff have to come in contact with patients, and interpersonal relationships are very crucial. Sometimes abilities to communicate and deal with people are more important than paper qualifications of the candidates.

HR and Legal issues go together. Legal aspects are so complicated it is best left to deal with CAB in the first instance, ACAS for rules and procedures, and respective organisations for medical protection for nurses and GPs.

The aspects of legal issues are not covered here.

A general list for a first-time manager to focus on would be:

1 Meet all staff – entire team – including the cleaners and caretakers during the course of the first few days to find out what they love about their jobs and challenges they face. Approach with the view **'How may I help you?'** to do better.

2 Read their CVs (Résumés) and previous reports and thank them for their contributions to the surgery.

3 Always find one who can be trusted and who will be your eyes and ears and plan to groom them as admin assistant in time, if the vacancy is not filled.

4 Find out about meetings and, if no formal ones are arranged, plan to do so once a month.

5 Recognise and appreciate their input to the meetings, which should be kept short and action points clearly stated for the future.

6 Get training or read about performance assessments and feedback sessions.

7 Ensure that issues on race, colour, gender, age, etc. are sensitively handled and state categorically that individuals will be assessed on their performance and positive attitudes they display for the good of the surgery.

8 Have clear communications so that all understand. Need for transparency is crucial.

9 Employees watch everything the PMgr says and does; hence, try to be the most ethical role model.

Manager's integrity and credibility are crucial for building a strong, trusting and successful team for the surgery management.

9.1 Job Specifications and Job Descriptions

For convenience Job Specifications and Job Descriptions for each job are combined together and **there is no Section 9.2**.

In order to get the right staff, the first step of recruitment is of paramount importance. This involves having correct job specifications – person's specification, and job descriptions.

Job descriptions should clearly state for all jobs, apart from the description of the job:

Title of the job

Locations(s)

Hours

Person's title

Reporting to

If one were to check these details for the surgery staff on the web, one would find so many requirements and skills. In the case of having a PMgr or nurse to do the job the surgery would have to pay salaries 'like top brass'. A receptionist's salary may vary from minimum basic wage per hour to, say, £12 per hour, if she is good. When she is so good, then a promotion is the only way to keep her and compensate her accordingly. Lot of the above descriptions have to be toned down to meet the requirements of surgeries managed by a single or even 6 GP partners without forsaking the crucial elements; the salary offered has to compensate even these minimal expectations.

The details given below are toned down and more realistic versions of what is needed in the surgery work; for each type of staff – the job (person) specification is mentioned first followed by the job descriptions.

9.1.1 Receptionists
9.1.1a Job Specifications

To get a job as a receptionist in a GP surgery the basic requirements are:
- Good personal skills – should keep a calm, courteous, friendly, yet professional

look and behave with great sensitivity to patients' needs.

- Good organisational skills – able to prioritise, time management and multi-tasking; very confidential.

- A minimum educational qualification – probably GCSE.

- Some computing knowledge – Microsoft Word, Excel and a database application, and proficient in spoken and written English language.

- Desirable but not essential is ability to speak one of the ethnic languages to deal with patients.

9.1.1b Job Description – Receptionist

A receptionist job description will vary from one surgery to another, but generally, duties, roles, and responsibilities of receptionists include:

- Meeting, greeting, and welcoming visitors.
- Entering visitors' details into the visitors' log book.
- Assist visitors in filling out visitors' passes, and issuing of visitors' pass.
- Assisting new employees as well as old ones in some cases with provision of ID badges, time sheet, rotas, photocopying, sending fax messages, posting notices and mail distribution.
- Taking incoming telephone calls, dealing with such calls promptly in a professional manner, and redirecting appropriate calls to other individuals or departments within and outside the establishment.
- General administrative duties including photocopying, invoicing, collecting cash and other forms of payments from customers if necessary, filing, booking and organising board and or meeting rooms, ordering stationery, dispatching and accepting mail and courier services (parcels).
- Ordering taxis for visitors.
- Excellent telephone manners.
- Switchboard experience.
- Use of photocopier, scanner and fax machine.
- Flexibility with work time.
- Good stress and anger management ability.

The title of the job, locations, if receptionist has to work in two split practices, hours of work and the person to whom the receptionist would report should be clearly stated.

9.1.2 Senior/Special Receptionist/Administration Manager

Depending on the size of the surgery and the ability of the Senior Receptionist, extra duties may be specified. Also, the surgery Partners may decide to have a separate Senior Receptionist and a separate Administration Manager. The details given below could be used for both with some adjustments to duties.

9.1.2a Job Specifications

To get a job as a receptionist in a GP surgery the basic requirements are:

- Good personal skills – should keep a calm, courteous, friendly, yet professional look and behave with great sensitivity to patients' needs; ability to deal with staff including very difficult but efficient ones.

- Good organisational skills – able to prioritise, time management and multi-tasking; extremely confidential and ability to think on 'one's feet'.

- Able to motivate the team and a good team player.

- A minimum educational qualification – probably GCSE; preferably 'A' level or even a graduate.

- Some computing knowledge – Microsoft Word, Excel, and a data base application and emails, and proficient in spoken and written English language.

- Desirable but not essential is the ability to speak one of the ethnic languages to deal with patients.

9.1.2b Job Description

Title: Receptionist/Administrator

Location(s):

Hours:

Reports to: PMgr

Summary: To work with other receptionists and healthcare professionals to provide a quality service to patients. Provide the first point of contact for patients and other stakeholders/visitors (either face to face or on the telephone) and provide administrative support to PMgr.

Duties:

1 Handling telephone and face to face requests for appointments and making the appointments on the computerised appointments system.

2 Directing patients to the appropriate healthcare professional within the Practice, e.g. Doctor, Specialist Nurse, Nurse Practitioner, Practice Nurse, Healthcare Assistant.

3 Booking in patients when they arrive at the surgery.

4 Helping new patients register with the surgery – providing the necessary paperwork and checking returned paperwork is complete.

5 Advising patients of the results of routine tests.

6 Receiving and checking repeat prescription requests. Printing repeat prescriptions.

7 Giving completed prescriptions to patients and to local pharmacies that collect them.

8 Calling patients to arrange for routine appointments, e.g. for immunisations, asthma checks, diabetes checks etc.

9 Taking phone messages and passing calls from patients, hospitals etc. to other colleagues.

10 Responding to patient requests for information about other NHS services.

11 Receiving and documenting payments for non-NHS services such as taxi medicals, HGV medicals, travel claim forms, some travel vaccinations, circumcisions etc.

12 Registering new patients and removing patients who have left on the computerised record system.

13 Checking consulting rooms each morning – turning on computers, checking couch roll etc.

14 Monitoring travel vaccination requests.

15 Providing information to the Midwife on newly pregnant patients.

16 Checking fridges, lights, windows, computers etc. at the end of each day.

17 Straightening/tidying the waiting room at the end of the day.

18 Keeping leaflets tidy and stocked.

19 Setting the surgery answer phone.

20 Photocopying, scanning and filing of paper records.

21 Ordering: this may be stationery and office supplies, consumables or medical/clinical supplies ordered under the supervision of one of the Nursing staff.

22 Receiving and checking deliveries.

23 Monitoring fridge temperatures.

24 Booking patient transport (occasional).

9.1.3 IMT-Computing Specialist

9.1.3a Job Specifications

To get a job as an IMT specialist in a GP surgery the basic requirements are:

- Good personal skills – should keep a calm, courteous, friendly, yet professional look and behave with great sensitivity to patients' and staff needs;
- Good organisational skills – able to prioritise, time management and multi-tasking; extremely confidential and ability to think on 'one's feet'; able to motivate the team and a good team player;
- A minimum educational qualification – probably 'A' level, preferably a graduate;
- Sound computing knowledge – Microsoft Word, Excel and a data base applications, hardware and software knowledge, emails and proficient in spoken and written English language;
- Desirable but not essential is ability to speak one of the ethnic languages to deal with patients.

9.1.3b Job Description

Title: IMT Specialist or support

Location(s):

Hours:

Reporting to: PMgr

Summary: To provide IMT support services to one or two practices pertaining to all computer software, operation, training, communication systems, making timely input of data for clinical points through the link system with the Health Authority/PCT and monitoring the target achievements in the various clinics under New Contract.

Duties:

1 Become thoroughly competent with the computer system used in the Practice – a Link system has to be used for all data records so that the Health Authority can access Link system information and management.

2 Train the receptionist staff, GPs, Practice Nurses and HCA on areas pertaining their use.

3 Maintain close links with the computer software supplier regarding problem solving in various areas.

4 Assist GPs, nurses and staff in computer related issues – operation, training, problem solving.

5 Send information for action by the Practice. Liaise with PCT/HA regarding various patient details – registrations, deductions, counts, list sizes, waiting for approval, acknowledgements etc.

6 Patient registrations, patient transfers, patient deductions.

7 Patient Amendments: Change of addresses.

8 All types of claims: Prescriptions, immunisations, vaccinations, night calls, minor surgery.

9 Contraceptive Services Target & Quality Payments: Pathology Links, scanning of documents.

10 Data storage and security, cervical cytology, upload/download, Read Codes usage/training.

11 Clinics data analysis and template set-up for the computer system listed in '3' above.

12 Computer software, applications, printing prescriptions, update of records, all forms of report searches etc.

13 Ensure computer systems and communication equipment incl. telephone, fax, copiers and scanners etc. used in the Practice are in good working order and seek prompt assistance as required.

14 Ensure when changes to offices or systems are made in either of the two practices.

15 Assist the Practice and the Practice Manager in highlighting areas for development.

16 Up to date records should be kept and even though claims are minimal due to Global sum the facilities for computer system and communication equipment are in place. To enable this, ordering of equipment and consumables have to made and ensure the receipt of items/equipment, their installation and commission, as necessary.

17 Training, operational problems and solutions from Torex/BT/computer

software supplier as appropriate.

18 Payment, for audit purposes all records should be kept up to date and readily available for inspection by PCT/HA.

19 The clinical points achieved each month should be checked and compared with targets aimed. Steps should be taken quickly to ensure input of data using ISIS and other procedures.

20 In times of dire emergency, due to staff absenteeism, for the effective functioning of the surgery, assistance in the reception work would be crucial and should be undertaken.

21 The above job description will be subject to periodic review and amendments in consultation with the post holder.

9.1.4 Medical Secretary

9.1.4a Job Specification

To get a job as a Medical Secretary in a GP surgery the basic requirements are:

- Good personal skills – should keep a calm, courteous, friendly, yet professional look and behave with great sensitivity to patients' and staff needs.

- Good organisational skills – able to prioritise, time management and multi-tasking extremely confidential and ability to think on 'one's feet'; and a good team player.

- Good knowledge of medical terms and skilful inn taking dictation and ability to do shorthand would be a distinct advantage.

- A minimum educational qualification – probably 'A' level, preferably a graduate.

- Sound computing knowledge – Microsoft Word, Excel, a data base applications, emails and proficient in spoken and written English language.

- Desirable but not essential is the ability to speak one of the ethnic languages to deal with patients.

9.1.4b Job Description

Title: Medical Secretary.

Location(s):

Hours: per week or Part-time or Full-time

Reporting to: PMgr.

Summary: To provide all Medical Secretary services pertaining to one or two practices.

Duties:

Mail:

- Open mail and sort out insurance letters, DSS forms, solicitors' letters etc. and log in;
- Pass relevant ones to the receptionist to obtain notes to be given to the GPs;
- On receipt of completed forms from the GPs, check that all relevant sections are duly completed, signature, date, account number etc. before sending these to the appropriate parties;
- Check and send for appropriate fees for the reports and non-NHS services as per list supplied and in those cases, where applicable, proceed with report/copies on receipt of money from the requesting party. Log in the payments requested and those received with dates;
- Do not issue reports to a third party without consent form from the patient.

Secretarial:

- Take dictation as and when GPs require it;
- Type letters/correspondence from audiotape messages given by GPs;
- Records and documentation: Maintain up to date records/files for all correspondences with;
- Deal with any queries raised in the letters for giving report/copies of records;
- Log out all mail to be sent to various parties after taking copies for files.

Routine issues:

1. Patients, solicitors, Health Authority, minutes of the meetings, pending issues;
2. Fees charges/received, cheques given to Practice Manager;
3. Complaints and associated correspondence;
4. Duty rota, health call (for doctor on call lists), GPs' absence;

5 GPs' correspondence, messages, contact details – tel. & mobile numbers.

6 Appointments;

7 Special matters;

8 Miscellaneous;

9 Assist in reception area, as and when necessary;

10 Be aware of targets for cervical smears and child immunisation. Liaise with the Practice – special appointments; house visits and private patient appointments;

11 Research statistics for GPs and their personal projects, disease incidence, 'at-risk' register and age/sex register, any other information for the Practice Nurses and ensure that all required forms are submitted on time to meet the targets;

12 Check for meetings with District Health Authority (now PCT) and Local Medical Committee and ensure relevant documents are available for the meeting;

13 Liaise with person in charge of IT support to ensure that all records are updated in the Link System, where applicable;

14 Any other assignments that may be required and agreed with the Practice;

15 Key Objective is to have minimal backlog of work in the practice in terms of updating records, claims, complaints and all issues affecting the performance of the Practice;

16 Act as Practice Manager in his absence, if there is no Administration Manager.

17 The above job description would be subject to periodic review and amendments in consultation with the post holder.

9.1.5 Nurse

9.1.5a Job Specifications

To get a job as a Practice Nurse in a GP surgery the basic requirements are:

- Good personal skills – should keep a calm, courteous, friendly, yet professional look and behave with great sensitivity to patients' needs. Ability to deal with staff including very difficult but efficient ones;

- Good organisational skills – able to prioritise, time management and multi-tasking, extremely confidential and ability to think on 'one's feet'. Able to motivate the team and a good team player;

- A minimum educational qualification – probably a graduate with nursing specialty subjects;

- Some computing knowledge – Microsoft Word, Excel, a database application and emails, and proficient in spoken and written English language;

- Desirable but not essential is the ability to speak one of the ethnic languages to deal with patients.

9.1.5b Job Description

Title: Practice Nurse

Location(s): of practice(s)

Agenda for Change (AfC) banding: 5

Hours of duty: specify hours for part-time or full-time

Responsible to: For Administration – PMgr

For all Clinical – Senior Partner

Summary:

The post holder is responsible for the delivery of basic practice nursing services care to the practice population. Supported by other nurses within the practice, they will deliver care within the boundaries of their role, focusing upon encouraging patients to be healthy, monitoring of long-term conditions, health prevention and screening activities. They will work collaboratively with the general practice team to meet the needs of patients, supporting the delivery of policy and procedures, and providing nurse leadership as required.

Duties: These are not listed in detail, as an RGN grade 5 nurse would be expected to be trained in the following skills – (refer to RGN website):

- Clinical practice – sound knowledge of procedures
- Communication – oral and written
- Delivering quality service
- Team working
- Risk management
- Information processing – Read Codes, databases etc.
- Learning and development – self and any trainee nurse
- Equality and Diversity Codes and procedures

- Health promotion
- Clinical Governance issues

9.1.6 Practice Manager
9.1.6a Job Specifications

To get a job as a Practice Manager in a GP surgery the basic requirements are:

- Good personal skills – should keep a calm, courteous, friendly, yet professional look and behave with great sensitivity to patients' needs. Ability to deal with staff including very difficult but efficient ones. High level of motivation is a positive point;
- Good organisational skills – able to prioritise, time management and multi-tasking; extremely confidential and ability to think on 'one's feet'. Able to motivate the team and a good team player;
- A minimum educational qualification – probably a graduate with specialty subjects;
- AMSPAR or Diploma in Practice Management is desirable but not essential. Some previous computing knowledge – Microsoft Word, Excel, a database application and emails, and proficient in spoken and written English language;
- Desirable but not essential is the ability to speak one of the ethnic languages to deal with patients;
- Strategic planning and business skills;
- Accounting skills and budgeting awareness;
- Management experience is more important. Both AMSPAR and the IHM offer their members further training opportunities and professional recognition. (Refer to websites)

9.1.6b Job Description

Title: Practice Manager

Locations(s): Practices addresses

Hours: state hours or Part-time (small practices) or full-time

Responsible to: Senior Partner

Summary: Practice manager, runs the business side of a GP surgery or health centre.

The PMgr would be responsible for managing the practice's staff and budgets, developing its business strategy, and making sure that everything runs smoothly.

Duties would typically include:

- Recruiting, training and supervising medical receptionists and secretaries;
- Dealing with accounts and budgets, paying wages and making sure the practice meets its financial targets;
- Organising duty rosters for doctors and clerical staff;
- Managing the reception and appointments system;
- Managing manual and computerised medical records systems;
- Controlling stocks of equipment, stationery and drugs;
- Arranging the building's cleaning, maintenance and security;
- Organising and attending practice meetings;
- Monitoring prescriptions;
- Contact with outside organisations such as local NHS trusts and primary care groups, and local authority social services departments.

9.1.7 Healthcare Specialists

The specifications and descriptions should be similar to the nurse but with considerably less responsibilities as the area they might be focusing on would be a narrow field. The details have to be modified to suit surgery requirements.

9.3 Job Appraisals

One can find via Google a job appraisal format. Here PCT format and one used in a specific surgery, applicable to most surgeries, are included. PCT format is mainly generic – encapsulating the requirements ranging from a very small surgery to a large Health Centre and surgeries have to tailor their needs from the details. The specific one focuses on the small to medium – up to 8 GPs in a practice operating on two locations.

9.3.1 PCT Formats

Introduction to an Appraisal Document

Preparation involves the appraisee writing answers to standard questions on the previous year's achievements, areas for development, and future objectives. This is sent to the appraiser to read. The appraiser then lists items he or she wants to discuss, having read the appraisee's points. The meeting is held and a written summary is made by the appraiser and signed by both parties. A form for training needs is completed and sent to the Personnel Department. The rest of the document is confidential to the two people involved. Most of the areas are listed.

Section A

Completed by the appraisee and given to the appraiser at least one week before the meeting.

Part 1 – Last Year's Achievements

What were your key result areas in the past 12 months, taking into account the agreed objectives from the last review meeting (if applicable)?

What do you feel your significant achievements have been?

How have they been achieved?

Have you taken on any temporary or new activities and responsibilities? What are they?

Part 2 – Areas for Development

- Which areas do you feel have not gone so well?
- Why has this happened and who or what could have helped you?
- How would you aim to improve these areas in the future?
- Which areas of the job do you dislike?
- Does this affect your performance in any way and, if so, how?
- Are there any areas of your job that you find particularly difficult?

- How can these be addressed?
- What skills have you got that are not being used in your current job?

Part 3 – Future Objectives

- What specific objectives would you like to set yourself for the next 12 months? Think about the job and also your personal development objectives.
- What additional job experience or areas of responsibility would you like to be given?
- What help do you think your immediate supervisor could give you?
- What could you do to help yourself?
- What training would you like to receive over the next year?
- What career aspirations do you have?

The appraisee is also asked to state any other comments or areas he or she wishes to raise during the appraisal discussion.

Section B

Completed by the appraiser and given to the appraisee at least four days before the meeting. "In addition to the points the appraisee wishes to raise during the discussion, the key areas I would like to cover are as follows:" (these are listed 1, 2, 3, etc.), the appraiser signs the section and gives it to the appraisee.

Section C

Completed by the appraiser and signed by both parties.

Performance Appraisal Summary Form

In addition to the points made in Sections A and B, a form is completed following the discussion to ensure that all the key areas are recorded comprising:

Section 1 – Other points raised in the discussion were: list points.

Section 2 – Objectives for the future: listed as 1, 2, 3, etc.

Section 3 – Training needs: this section only is photocopied for the Personnel Department; signed by appraiser, appraisee, Head of Department, and dated.

9.3.2 Surgery Formats

Part A – Factors assisting in overall performance objectively and establishing levels of proven performance. (Select only one from each criterion)

Part B – Assists in analysing steps to be taken by both the supervisor and the incumbent to sustain or improve performance in the future (mark each criteria with level of significance)

Part C – Assists in career progression and training consideration (comment as appropriate).

PART A

1. Quality of work:

Employee   Supervisor

- Always above average
- Can be accepted without checking
- Usually acceptable
- Frequently requires work to be done

2. Quantity of work (productivity):
- Normally performs additional assignments
- In addition to regular work
- Regular duties completed in time
- Meets expectations
- Requires improvement

3. Ability to meet normal workload:

- Can cope with extra peak loads
- Usually completes quickly
- Normally on time
- Frequently late

4. Accepting responsibility:

- Able to undertake new responsibility
- Performs regular duties adequately
- Performs responsibilities inadequately

5. Preventing or coping with problems:

- Sound judgment – able to use ingenuity
- Alert – use routine discretion in minor matters
- Anticipates problems but requires advice from supervisor for action
- Lacks foresight – usually caught unaware

6. Reliability (ability to work without supervision):

Employee   Supervisor

- Can be relied to work under difficult circumstances
- Keeps head even in crisis
- Works well on own
- Requires occasional checking
- Must be constantly supervised

7. Work habits (Punctuality, attendance):

- Always dependable – willing to go extra mile
- Generally displays dependability
- Occasionally poor work habits

- Frequently poor work habits

8. Job knowledge (rules, procedures, etiquette to patients):
- Thoroughly familiar and keen to learn next stage
- Very familiar and cooperative
- Adequate knowledge
- Insufficient knowledge

9. Ability to learn/process information on a computer:
- Able to use computers efficiently
- Has adequate knowledge
- Needs constant supervision
- Has limited skills

10. Clinical skills: (for nurses only)
- Able to use skills effectively
- Has adequate knowledge
- Has limited skills

Employee   Supervisor

11. IT skills: (for IT supervisor)
- Able to use computers efficiently
- Has adequate knowledge
- Needs constant supervision
- Has limited skills
- Sound appreciation of procedures
- Sound appreciation of claims
- Proactive approach for claims
- Computer training of other personnel

Supervisor – Summary comments: (comment on performance, results and progress)

Overall performance rating:

- Exceeds expected output
- Meets job expectations
- Areas for improvement identified
- Unsatisfactory – falls short of minimum performance

PART B

Level of significance (H = High; M = Medium; L = low).
  Employee   Supervisor

1. Interpersonal skills:

Ability to relate to others – staff and patients; cooperation;
Being an effective team member.

  Employee / Supervisor

2. Communication:
- Express clearly and understand others
- Ability to listen and learn from others
- Ability to recognise formal communication
- Ability to recognise informal communication

3. Self-improvement:
- Acquire and utilise additional skills
- Seek additional responsibilities

4. Perseverance:

- Ability to complete tasks despite difficulties
- Ability to adjust priorities

5. Efficiency:

- Effective time management skills
- Ability to work quickly without making mistakes or needing supervision

6. Commitment:

- Positive, enthusiastic/optimistic approach
- Pride in working towards surgery objectives

7. General:

- Strengths: list areas
- Weaknesses: list area
- Areas for improvement: list areas.

PART C

1. Development plan for improvement:

Objectives

Supervisor's commitment to action

Budget approved

Target date for completion

    a.
    b.
    c.
    d.
    e.

2. Job Interests:

Employees interest Supervisor's interest

3. Comments on appraisal meeting

Employee/Supervisor

- Thoroughness
- Adequate time
- Location
- Openness

Signatures:

Employee	**Date**
Supervisor	**Date**
Manager	**Date**

9.4 Staff References

These are required to be given when an employee leaves the company. In the olden days there were no problems giving a reference sometimes masking certain shortfalls. It is not uncommon to give a glowing reference to a troublesome employee to get rid of him.

However, these days there are issues of litigation in the extreme for making a false claim. Equally an employee may take the employer to court and in this aspect even CAB has to act in favour of the client and they are not required to know both sides of the case. These have put strain on the part of the person required to give a reference, and they may play safe and not raise any contentious issues at all.

It is always a pleasure to give a reference to a very good employee, even though he/she is leaving for a better career or pastures, which one should never stop. Equally, loaded comments or using puns should be avoided, even though they used to bring a smile while reading.

The classic example was, when one Mr Jones was a skiver and the employer could not get any work done by him, the employer used a pun and wrote, "He would be a very lucky person to have Mr Jones working for him." During these days of political correctness such beauty in expressions is lost forever.

When giving reference it is better to be:

Very formal and it is customary to give it in a typed document;

Always date the letter;

Address to the person in the organisation – either by title or name if known – use surnames only – never first names;

Give the full address and post code;

Give a reference – as 'Re: so-and-so' – name of person to whom reference is sought;

Close the message with 'Yours faithfully' – if the name of the person is not known, 'Yours sincerely – if surname is known';

The body of the references are only given for a select few employees. For other staff the message given below could be modified as required.

9.4.1 Receptionist

"To whom It may concern

I have known Ms …… for nearly (so many) years and she joined as a Receptionist but quickly learnt the ropes. She is good in dealing with patients and does not lose her cool when intimidated by some patients.

She is good in computing and does not make errors in typing or in coding. She is adept in dealing with colleagues, junior staff, patients, public and her superiors – GPs and Partners. She is extremely competent and thinks on her feet. She had in certain cases deputized for Senior Receptionist in SR's absence. The jobs are safe with her in terms of completion on time and quality of work. She needs minimal or no supervision.

We would be extremely sorry to see her leave."

9.4.2 A Competent Nurse

"To Whom It May Concern

I have known MS, of for nearly (so many) years. She has been Practice Nurse in our surgery helping out in the two split surgeries in (say the area of the country).

She is very methodical, thorough and heavily focused on patient care. She strictly follows the nursing protocols to give the best medical care. She is self-motivated and totally committed to the surgery and patient care. She exudes considerable skills and aptitude and is extremely self-disciplined.

She seeks to improve her skill continually by attending various courses with the sole aim of improving her service to the patients. She is skilful in communicating and able to deal with all ethnic and cultural groups, young and old.

She also has a special talent to deal with difficult patients. She gets on well with the GP's, receptionists and all support staff. She is a good team player.

I have no hesitation in stating that she will do only too well in the course that she is planning to undertake shortly.

We all would be extremely sorry to see her leave us."

9.4.3 Practice Manager

(Used He when it should be He or She; change, as needed)

"PMgr joined us …… and he is a very valued member of the practice. He has flair in dealing with the staff, partners, patients, HA, PCT and other outside Personnel.

He has built a good team of staff and reduced the staff turnover. He has a sound appreciation of the New Contract and able to deal with PCT on payments due for the surgery.

He has improved the working and the atmosphere of the practice significantly. He is very focused on the financial aspects of the practice. He is pleasant and able to communicate effectively with all personnel.

We all would be extremely sorry to see him leave us."

9.5 CVs

CVs (Résumés in USA)
9.5.1 UK Format

This format is usually two to three pages listing:

Name, address and contact details.
Educational qualifications from young age to current.
Work Experiences.
Experience – jobs with tile, reporting to, responsibilities and achievements.

Personal information – hobbies, special interests, marital status.

Presently age and marital status or even title – Mrs or Ms need not be stated but employers may ask and it is better to include these.

Even though discriminations of all sorts are not legal and NHS may proudly state this, it is difficult to stop interviewers straddling these areas with their subtle questioning. Interviewees, unless very offended, may not take the issue further and treat it as a way of life and move on to seeking the next interview with other firms. Even if the issue is taken further via CAB or legal route, that particular job is lost and the candidate may have to spend months to get any satisfaction from the complaint. It is better to move on.

A slightly different format to above is shown below – for a specific job the details for each applicant have to be filled in as appropriate:

Name in capitals:

Email address:

Tel (Mobile): (landlines rarely used)

PROFESSIONAL PROFILE: A general summary of career and ambitions.

KEY SKILLS:

- Customer service or similar
- Highlight communication skills, sensitivity etc.
- Problem solving
- Mention working as a team
- Organisation
- What areas managed effectively, cost savings made etc.
- Languages: Fluent in English and any other. Crucial to know very well spoken and written English to deal with patients; also any ethnic language as role of interpreter would be a bonus.

CAREER HISTORY:

List all job experiences in the above details, starting with the latest.

For each of the above experience state the following:

- From start date to leaving date
- Organisation
- Position
- Reporting to
- Responsibilities

TRAINING:

Any special training, courses attended with certificates received etc.

EDUCATION:

Details of schools, GCSE/O Level; A level results or equivalent; university qualifications; special computing courses, etc.

HOBBIES: Extracurricular activities, etc.
PERSONAL: Date of birth, marital status.

Limit to 2, maximum 3 pages, as it would require a dedicated reader to afford time to go through the details.

If a CV runs to too many pages then usually an intermediary would be asked to select a few CVs for interview. If such a situation were to arise, then a candidate would be at a great disadvantage. Especially during the formative years of one's career, it is recommended to limit a CV to 1 or maximum 2 pages. The aim is for the PMgr to see the applications for all staff jobs and GP Partners to see all applicants CV for the PMgr post.

9.5.2 USA Format

The résumé usually has to be one page, as the people are so pushed for time, they would 'bin' any CVs running more than one page, especially if the response is good. So aim to catch the top man who might conduct the interview.

Adjust font sizes but not less than 10. Preferably 11 for the body of the résumé, header and footer may be font size 9.

A typical format is given below for a PMgr job:

Header: Name – block capital; email and mobile telephone no.

Position Sought: Practice Manager – part-time or full-time – short-term or long-term – to suit surgery needs.

Summarises previous experience, which could be related – man management, finance, H&S, HR etc. if applicable.

Summary: Over xx years of increasingly responsible, diversified experience in Senior Management in large corporate organisations in (state name) responsible for (state position and number of staff reporting) etc.

Skills: (the bullet presentation lists the key areas which should interest the employer)

* Operations
* Marketing
* Financial/Computing
* HR
* Management

Include areas of experience in key words under each heading as applicable:

Quality control, sales, new products, accounts, budgets, staff issues, Microsoft packages

Experience:

List all job experiences in the above details, starting with the latest.

For each experience state:

- From (date) to (date)
- Organisation
- Position
- Reporting to
- Responsibilities (particularly, for the post of Practice Manager, the dimension of previous jobs – financial – value of direct control e.g. for 2 M GBP etc.; and for staff – responsible for 15 staff etc.)

Personal:

- Date of birth:
- Marital Status: If married, state so.

- Qualification: Degree, university, country (year);
- Training:
- Hobbies and awards:

GP and nurses' applications have to run into 2-3 pages due to the depth of experience. The formats given above, apply to all other jobs in a GP surgery.

Nothing would be gained by inflating one's experience or qualifications; it is better to be succinct and to the point. The interview would cover the areas the interviewer wants to clarify. The one-page format packs lot of skills and key words which would separate such a résumé from others.

Also, do not have strong issues about not declaring Miss, Mrs and also the date of birth. These are bound to come out. Instead aim for giving these and maximise discussions on the job selection by the interviewer.

The key objective of a CV/résumé is to get an interview. Hence, focus attention and attract the reader's interest so that an interview results.

Search with Google for more about the formats for CVs.

A USA format CV is given for the author.

V Subramanian (Mani)

Position Sought:

Practice Manager – Part-time or full-time – short term or long term – to suit surgery needs.

Summary:

Over 4 years of Practice Manager experience in a busy N. London practice/Birmingham and over 25 years of increasingly responsible diversified experience. Manufacturing, Import/Export and Trading experience on a range of products. Technical, Financial, Senior Management experience and Overseas Operations for UK and US companies.

Skills:
* *Plant & Operations*
* *Marketing*
* *Financial/Computing*
* *GP Practice Management*

17 UK plants	Intl. Markets	Capital Budgets. P&L	Prac. Manag.
R&D Budgets	Joint Ventures/ Collabor	Accounts	Torex /Vision Systems
Quality Control	Project Evaluations	Word, Excel, P/point	PCT/HA/MPS liaison
Training & Dev.	Import/Export proceed	Microsoft pkg	New Contract; C&B; PBC

Experience:

8/04 to date: BMSD Consultancy Ltd, Company Secretary (my wife's computing consultancy company).

2/05 to 7/05: **Practice Manager**, Old Mill Surgery, Edgbaston, Birmingham (short term assignment to help out)

Familiar with Choose & Book, Agenda for Change, PBC etc., 2500 patients.

Single Partner and 1 locum GP, 2 nurses and full clinics.

3/01 to 11/04: **Practice Manager** – inner city GP surgery management of 6 GPs; 10,000 patients; 2 split surgeries; 20 staff; 3 PCT nurses; 8x2 Clinics; Haringey PCT; Torex Comp. System; Training, Management, Clinical governance/adherence, audits, quality checks, writing manuals for staff/GP use; site development; Liaise with PCT/HA; maximised income; enhanced services and increased clinics for patient care. Sound knowledge of New Contract, Protocols and seeking maximum quality/admin. points.

11/99 to 7/03: **Subtech Ltd (own company)** – computing contracting/trading/technical consultancy.

1/95-10/99: **M J Exports (UK) Ltd – subsidiary of MJ Exports Ltd, India**.

An Import/Export company with a turnover of US $12 million per year on a range of products.

Management of orders, deliveries, **Finance, Legal, Company Secretarial**, L/Cs, accounts etc.

General Manager – responsible for UK Operations. Reporting to the Chairman of the Group.

5/92-12/94: **Voyager Emblems Inc., NY, USA**. (Subsidiary plants in Canada,

India and Australia).

Managed 100% owned Indian plant in Pune along with key operations in US & Canada.

Plants & continual liaison with Australian Plant.

Director of International Operations – Reporting to the President of the Company.

4/84-4/92: **Independent Consultant in UK. Technical, Marketing and Financial.**

10/72-12/83: **Plant & Operations Management**

* Carborundum Universal Ltd, Madras, India. Project Manager, reporting to the Exec. Director.

* The British Aluminium Co. Ltd (BA)/Alcan International UK Ltd

10/68-9/72: Ph. D in Metallurgy – Wales; Management Studies – Wales.

5/65-9/68   Plant Metallurgist, BA, Wales.

7/62-4/65   Foundry Technologist, Cast Iron, Steel & Non-Ferrous, Coal Mining Machinery Plant, India.

Personal:

Date of Birth: 18 Sept. 1940

Marital Status: Married

Qualification: BE (Metallurgy) India; Ph. D – Wales; Management (Wales)

9.6 Recruitment

9.6.1 Checklist for all Admin Staff Appointments

Generally most of the entrants to receptionists' vacancies may be school leavers, or might not have been to university, depending on their ages. The CV may indicate the education, work experiences, hobbies and some personal details. References might not be listed and given only after the interview. However, the surgery has the right to some further information and they must ascertain this and be satisfied before appointing anyone.

These requirements are necessitated due to the large movement of people into the

UK from Europe, purely as member states and from outside Europe, due to previous Commonwealth countries status; on these people several restrictions are applied. Then there are the people coming as **'students enrolling in various short courses but seeking entry status and benefits'**.

The checklist should include the following:

- Qualifications – University and main course subjects with certificates, if any;
- Other vocational courses;
- Previous experience, no. of years worked, the capacity, reporting to;
- Training – no. of years and status or certificates obtained;
- Ability to speak in English to patients; if not then GPs to be notified;
- Nationality – check passport;
- Work permit status – students only 20 hours per week during course time and normal hours during college/university holidays. They should work in non-clinical fields only;
- References;
- Ask them to state whether there are any other issues the surgery should know about;
- Age, pregnancy status should not be queried but if the person volunteers then it should be noted. Asking generally about any urgent medical condition needing hospital visits or attending any clinics may make them volunteer information on pregnancy or any serious illnesses;
- It is preferable these are listed in a form for the candidate to write down the responses.
- Record their answers to other questions at the interview, as it may be useful at a future date.

9.6.2 Checklist for Nurse Appointments

Generally most of the entrants to nurses' vacancies would usually be graduates with nursing training or as special qualification. The CV may indicate the education, work experiences, hobbies and some personal details. References may not be listed until after the interview.

However, the surgery has the right to some further information and they must ascertain this and be satisfied before appointing anyone. These requirements are necessitated due to large movement of people into UK from Europe purely as member states and from outside Europe due to previous Commonwealth countries status; on these people restrictions are applied. Then there are the people coming seeking entry status and benefits.

The checklist should include the following:

- Qualifications – University and main course subjects with certificates, if any;
- Other vocational courses/training with certificates;
- Previous nursing experience, no. of years worked, the capacity, reporting to;
- Nurse training – no. of years and status or certificates obtained;
- Member of Royal College of Nursing or similar approved bodies – a must. The Registration certificate should be produced; if not, then it had to be brought to the surgery, before any appointment be offered subject to other issues being satisfied. RCN number to be given in the meantime;
- Medical protection – MPS/MDU if applicable or RN coverage;
- Ability to speak in English to patients; if not, then GPs to be notified;
- Nationality – check passport;
- Work permit status – students only 20 hours per week during course time and normal times during College/university holidays. The onus is on the candidate to get permit from Home Office for foreign nationals;
- References preferably one should be from the GP Partners, if the candidate has worked as a nurse in a GP practice in UK;
- Special chronic disease management skills – CHC, diabetes, CHD, asthma, HT, mental health, gynae, family planning, minor surgery, etc.;
- Ask them to state whether there are any other issues the surgery should know;
- Age, pregnancy status, should not be queried but if the person volunteers then it should be noted. Asking generally about any urgent medical condition needing hospital visits or attending any clinics may make them volunteer information on pregnancy or any serious illnesses;
- Previous or current regulatory or disciplinary investigations, in UK or abroad, with results to date and evidence of current status;
- Clearance letter from GMC or PCT or such bodies;
- Criminal Records Bureau (CRB) clearance;
- It is preferable these are listed in a form for the candidate to write down the responses;

- Record their answers to other questions at the interview, as it may be useful at a future date.

9.6.3 Checklist for GP Appointments

Generally all entrants to GP vacancies would have to be medical graduates with MBBS degree along with MD or equivalent and PhD research experience along with medical internships. The CV might indicate the education, previous GP work experience, hobbies and some personal details. References might not be listed and given only after the interview.

However, the surgery has the right to some further information and they must ascertain this and be satisfied before appointing anyone. These requirements are necessitated due to large movement of people into UK from Europe purely as member states and from outside Europe due to previous Commonwealth countries status; on these people restrictions are applied. Then there are the people coming seeking entry status and benefits.

The checklist should include the following:

- Qualifications – MBBS, MD or equivalent. PhD on related medical field;
- Other vocational courses/training with certificates;
- Previous GP experience, no. of years worked, the capacity, reporting to;
- GP training – no. of years and status or certificates obtained;
- Member of General Medical Council (GMC), Royal College of General Practitioners (RCGP) or similar approved bodies – a must. The registration certificate should be produced; if not, then it has to be brought to the surgery before any appointment be offered subject to other issues being satisfied. RCGP, GMC numbers to be given in the meantime;
- Medical protection – MPS/MDU membership to be evidenced;
- PCT performers' list;
- Ability to speak in English to patients; if not, then GP Partners to be notified;
- Nationality – check passport;
- Work permit status – students only 20 hours per week during course time and normal times during College/university holidays. The onus is on the candidate to get permit from Home Office for foreign nationals;
- References – preferably one should be from the GP Partners, if the candidate has worked as a GP in the UK;

- Special chronic disease management skills – CHs, diabetes, CHD, asthma, HT, mental health, gynae, family planning, minor surgery etc.;

- Ask them to state whether there are any other issues the surgery should know;

- Age, pregnancy status, should not be queried but if the person volunteers then it should be noted. Asking generally about any urgent medical condition needing hospital visits or attending any clinics may make them volunteer information on pregnancy or any serious illnesses;

- Previous or current regulatory or disciplinary investigations, in UK or abroad, with results to date and evidence of current status;

- Clearance letter from GMC or PCT or such bodies;

- CRB clearance;

- It is preferable these are listed in a form for the candidate to write down the responses;

- Record their answers to other questions at the interview, as it may be useful at a future date.

9.6.4 Advertisements

In weekly papers specifically focused for GP surgeries, like *Pulse* and *GP magazine* and on the web – *First Practice Management* – one can get an idea of the type of adverts to place for any vacancy in the surgery.

Unlike large practices, salaries need not be specified for vacancies in smaller surgeries, leaving the details during the discussion between the candidate and the PMgr and/or GP partner.

Government agencies like Job Centres rarely provide suitable candidates and it is a waste of theirs and the surgery's time and effort.

Networking usually results in better candidates for the vacancy but as per legal requirements an adverts have to be placed for GP/Locum/Nurse vacancies.

The adverts should list some basic information and a few formats for the vacancies are given below:

Surgery Details

Vacancy

9.6.4.1 Receptionists

"We are a busy 6 partner GP Surgery based across two sites. We are looking for a part-time receptionist for 20 hours per week spread over 5 mornings at our surgery 1.

The successful candidate will have excellent customer service skills and be expected to work some evening sessions (to 7:00pm). There is also an opportunity to work additional hours at our Surgery 2 site should you be looking for more hours per week."

9.6.4.2 Administration Manager

"We are a busy 8 partner GP Surgery based across two sites. This is a newly developed role to work within our reception team and to spend time working alongside the Practice Manager with various tasks when required. Your role would be to oversee the reception team at either site, reception duties when needed, all administration work involved in ensuring the smooth running of the front of house. This is a varied and challenging position and would require someone who is flexible, works well in a team, is a forward thinker and can thrive in a busy environment. Hours are 8am – 4pm Monday to Friday."

9.6.4.3 Health Care Assistant (20 hours per week)

"An opportunity has arisen for an enthusiastic and flexible Health Care Assistant to join our Practice nursing team. The successful applicant would be working approximately 20 hours per week plus additional hours should these become available. Previous experience as Practice HCA is essential. Phlebotomy trained would be an advantage but not essential. This position will be subject to a CRB check. Previous experience, as practice HCA, is desirable but not essential."

Duties:

- Measurement of height and weight
- Phlebotomy
- Urinalysis
- Blood pressure monitoring
- Temperature and pulse recording
- Peak flow measurements
- Venepuncture
- Wound care
- New patient health checks
- Lifestyle advice

- Preparation for minor surgical procedures
- Stock control and ordering

Previous applicants within the last 3 months need not reapply.

9.6.4.4 Practice Manager

"We are a friendly, five partner training practice based in the attractive rural village of (name village and county). We provide GMS medical services to nearly (state list size) patients from a new single, purpose-built surgery.

Due to the retirement of our current Practice Manager, we are looking for an enthusiastic, dynamic Practice Manager preferably with a proven record in general practice although not essential.

The successful candidate should be able to demonstrate sound leadership skills and have the ability to lead the delivery and development of services along with our five GP partners and supportive clinical and administrative team.

The candidate should ideally have a sound understanding of IT, GMS, QOF and CQC requirements.

The post would be for a minimum of 25 hours per week.

Salary is negotiable and according to qualifications and experience, £36,500 to £45,500 pro rata (state, if rate applicable).

Closing date midday on (dd/mm/yy).

Interviews anticipated (dd/mm/yy).

For an informal talk, to learn more about this exciting opportunity, please contact, giving the name and telephone number for the applicants to speak and get any queries clarified before applying."

9.6.4.5 Practice Nurse

A typical advert placed via recruitment agency might look as below:

Locum/Temp Nurses

Career Area:

Job Category:

Practice Nursing Grade Type:

Nurse Grades Grade:

Unspecified Region: North West

Area: Greater Manchester

Salary: £15 to £20 per hour

Posted: dd/mm/yy

Start Date: ASAP

Recruiter: AN N Other

Job Ref: SPN24/Ealing

We are currently recruiting for a Practice Nurse in Greater London area on an ongoing basis.

Hours to suit.

Must have EMIS Web experience.

9.6.4.6 Salaried GP/Long-Term Locum

"Due to retirement of our Senior Partner, we are looking for an enthusiastic salaried GP to join our team of 6 Doctors, 4 Nurses, 1 Nurse Practitioner and an HCA across two semi-rural sites.

- List size 11,200
- No OOH commitment
- Friendly, supportive clinical team
- Excellent administrative support
- Regular clinical meetings
- High QOF achievement

Informal enquiries welcome; position to commence mm/yy; please telephone Dr. J Blog on: 020 8123 4567 for further information or to arrange an informal visit.

Closing date to be given.

Please send CV with covering letter by post or email to (name, designation, address and email address)."

9.7 Disciplinary Procedures

The details of disciplinary procedures and the Employment Acts to protect the Employees and Employers are summarised, leaving the reader to check further details via Google when necessary.

The very fact that the Practice Manager (PMgr) needs to look at these procedures means there have been serious failings on the part of the employee, PMgr and the Surgery Management i.e. Partners. Nipping the problem in the bud is a safe motto to follow.

To enable this, the PMgr should highlight areas which the staff should follow, observe their actions so that if they deviate from good practice they could correct themselves before precipitating the situation. Often irritating issues are unnecessarily blown up due to attitude and perception problems and procedures not strictly adhered to.

I feel in the main, there are no bad employees, only bad management. If this principle were instilled in the PMgr's mind, then the PMgr would strive to focus on issues relating to staff behaviour at the outset and avoid time consuming and often costly problems for the surgery by having to go through the disciplinary route.

The PMgr being right is not as important as being smart, and should minimise staff problems, which usually is a great distraction to all GPs and other staff.

Having procedures written down and distributed to staff at the time of joining the surgery is a crucial step but PMgr responsibility only starts there. PMgr has to be in a state of constant vigilance and question whether more could be done to help the staff in areas of training, time keeping, etc.

PMgrs generally fail in keeping written records and show favouritism, which other staff perceive quickly. There are so many rules and regulations, as can be evidenced at the ACAS site, for various issues, that a receptionist may be daunted at the document and may put it aside without reading any of it. There is no point in questioning why they did not read or observe.

A good PMgr should understand these human traits, and to make them read, he should issue a memo listing only 6-8 simple points that generally create problems of conflict i.e.:

- Timekeeping
- Absence
- Health and safety
- Use, often misuse, of organisation facilities
- Discrimination, bullying and harassment

- Personal appearance
- Gross misconduct liable for dismissal

Whereas GPs have MPS or MDU and Nurses RCN for legal protections, and the PMgr can join these organisations for a nominal fee, other staff do not have any, nor could they pay fees to join due to the receptionists' low salaries. The only option for them is to contact the local Citizens Advice Bureau (CAB) for advice should a problem arise. When unfair dismissal arises, it is usually better for junior staff to move on than what ACAS advices because they can ill afford to carry on without employment and earning, and despite all the rules and protection offered, few would contemplate lengthy action with the Surgery Partners.

The junior staff should understand, right at the outset, that good behaviour is their only protection in keeping their job.

On issues of discrimination and sexual harassment, staff must follow CAB and ACAS advice as these are quite serious and a lot more is at stake than just employment and earnings.

Disciplinary procedure is sometimes the best way for your employer to tell you when something is wrong. It allows them to explain clearly what improvement is needed and should give you an opportunity to put across your side of the situation.

Clear and consistent disciplinary procedures are good practice in the workplace. They help to promote fairness and consistency in the treatment of individuals.

A tribunal will consider whether a fair procedure has been followed as evidence to support its decision. The disciplinary procedure should state in writing, the type of disciplinary action and penalties, which can result from unacceptable conduct or performance.

Disciplinary procedures should not be seen primarily for imposing sanctions. They should be seen as a way of helping and encouraging the employee to make improvements to the standards and conduct at work.

It is good practice to attempt to solve the problem in a less formal manner in the first instance. If this approach fails then the more formal disciplinary procedure may be appropriate.

The legal obligations of the employer

The Employment Rights Act 1996 requires the employer to provide written information to their employees about certain aspects of the disciplinary procedure. More details on Employment Act are given later in the section.

Codes of practice

ACAS are empowered to produce codes of practice on disciplinary rules and procedures. The codes provide employers with practical guidance on how to draw up and effectively operate disciplinary rules and procedures.

ACAS guidelines on what should be included in disciplinary proceedings:

- State the type of action and penalties, which can result from unacceptable contact.
- Have a clear timetable for dealing with disciplinary matters.
- Give full details of the disciplinary offence. Investigate the alleged disciplinary offence before disciplinary action is taken.
- If suspension of the employee during the investigation is considered necessary, it should be on full pay and for as short a period as possible.
- Allow the employee to be accompanied by colleague or union representative.
- Allow workers to put their case before a decision is made. Unless in the case of gross misconduct, do not dismiss on first offence.
- Provide the worker with the right of appeal. Indicate the type of offence that would be considered gross misconduct.

A typical disciplinary procedure will have the following stages:

- A formal, oral warning in the case of a minor offence.
- A written warning for subsequent minor offences or a more serious offence.
- A final written warning for further misconduct. The warning should make it clear that dismissal may follow failure to comply.
- Dismissal with appropriate notice will follow if there is insufficient improvement.

Misconduct:

Conduct which is sufficiently serious to require disciplinary action. In order to warrant dismissal, misconduct must be extremely serious, or repeated on more than one occasion. Misconduct can include persistent lateness, unauthorised absence and failure to meet known work standards.

Gross misconduct:

This is the term used for serious misconduct, which may lead to instant dismissal (that is, summary dismissal). Acts that constitute gross misconduct are those resulting in a serious breach of contractual terms and will be for the organisation to decide in the light of their own particular circumstances. They might include the following:

- Theft, fraud or deliberate falsification of records.
- Physical violence.
- Serious bullying or harassment.
- Serious insubordination.
- Serious incapability brought about by alcohol or illegal drugs.

Employers should give their employee plenty of examples of what they consider to be gross misconduct to ensure that they understand the type of behaviour they consider unacceptable.

In the case of gross misconduct employers should suspend workers (on full pay) and carry out an investigation.

Employments Act

Some details are listed below for the reader to know about the Act; read more about it by searching via Google. This should cover not only the Acts but also their impact assessments, when relevant.

- Employment Act 2008
- Employment Law Changes 2010, 2011 and 2012

Impact Assessments:

- Employment Bill impact assessment: part 2 – dispute resolution review.
- Employment Bill impact assessment: national minimum wage enforcement.
- Employment Bill impact assessment: cadet force adult volunteers.

- Employment Bill impact assessment: amendment to trade union law.
- Employment Bill impact assessment: employment agency standards enforcement.
- Employment Bill: impact assessments.

The Employment Act 2008 is comprised of 23 sections and the main provisions are as follows:

Sections 1-7 – changes to the law relating to dispute resolution in the workplace.

Sections 8-12 – changes to the enforcement of the national minimum wage (NMW).

Section 13 – clarifies that Cadet Force Adult Volunteers (CFAVs) do not qualify for the NMW.

Section 14 – broadens the type of expenses that can be reimbursed to voluntary workers without triggering eligibility for the NMW.

Sections 15-17 – make the following amendments to the employment agency standards enforcement regime.

Top 10 employment law changes in 2010:

Increase in the Default Retirement Age

The current Default Retirement Age (DRA) stands at 65.

Equality Act

The Equality Act will become law in October. The Act introduces ground breaking new laws which will help narrow the gap between rich and poor; require businesses to report on gender pay; allow businesses to positively discriminate in recruiting and promoting people from under-represented minority groups (as long as they are as well qualified for the job as the other candidates); and significantly strengthen and harmonise UK anti-discrimination law.

Equal rights for agency workers

The right to the same pay, holidays and basic conditions of employment as permanent staff doing the same kind of work after serving a twelve-week service qualification period.

Additional paternity leave

Additional paternity leave will be introduced in April 2010, but it will only apply to parents of babies born on or after 3 April 2011. Currently, employed fathers are entitled to two weeks paid paternity leave and mothers to 52 weeks maternity leave (of which up to 39 weeks are paid). Under the new law, mothers would be able to transfer the final 26 weeks of their maternity leave to the father once the mother has returned to work.

Statutory payments (for current figures, please check websites)

In April, the *weekly earnings threshold* for statutory adoption, maternity, paternity, and sick pay will increase from £95 to £97. And statutory adoption, maternity, and paternity pay and maternity allowance will increase from £123.06 per week to £124.88 per week. (NB. the rate of statutory sick pay will remain at £79.15 per week.)

- **Fit notes replace sick notes**
- **Union rights**
- **Unfair dismissal**
- **Independent Safeguarding Authority**

Starting November 2010, new workers and those moving jobs, who want to work with children or vulnerable adults must register with the Independent Safeguarding Authority – **Time to train initiative** – please check Google and read about it.

10. PAYE

All details for PAYE (Pay As You Earn) can be obtained from the HMRC website. However some essential points are mentioned as staff will have queries on general issues and the following should serve as a useful reference.

PAYE is the system that HM Revenue & Customs (HMRC) uses to collect income tax and national insurance contributions (NICs) from employees' pay. The employer deducts income tax and NICs from employees' pay each pay period (which could be monthly, fortnightly or weekly) and pays employers' Class 1 NICs if they earn above a certain threshold. Employers pay these amounts to HMRC monthly or quarterly.

Employers should provide HMRC with details of payments made to employees together the tax and national insurance contributions deducted when or before the payments are made to the employee.

The employer will normally be sent a notice of coding (form P2) by HMRC each tax year in January/February. Your employer is told your code number but not how it has been calculated. This is important because it means that the employer is not able to check, if a code is correct.

It is up to the individual to check that the code is correct!

Overtime, bonus, ex-gratia payments

Overtime and bonus will be regarded, as part of earnings and NI and Tax is due.

However, for ex-gratia payment (made for work not related to usual employment) is not liable for NI but liable for Tax.

Most PAYE codes have a number followed by a letter:

- The number tells the employer how much tax-free pay you are allowed.
- The letters also have a specific meaning (see below)

The number tells the employer how much tax-free pay you are allowed (but please see special case for 'K' code below).

The last digit of your tax-free pay is removed to create the code (so a £8,105 personal allowance becomes the digits 810 in the code).

For example, if your code number is 240, you are entitled to tax-free pay of £2,400.

Therefore, you can earn £200 each month (£2,400 divided by 12 months) before any tax is deducted. Any pay above that will be taxed.

Using the tax tables provided by HM Revenue and Customs, or an approved computer programme, your employer works out how much tax is due, deducts it from your pay, and pays the rest to you. The tax is paid over to the Tax Office.

'L' refers to the normal personal allowance for those under 65.

'P' refers to the normal personal allowance for those 65 to 74.

'Y' refers to the normal personal allowance for those 75 or over.

'T' refers to circumstances where there are other items that require HMRC to look at your tax code, for example the income-related reduction to the Personal Allowance for those with income above £100,000

The 810L code means that you are entitled to the full tax-free personal allowance for 2012/13 of £8,105. 810L is the right code for your main job in 2012/13, if you are under 65, don't have any taxable benefits in kind from your employer (such as a company car or medical insurance) and have no untaxed sources of income or unpaid tax which is being collected through your PAYE code.

10.1 Software Packages

Every surgery will have a software package for Payroll and the package will be quite versatile and comprehensive in its application. The representative from the supplier company would train the PMgr about how to use the system — setting up weekly and monthly pay, PAYE codes, pension payments — and would also explain after the system calculates and inputs tax and NI for both employee and employer contributions.

It is important that the staff data is input correctly at the outset and payroll set up for monthly pay. The rate per hour should also be input.

Each month it may take about 30 min. to prepare the payroll and get printouts of the salary for the month for each employee including the GPs.

P60, P45, P35, P14 and P11D all would be automatically computed, when the year-end approaches.

Payments to HMRC for Tax and NI Employer and Employee payments would be computed from monthly figures input.

All pension payments would also be computed and data sent to NHS Pensions Agency automatically.

Agency staff, temporary staff and locum staff details could also be input and various amounts calculated in the system.

Payroll packages work very well and rarely any problems were encountered; and even if it did, immediate help is always at hand from the software supplier.

10.2 Tax and NI

HMRC website gives the details for both employers' and employees':

- Tax tables for monthly and weekly pay
- NI due on the income earned weekly or monthly

Go to the HMRC site.

Select 'Employers (blue)' and 'Employees (red)'.

- In the new screen – Input PAYE Tables for the year e.g. 2014-15.
- Search.
- New screen – Rates and thresholds for employers.

Current thresholds and rates are given for:

- PAYE
- NICs
- Statutory Payments
- Mileage payments
- National Minimum Wage
- Student loan repayments
- Cars
- Maternity rates etc.

The PAYE software also calculates the NI for employer and employees contribution for the monthly salary received.

The Payroll package used would automatically calculate and deduct NI payments but the PMgr should be aware of these details on the HMRC site.

Please take a printout, for each year, of the tables pertaining to the staff, without naming the staff, adjacent to the appropriate figures – confidentiality issues.

10.3 Employer Annual Return

P35 and P14s

Employer Annual Return is due by 19 May following the end of the tax year and consists of:

- A P14 form for each of the employees.
- P11 or equivalent record.
- A P35 form, which summarises the end-of-year payroll totals for all the employees in the surgery.

Expenses and benefits: form P11D (b) must reach HMRC by the filing date of 6 July.

10.4 Forms

10.4.1 P45

One gets a P45 from the employer when one stops working for them. It's a record of one's pay and the tax that's been deducted from it so far in the tax year.

It shows:

- Tax code and PAYE (Pay As You Earn) reference number
- National Insurance number
- Leaving date
- Earnings in the tax year
- How much Income Tax was deducted from one's earnings

A P45 has four parts – Part 1, Part 1A, Part 2 and Part 3. Your employer sends Part 1 to HMRC and gives you the other three. When you start a new job, or claim Jobseeker's Allowance, you give Part 2 and Part 3 to your new employer or to the Job Centre. You keep the remaining one – Part 1A – for your own records.

Your employer should automatically give you a P45 when you stop working for them. If not, ask for it – you're entitled to it by law.

10.4.2 P46

If you don't have a P45 because, for example, you're starting your first job or taking on a second job without giving up your other one, your new employer may give you a form P46 to complete.

It contains important information that affects the amount of tax you'll pay, such as whether:

- This is your first job
- You've been claiming Jobseeker's Allowance or Employment and Support Allowance
- You've got another job
- You're paying off a student loan

Some employers may not give you a P46 to complete, but will ask you for the relevant information to allocate a tax code and work out the tax due on your first pay day.

HMRC will process the P46 or the relevant information passed on from your employer. It's important that you complete the P46 or provide the relevant information your employer has asked you for as soon as possible before your first pay day, so your employer knows which tax code to use.

10.4.3 P60

Your P60 is the summary of your pay and the tax that's been deducted from it in the tax year. Your employer should provide you with a P60 to keep as a record at the end of every tax year (which runs from 6 April to 5 April the next year).

If your employer doesn't give you a P60 at the end of the tax year, ask for it – you're entitled to it by law if you are still working for the employer on 5 April.

10.4.4 P11D

Your employer uses a P11D to HMRC about the value of any benefits in kind they've given you during the tax year.

This means benefits or expenses that effectively increase your income, such as:

- A company car
- Private medical insurance
- Interest free loans

Your employer will only declare them if you've earned at least £8,500 in the year, including the value of the benefits. They will work out how much each benefit is worth, record it on the form and send it to HMRC. They'll also give you a copy, which you'll need for your records or if you complete a Self Assessment tax return.

If you apply for a loan or mortgage, banks and building societies will accept a P11D as proof of extra income.

10.4.5 Lost P60

If you've lost your P60 your employer can issue you with a duplicate. Since 2010-11 your employer no longer needs to show on the P60 that it is a 'duplicate'.

10.4.6 Completing a P46 if you've lost your P45

If you've lost your P45, you won't be able to get a replacement. Your new employer may give you a form P46 to complete or ask you for relevant information to pass on to HMRC so that they can give you a tax code for your new employment.

10.4.7 P11D

Your employer doesn't have to give you a copy of the P11D. But the law says they must tell you what details they've included on the form – even if you've left the job. It's usually easier for them to give you a copy of the form when they send it to HMRC.

If you lose your copy, your employer should be able to let you have another one. If they can't, ask HMRC for a copy.

10.5 NHS Pensions

For the standard pension calculator – NHS Pension Scheme (Amended 1 April 2008), please check the website for latest rates.

Standard pension:

When one retires from the NHS Pension Scheme (Amended 1 April 2008) one will get a pension and tax-free lump sum.

The annual pension will be 1/80 of the best of your last 3 years' pensionable pay for each year of Scheme membership.

Part years of membership will also count towards pension.

This will usually be paid for the rest of your life. The lump sum will normally be 3 times yearly pension, but married men with membership before 25.3.72 may get a smaller lump sum.

There are some limits on the amount of membership that can count for benefits.

These are:

- Not more than 40 years at age 60 if those years were worked before 1 April 2008
- Not more than 40 years at age 55 for special classes*
- Not more than 45 years altogether

One cannot be a member if one has attained age 70 by 31 March 2008 or age 75 since that date** (65 for special classes):

*Special classes are Scheme members in certain employments who joined the Scheme before 6.3.95.

Pensions taken before normal retirement age – actuarially reduced pensions

If a pension is taken before the normal retirement age (60 years old for most members of the NHS Pension Scheme, 55 years old for special classes), the pension and lump sum are reduced to take account of the fact they are being paid earlier than normal.

This reduction is called **'actuarial reduction'** and is set by the Secretary of State on the advice of the Scheme Actuary.

11. Finance

The accountant would do all the necessary paperwork relating to preparing the year-end accounts for the practice. However, the practice has to ensure all the financial transactions, payments received and made, are correctly logged and receipts and documents filed for the accountant to prepare the year-end account.

11.1 Mortgage details

The mortgage for the surgery buildings and any property used for surgery purposes e.g. GP's private flat, if adjacent to the surgery and used for surgery purposes, can be included in the accounts.

11.2 Loans and Interests

All paperwork relating to any loans received and associated interests from banks, building societies or any other lender have to be kept in files for the use of the accountant.

11.3 Hire Purchases and Interests

All paperwork pertaining to any hire purchases, lease of cars along with interests paid has to be kept in files for the accountant.

Finance is a very tempting area and misappropriations can occur quite easily. Avoid charging for cars, buildings etc. for family, even when the family members are involved as staff in the surgery. Partners' expenses are allowed and mostly at cost.

All expense payments to relatives, siblings etc. have to be avoided.

The NHS depends on GPs' trust and that trust has to be earned.

The PMgr is also not absolved from malpractices when it comes to finance e.g. through Petty Cash expenses or costs of equipment, furniture costs etc.

The partners should not put the Accountant in a compromising position, ever to falsify the surgery accounts.

12. Superannuation

Superannuation and Seniority Payments

The details for these two NHS payments can be checked via NHS websites. However, the PMgr needs to have some understanding of the payment methods and amounts, as GPs normally will ask general queries about quarterly payments received. The PMgr has to highlight any shortfall in payments immediately so that the shortfall can be rectified by the PCT.

12.1 Superannuation

Under the new GMS contract, GPs' superannuation contributions will be calculated on actual NHS profits. This is a major change to the scheme, which will affect both GMS and PMS GPs.

Profit is total income less total expenses. For the first time a practice's expenses will now have an impact on superannuation. It will be more important for practices to ensure expenses are controlled.

Increase in Employee Superannuation Contributions

The 'employee' contribution, presently 6%, changes to:

NHS Earnings	%
Up to £19,165	5
£19,166 to £63,416	6.5
£63,417 to £99,999	7.5
Above £100,000	8.5

Most GPs are therefore seeing an increase in employee contribution of between 1.5% and 2.5% when calculated on their NHS earnings, without any increase in any

NHS benefits.

Added Years –

Enabling GPs to purchase up to £5,000 in additional pension.

Dynamising –

Based on the increase in the retail price index plus 1.5%.

Extra Lump Sum

On retirement GPs presently receive a tax-free lump sum equivalent to three times their annual pension. It would be possible to commute an additional part of the pension in exchange for an increased lump sum, up to certain limits.

Abatement

GPs who retire before age 60 suffer an abatement of their pension if their total earnings, including their pension, are more post-retirement than they were before.

Currently the PCO are making deductions for superannuation. It must be stressed that this is only a payment based on an estimate of your profits. Once the actual profits have been calculated one may have an increased contribution to pay or receive a refund on superannuation.

Practices need to ensure that provisions are made for payment of the balance of superannuation. It would be advisable when practices receive achievement payments for the QOF, they put aside the amounts due for superannuation.

12.2 Seniority

Seniority payments are payments to a contractor in respect of an individual GP provider (a partner, single-handed practitioner or a shareholder in a limited company that is a GMS contractor). The payments reward experience and are based on the GP's number of years of reckonable service.

Calculating your seniority payments

Any GP provider who has at least two years of service as a GP provider will be eligible for seniority payments.

There are four stages in calculating the seniority payment to which one is entitled.

Stage one – calculating reckonable service

Stage two – seniority and qualifying dates

Stage three – calculating the full annual rate of seniority payments

Stage Four – Average Adjusted Superannuable Income

Seniority factor

Seniority factor payments were introduced as part of the new General Medical Services (nGMS) contract in 2004 and were designed to reward GPs' experience.

They are part of an individual GP's pay although they are paid to the practice. The payment that a GP receives is based on a scale and is dependent on:

- A GP's years of reckonable service

- A GP's 'qualifying income fraction' – this determines the proportion of the seniority payment that a GP receives and is a fraction of their NHS profits (excluding any seniority payment) compared to the national superannuable income.

GPs earning less than a third of the national superannuable income are not eligible for seniority payments. GPs earning between one third and two thirds of the national superannuable income receive 60 per cent of the payment. GPs earning two thirds or more of the national superannuable income receive 100 per cent of the payment.

The final seniority factor for a given year can only be calculated once the average superannuable income for all GPs is known. As it often takes a long period of time for this data to become available, an interim seniority factor is calculated which enables primary care organisations to make payments before they have the data to calculate the final seniority factor.

The Technical Steering Committee, that has representatives from the General Practitioners Committee (GPC), NHS Employers and the Health Departments for England and Wales, publishes the interim and final seniority factors for General Medical Service (GMS) contractors. For more information visit the Health and Social Care Information Centre (HSCIC) website.

2014/15 phasing out of seniority payments

It has been agreed that seniority payments will cease on 31 March 2020. In the meantime, those in receipt of payments on 31 March 2014 will continue to receive payments and progress as currently set out in the SFE (Statement for Financial Entitlement – in the past before 2004 Red Book). There will be no new entrants to the scheme from 1 April 2014. The current qualifying arrangements will continue for those currently in receipt of payments.

It is the joint expectation that the agreed changes to seniority payments will result in the quantum of seniority payments from the seniority pool falling by 15% each year from 2014/15 to 2019/20. In the event that this reduction is not delivered in any year, NHS Employers and GPC will agree action to achieve this. All funding released will be added into the global sum with no Out of Hours deduction being applied.

2014/15 interim factors

The 2014/15 interim seniority factors are £96,097 in England, £84,012 in Wales, and £87,707 in Northern Ireland, and will be used by NHS payment agencies to determine the level of the seniority payments for 2013/14. More information can be found on the HSCIC website (http://www.hscic.gov.uk/)

12.3 CCGs and the Changes

It is important to establish the correct employment status for a worker from the outset. Wrongly identifying a worker as self-employed when in fact they should have been treated as employed can leave the engager facing large tax and NI liabilities. Therefore, the employment status of individuals engaged for CCG posts should be carefully considered to ensure it is correct under current legislation.

Where a GP's role in the CCG is classed as employment rather than self-employment, there are a number of areas, which need clarification:

1 TAXATION
2 TAX RELIEF ON EXPENSES INCURRED
3 NATIONAL INSURANCE CONTRIBUTIONS
4 SUPERANNUATION

From April 2013, all CCG earnings for GPs carrying out work for a CCG will be fully superannuable, providing that the CCG is an NHS employing authority under the terms of the NHS Pensions regulations.

5 SENIORITY

Under current seniority calculation rules there will be an effect on the amount of seniority that a GP is entitled to when working under an employed rather than a self-employed arrangement and this needs to be fully understood.

13. Depreciation

Depreciation and Disposals

13.1 Capital Allowances

One can claim capital allowances, if one is running a limited company or if one is self-employed.

The accountant will deal with these when he prepares the final accounts for the year. Only general comments are made to explain the terms.

Buying an asset, for example, a car, tools, machinery or other equipment for use in business, one cannot deduct the expenditure on that asset from trading profits. Instead, one may be able to claim a capital allowance for that expenditure. If one has chosen to use the cash basis to calculate the profits one can only claim capital allowances on cars.

Capital allowances are also available for certain building-related capital expenditure, for qualifying capital expenditure on qualifying research and development, for donations of used business assets to charity, and certain other capital expenditure.

The aim is to give tax relief for the reduction in value of qualifying assets that one buys and own for business use by letting one write off their cost against the taxable income of the business.

Partnerships:

If the business is a partnership, one needs to claim capital allowances on assets owned by the partnership collectively in the Partnership Tax Return, not in the returns for individual partners. The most commonly claimed allowances are for plant and machinery. Note: That special rule applies on plant and machinery that is owned by one of the partners but used in the partnership's business.

Claims should be made on the Partnership Return. These should be made within 12 months after the 31 January filing deadline for the return.

First-year tax credits:

There are also some special rules that allow companies to surrender losses attributable to allowances claimed on expenditure on certain specific energy-saving or environmentally beneficial plant or machinery, in return for a cash payment.

Find out more about first-year tax credits from the website.

Writing-down allowances (WDA):

WDA are annual allowances that one can claim to reduce or 'write down' any remaining balance of capital expenditure on plant and machinery that one has not already claimed a capital allowance for, referred to as a 'pool' of 'unrelieved' expenditure. There are two rates of WDA for plant and machinery, the rate for the main pool, 18%, and for the special rate pool, 8%.

Small Pools Allowance (SPA):

The WDA for small pools, sometimes referred to as the 'SPA', allows one to write off either the main or special rate pool or both of them if the balance in that pool is £1,000 or less.

Time limits if you haven't made a claim

If one discovers that a claim has been missed, after one has sent in Company Tax, Income Tax or Partnership Return, then one can request an amendment. However, there are certain time limits on this.

13.2 Depreciation

Depreciation is a systematic and rational process of distributing the cost of tangible assets over the life of assets. Depreciation is a process of allocation.

Cost to be allocated = acquisition cost - salvage value

Allocated over the estimated useful life of assets.

Allocation method should be systematic and rational.

Depreciation methods based on time:

- Straight-line method
- Declining balance method
- Sum-of-the-years'-digits method (not normally used in small GP surgeries)

Depreciation based on use (activity)

Depreciation = (Cost - Residual value)/useful life.

In a GP Partnership practice, the items bought are of small amounts running to less than £10,000; computer and communication equipment may be far less and the useful life is about 3 years, for telephone equipment 5 years. So the depreciation to be applied would be 33 1/3 % for 3 years and 20% for 5 years.

Distinguish between depreciation from capital allowances. Depreciation is an accountancy concept, used to spread the cost of an asset over its useful life in the business. The rate used will depend therefore on an estimate of that useful life, so computers might be depreciated at 25% or 33%, or at a lower rate if their useful life is expected to be longer. This might be on a straight-line basis (same amount each year) or reducing balance (25% of 100%, then 25% of 75% and so on). It depends on the asset, and there is an element of choice and subjectivity.

Because of that subjectivity, depreciation is not allowable for tax purposes, and is replaced by capital allowance. First year allowance for plant & machinery in 2006-7 (small businesses) is 50% – was 40% last year – and 25% thereafter, on the reducing balance basis. Other rates apply for various different assets.

Fixtures and Fittings

Generally a fixture is understood to be any item that is bolted to the floor or walls, and a fitting to be any item that is free standing or hung by a nail or hook. The accountant would deal with the complicated computations for depreciation.

Motor Vehicles

The mileage rate is only available for journeys, or any identifiable part or proportion of a journey, that are wholly and exclusively for business purposes. It is not available for private journeys, such as travel from home to work, or for journeys that serve both a business and a private purpose.

If a GP keeps a mileage log of car expenses, the maximum he can claim is 45p per mile (for the first 10,000 miles and 25p for over 1,000 miles). No other allowances can be claimed including fuel costs, insurance and road tax. The mileage rate does not include incidental expenses incurred in connection with a particular journey, such as tolls, congestion charges and parking fees. These will be allowable as a deduction where they are incurred solely for business purposes.

Capital allowances on cars are available and the HMRC site does give details for the current year.

All motor vehicles used for the surgery, vans and even GPs' personal cars are all to be included in the accounts.

13.3 Disposals

'Disposal' means to relinquish ownership of an asset in a conclusive manner by sale, exchange, transfer, involuntary conversion, abandonment, or donation.

When things like communication equipment is sold or disposed of the final value would be in double-digit figures. For the sale of used cars the value would be higher, and this affects the computation of depreciation; usually the accountant would be able to deal with these quite easily when preparing final year accounts.

14. Nurses

Practice nurses have become significantly more skilled over recent years and are now providing some services to patients that were previously delivered by GPs. This is as a result of the training and development initiatives within the nursing profession, leading to the creation of roles such as nurse practitioners and independent nurse prescribers.

Much of their work involves managing the care of patients with long-term conditions and running a wide range of extended service clinics in the practice including:

- Long-term conditions – asthma, diabetes, blood pressure monitoring
- Cytology services
- Family planning
- Stop smoking
- Childhood and travel vaccinations

14.1 Duties

The post holder is responsible for the delivery of basic practice nursing services care to the practice population.

Supported by senior nurses within the practice, they will deliver care within the boundaries of their role, focusing upon supporting patients to be healthy, monitoring of long-term conditions, health care and illness prevention and screening activities.

They will work collaboratively with the general practice team to meet the needs of patients, supporting the delivery of policy and procedures, and providing nurse leadership as required.

More detailed duties are listed in the Job Description (see Section 9.1.5).

14.2 Patients

Dealing with patients

Nurses usually should have had plenty of exposure during their training prior to qualification. It is imperative that they deal with patients with kindness and sensitivity. They should never give way to impolite and rude behaviour even under intense provocation. They should give a sympathetic hearing to patients' comments and help them in all ways possible.

Should a patient be late for an appointment, like a GP, the nurse must never ask the patient to make another appointment as a punishment. Despite the nuisance value and delay it may cause, it would be expected of her to see the patient before the session ends. Complaints against nurses should be a rarity and they must ensure they are not at any time on the receiving end.

It is not uncommon for nurses sometimes to refuse to do ear syringing even though it is part of their duties. Due to personality clashes with a particular GP they may not fully co-operate in doing clinics with that GP. Then it would be a disciplinary issue for the PMgr to address, but a sensible nurse should avoid these situations and comply with the surgery rules. It would also be expected of the particular GP to make changes to his behaviour to enable a smooth functioning of the surgery.

14.3 Training

It is unusual for a nurse be involved in any induction training in a surgery, unless a GP can afford the time. What usually happens is that a new nurse might assist the GP during some surgery sessions or clinics for him to comment on her performance.

The PMgr, however, can deal with the administrative aspects of her work and these generally form the main basis of her induction training.

If suitable courses were to be conducted in PCT, RCN or other outside agencies, she might be sent to such courses, as part of her training in surgery procedures.

14.4 Emergencies

Emergency medications:

Some areas are mentioned for information and awareness of surgery staff but the nurse would have a comprehensive list of emergency situations that may arise. More details can be obtained from the website given below.

Life-threatening medical emergencies:

- Cardiac arrest
- Anaphylaxis

Potentially life-threatening emergencies:

- Asthma and bronchospasm
- Severe upper airway obstruction
- Acute pulmonary oedema
- Arrhythmias
- Hypoglycaemia
- Convulsive status (convulsion for longer than 10 minutes)
- Meningitis and/or meningococcaemia (suspected)
- Septicaemia (suspected)

Non-life threatening emergencies:

- Nausea and vomiting
- Severe acute pain
- Migraine (adult)
- Painful wounds
- Palliative care emergencies
- Psychiatric emergencies (adults)
- Contaminated wounds

Oxygen

Oxygen is essential for managing emergencies and its availability is a requirement for general practice accreditation. Oxygen cylinders can be hired and refilled from a medical gas supplier. A size C cylinder (490 L) will last for 55 minutes at 8 L/min.

The following are required to administer oxygen:

- Adult and paediatric Hudson masks and nebuliser masks
- Nasal prongs
- Airways, and
- A bag valve-mask breathing system (e.g. Air Viva 3)

Equipment for managing emergencies

Appropriate supplies of IV infusion sets, cannulas, syringes, and needles are required. General practitioners should consider the following items for their practices:

- An Automated External Defibrillator (AED) with monitor and manual override. Although a defibrillator is not a requirement for practice accreditation, its absence may put a practice at clinical and medico-legal risk
- Pulse oximeter
- Portable packs to enable equipment to be taken for use offsite.

Equipment for the doctor's bag

The doctor's bag is very important and the contents of it vary according to the individual doctor and their pattern of work. GPs working in remote parts of the Highlands of Scotland will obviously have very different requirements from those working in the inner city.

Many GPs will no longer work out of hours but will still need to be able to assess and manage patients while out on home visits. Those working for out of hours organisations may have some, or all, of the necessary equipment and medications provided.

Most GPs will use a bag of some variety and the following should be considered:

- The bag must be lockable and not left unattended.

- Most medicines should be stored between 4° and 25°C. A silver-coloured bag or cool bag is more likely to keep drugs cooler than a traditional black bag.

- Consider keeping a maximum-minimum thermometer in the bag to record extremes of temperature.

- Bright lights may inactivate some drugs (e.g. injectable prochlorperazine) so keep the bag closed, when not in use.

- Lock the bag out of sight in the vehicle boot when not in use.

There are several key issues to be considered, like:

- Basic and administrative equipment
- Diagnostic equipment
- Other equipment
- Administrative issues
- Drugs

Managing emergency drugs in general practice

Drugs must be stored in a locked cupboard or a locked bag at less than 25°C. ADT and Syntometrine are stored in a refrigerator.

Schedule 8 drugs (opioids) must be stored in a locked, fixed, steel safe; although ampoules may be put in a locked bag for use away from the clinic.

All emergency drugs should be logged in a book or spread sheet that includes, date received, date administered, recipient, and expiry date.

Systems should be in place for checking drug stocks and expiry dates, and for auditing the log.

A separate book is required to log Schedule 8 drugs received and used.

14.5 Medicine Management

This is one of the crucial indicators which need to be continually reviewed for better patient management. The details to check are as below:

- All prescribers to be aware of what medicines the patient is taking;

- All nurses should be aware of this information;

- Practice has up to date emergency equipment and drugs – anaphylaxis is one condition that may constitute an emergency in the practice premises. Anaphylaxis refers to a rapidly developing and serious allergic reaction that affects a number of different areas of the body at one time. Severe anaphylactic reactions can be fatal. Most people experience allergy symptoms only as a minor annoyance. However, a small number of allergic people are susceptible to a reaction that can lead to shock or even death. Fortunately, anaphylaxis is rare. The death rate from anaphylaxis is about 1 out of every 2.5 million people per year;

- List of equipment and drugs available to deal with an anaphylactic emergency;

- The equipment and drugs are inspected regularly;

- The dates of emergency drugs are checked and those, which have expired, are disposed of safely. The system present should prevent out of date drugs on the premises, including those in GP bags;

- Random checks to be made on the drugs stored in the premises and in GP bags;

- Repeat prescriptions to be given within 48 hours in most cases;

- The practice leaflet should state this area of concern to the patients;

- Receptionists made aware of the repeat prescription policy – do's and don'ts;

- Medication review may not always be face to face with patients – even telephone or from records would be adequate;

- Patients with 4 or more repeat prescriptions to be reviewed once a year;

- All patients with repeat prescriptions have to be reviewed once a year;

- GPs, nurses or pharmacists can do the review.

- 3 actions agreed with the Prescription Advisor form PCT to be produced and actions agreed upon with the advisor. This performance has to be evidence-based.

- If the practice has any patient on injectable neuroleptic medication (a tranquilizing drug, especially one used in treating mental disorders), the system in place should identify the patients and follow up of those who do not attend;

- If patients receive injectable drugs from the hospital. Then GPs can exclude those patients from the system. It is recommended that the PMgr notifies the names of those patients to the Prescription Advisor lest any adverse fallout from the actions of those patients affect the GP practice;

- Food items should never be kept along with medicines even for a short time.

14.6 Protocols

There are innumerable protocols, from hand washing to treating a cardiac patient.

The lists can be accessed via Google.

The role of protocols becomes more and more important in the surgery work and protocol-based care enables NHS staff to put evidence into practice by following strict procedures.

Some protocols are listed below:

- B12 protocol:
http://www.wales.nhs.uk/sites3/page.cfm?orgid=739&pid=27764
- Protocol for the management of hypertension 2010:
http://www.wales.nhs.uk/sites3/page.cfm?orgid=739&pid=43202
- Protocol for depo provera:
http://www.wales.nhs.uk/sites3/page.cfm?orgid=739&pid=38442
- Protocol for nurse pill checking 2010:
http://www.wales.nhs.uk/sites3/page.cfm?orgid=739&pid=43205
Nurse pill reviews:
http://www.wales.nhs.uk/sites3/page.cfm?orgid=739&pid=32236
Nurse monitoring of maintenance therapy:
http://www.wales.nhs.uk/sites3/page.cfm?orgid=739&pid=32237
- Guidelines for chaperones in primary care:
http://www.wales.nhs.uk/sites3/page.cfm?orgid=739&pid=32238
- Ear irrigation policy:
http://www.wales.nhs.uk/sites3/page.cfm?orgid=739&pid=32239
- Treatment of anaphylaxis:
http://www.wales.nhs.uk/sites3/page.cfm?orgid=739&pid=32240
- Protocol – nurse review of patients with epilepsy:
http://www.wales.nhs.uk/sites3/page.cfm?orgid=739&pid=32453
- Treatment of patients with dysfunctional or absent spleen:
http://www.wales.nhs.uk/sites3/page.cfm?orgid=739&pid=33326
- Guideline for immunisation:
http://www.wales.nhs.uk/sites3/page.cfm?orgid=739&pid=33327
Allergic rhinitis:
http://www.wales.nhs.uk/sites3/page.cfm?orgid=739&pid=37940

- Administration of childhood vaccines:
  http://www.wales.nhs.uk/sites3/page.cfm?orgid=739&pid=41906

- Diabetes protocol:
  http://www.wales.nhs.uk/sites3/page.cfm?orgid=739&pid=41907
  Diabetes guidelines Nov 2009:
  http://www.wales.nhs.uk/sites3/page.cfm?orgid=739&pid=41963

- Asthma guidelines:
  http://www.wales.nhs.uk/sites3/page.cfm?orgid=739&pid=41964

- COPD guidelines:
  http://www.wales.nhs.uk/sites3/page.cfm?orgid=739&pid=41965

The above were selected to indicate the range of protocols one has to be aware off and follow rigidly.

14.7 Clinics

There are so many clinics, which surgeries could do, and not many do all the ones listed below (the bold ones indicate clinic services usually offered in most of the surgeries):

- **Adult Immunisations;**
- **Post and Antenatal – a double appointment required** – *sometimes by midwives*;
- **Asthma, diabetes, hypertension;**
- **Cervical Smear;**
- Check-ups for the elderly;
- *Child Health Surveillance – in conjunction with the Health Visitors*;
- **Child Immunisation – arranged by computer recall from the surgery**;
- Cryosurgery (treatment for warts);
- *Dietician – with a Doctor's referral – by Health Visitors*;
- Family Planning;
- **Health Promotion – anti-smoking, asthma, weight reduction, diabetes, and well-person checks;**

- **Minor Surgery** – including treatments for skin lesions, ingrown toenails and verrucas – a double appointment is necessary;

- **Mother & Baby;**

- **Phlebotomist (Blood Tests);**

- *Physiotherapist – with musculoskeletal problems – provides for first referral and follow-up consultations;*

- **Travel Clinic** – holiday immunisations for patients registered with the practice;

- **Vasectomies with GP's referral;**

- **Well Person Clinics, New Patient Clinics** – once registration is confirmed, attend clinic with the health questionnaire and a urine sample (bottle available at the Reception);

Delegation/Empowerment

The PHCT has developed nurse-run clinics to provide most of the care: –

- Hypertension clinic
- Cholesterol clinic
- Chronic heart failure clinic (including domiciliary care and a hospital discharge system)
- Stopping smoking clinic
- Diabetic clinic

Guidelines

There must be evidence-based guidelines, which all members of the PHCT must sign up to and have ownership of. Nurses cannot run clinics if doctors are all using different guidelines and medications.

Structured computer records

Structured computer records are essential so that everyone has easy access to information and the setting of standards and auditing of results is possible.

Diabetic Clinics

Initially, the estimated time to see each diabetic patient is about 20 min.

Consequently, a maximum of 6 patients need to be booked for the clinics.

PCT Nurse will notify any increase in number to receptionists and practice nurse.

As PCT Nurse – an H Grade nurse is able to do the clinic with no involvement of the GPs except for any discussions pertaining to fine-tuning of medication, it is imperative that their time is utilised more effectively and the practice nurses and receptionists do the preparatory and finishing work in-house.

The protocols for the clinic have been provided by the computer system provider – for each clinics e.g. diabetes, the various screens will appear one after another once the details for each screen are input.

The PCT Nurse will see all diabetic patients in the clinics. The details of insulin dependent patients, who are seen by hospitals and are under their monitoring, will be entered in the computer. GPs' roles are to utilise hospital services and follow hospital consultants' recommendations. (New contract stipulates what factors to be assessed and reported and does not expect GPs to do it).

Blood test results are needed prior to giving appointments to the PCT Nurse:

The details required to be determined, and recorded are:

- LFT
- HbAIC
- Fasting Lipid Profile
- Urea
- Creatinine

If the details are not available, then a blood test has to be done and results obtained prior to giving a clinic appointment with the PCT Nurse.

Patients are invited to come and pick up the blood test forms to be taken to the hospital. The practice nurse has to identify such patients and the receptionists have to telephone/contact them to come to surgery and pick up the blood test forms.

Once the results are obtained, then practice nurse has to put the data in the computer 'ASAP'.

Urine Sample:

All patients to give sample for urine test – to be done on the day (prior to clinic appointment) with the PCT Nurse.

Nurse's Folder

For any referral as required.
The following need to be provided in a folder for the PCT Nurse:

- Referral form for Dietician
- Referral form for Chiropodist
- Referral form for Retinopathy evaluation – nearest Optician (Hammonds Eye Clinic – 546 High Road, Tottenham).
- Diabetic Protocol – MS Rebecca Cheatle – PCT Nurse will assist with proving such a protocol.

Essential equipment and test units:

- Micro-albumin Test strips – need to be available in the consulting room
- Tuning fork
- Electronic BP equipment

Inviting patients – steps to follow by practice nurse:

Initially patients not seen for over 1 year.

Check whether the patient has had blood test results with all the relevant details listed in '5' above.
If yes – then make appointment for the PCT Nurse.
If not, then arrange for blood test as stated in '5' above.
Make a list of patients with name, surname and DOB and telephone number and give to the Senior Receptionist to arrange for appointments with PCT Nurse on the appropriate dates for the clinic.

Initially max. 6 patients per clinic (see 1 above).

Once patients not seen over 1 year have been called, then patients not seen over 6 months need to be called.

The Practice Nurse, with a GP and the PMgr, will have to assess the monthly performance for the diabetic clinic and make recommendations on improvements so as to meet the set targets and reach quality points predicted.

Clinical Guidelines

For full details of each clinical guideline and its associated publications please check via Google. Some topics are given below:

Falls:

http://www.rcn.org.uk/development/practice/clinicalguidelines/falls

Irritable bowel syndrome:

http://www.rcn.org.uk/development/practice/clinicalguidelines/irritable_bowel_syndrome

Pain in children:

http://www.rcn.org.uk/development/practice/clinicalguidelines/pain

Perioperative fasting:

http://www.rcn.org.uk/development/practice/clinicalguidelines/perioperative_fasting

Perioperative hypothermia:

http://www.rcn.org.uk/development/practice/clinicalguidelines/perioperative_hypothermia_inadvertent

Pressure ulcers:

http://www.rcn.org.uk/development/practice/clinicalguidelines/pressure_ulcers

Venous leg ulcers:

http://www.rcn.org.uk/development/practice/clinicalguidelines/venous_leg_ulcers

Violence:

http://www.rcn.org.uk/development/practice/clinicalguidelines/violence

15. GPs

GPs

GPs have enough help and advice from BMA, MDU or MPS, GMC, RCGP, PULSE and GP publications about their roles, procedures, protocols and management tips from time to time.

15.1 Duties

General practitioners, or GPs, provide primary and continuing medical care for patients. They take account of physical, emotional and social factors when diagnosing illness and recommending the required treatment. Patients may be referred to hospitals or other clinics for further assessment and/or treatment. Treatment using alternative medicines e.g. acupuncture, ayurvedic etc. are in vogue.

GPs may run specialist clinics within the practice for patients with specific conditions. They increasingly work as part of a team alongside other healthcare professionals, including community health doctors, to discuss care options for patients and their families and help patients to take responsibility for their own health.

1 Promoting health education in conjunction with other health professionals;

2 Organising preventative medical programmes for individual patients;

3 Discussing the development of new pharmaceutical products with pharmaceutical sales representatives;

4 Keeping up to date with medical developments, new drugs, treatments and medications, including complementary medicine;

5 Observing and assessing the work of trainee GPs and medical students and teaching at medical schools or hospitals;

6 Maintaining a portfolio of continuing professional development (CPD) activities.

The core work of a GP is all about '**listening**'.

Daily tasks could include:

- Holding consultations in the surgery
- Listening to patients and diagnosing and treating their symptoms
- Deciding on the right course of action for patients (could include hospital referral for specialised treatment)
- Administrative and management duties

GPs are also often involved in research and medical education, so you'll have to keep up to date with massive amounts of information from drug companies and medical journals. The study will never end in this job.

Typical work activities

Only a few are listed below and the Job Description for a GP and details of the duties are dealt with in Section 9.2.8.

- Responding to medical/health problems presented by patients including history taking, diagnosis, investigation, treatment and referral as appropriate.
- Maintaining confidentiality and impartiality.
- Commissioning healthcare by liaising with medical professionals in the community and hospitals.
- Providing specialist clinics for specific conditions or for certain groups, e.g. diabetes, smoking cessation and new babies.
- Meeting targets set by the government for specific treatments, such as child immunisations.
- Managing resources to service targets as effectively as possible, for example, using Choose and Book, the national electronic referral service.
- Using IT skills – some practices have one partner who specialises in the use of IT within the practice but all will be expected to have basic abilities for work such as maintaining patients' records using specific packages.

A GP is still responsible for:

- Keeping detailed records of all patients and the treatments they receive
- Hiring and managing staff
- Making major spending decisions on premises and equipment
- Liaising with other medical and health care professionals within their own surgery and beyond.

15.2 Patients

Patients have to be viewed as 'Customers' as their number determines the income given to the surgery by the PCT. However much some patients may test GPs' patience, the treatment to the patients must be civil, cordial and never discriminatory for whatever reason. Any complaints from them would do more harm to the surgery, even if the GP were right. Being right is not the key thing, being sensitive to the needs of the patients is. See Section 6.0 for further information on **'Patients as Customers'**.

15.3 Locum GPs

There is a lot of locum work within the following sectors nationwide:

- General Practice & Private Practice
- Hospitals
- Out of Hours Co-operatives
- Walk-in Centres
- Prisons
- Military Services.

Doctors choose to work as a locum:

- Agencies pay well
- Quick and simple registration

- Prompt and efficient payment
- Long and short term locum positions

Locums work within UK general practice in the following areas:

- Self-employed GMS practice Personal medical services
- (PMS) practice Private or non-NHS practice
- PCO-employed practice
- Out-of-hours providers
- Alternative primary medical services
- Employment through a locum's agency

Expectations of locums

Practices often have unrealistic expectations of locum GPs, and locums can be over-optimistic about how practices will treat them. False assumptions about hours, duties and payment frequently taint the relationship. Practices expect different things from locum GPs, and likewise locum GPs expects certain things from practices.

Solution – submitting a NASGP booking form outlining the job to be done, insisting on signed contracts with practices and ensuring that the practice has adequate protection to cover your own liabilities.

Information about practice-based services and secondary care and support services outside the surgery is essential to deliver the best care.

Solution – a locum information pack. But someone has to create it and keep it up to date. Insist that practices recognise their responsibility to reduce enforced underperformance.

A new locum might need longer time to consult than the partners. Also, locums should make sure know how the practice reviews repeat prescriptions. If the system is unsafe, locums should say **'NO'** and consider who needs to know that there is a problem.

A locum might hold a conscientious objection to a particular treatment or procedure, e.g., abortion. It is important that patients do not get stuck in the middle of a moral debate. Nor should everyone's time be wasted because patients are booked for procedures locums aren't qualified to perform.

Practices often expect locum GPs to perform tasks, such as signing repeat prescriptions, which are risky, if you don't know the patient. Locums must make clear, before starting, what they would and won't do, and what you can and can't do.

Performance feedback is essential for good risk management, and locums should demand it.

Written Agreement

When a locum GP is engaged by practices, the parties use a written agreement that sets out the terms of their engagement. Practices vary considerably in the way they are organised, and in terms of what is considered a standard working day. Using a written agreement ensures that both parties' expectations are clearly set out and should help to create a successful working relationship. There is also the added benefit of ensuring that the locum is working within their range of experience.

The agreement is normally made between the locum and the practice manager or someone with delegated authority to negotiate (deputy manager). However, receptionists should also be made aware of the exact terms of the agreement (though not necessarily the financial arrangements), particularly in relation to agreed workload.

Arrangements for termination of the agreement

Arrangements for the termination of the agreement made should be included, particularly if the locum is engaged by the contractor on a longer-term basis. Where such arrangements are outlined within an agreement, they would often include the following:

Details of how the parties could decide to terminate the agreement i.e. by mutual agreement, or by providing a certain length of notice (acceptable to the locum and the contractor).

If the contractor terminates the agreement before the agreed period of notice, then the details of the fee claimable by the locum (for example, this fee could be based on the difference between the notice actually given and notice that should have been given according to the terms of the agreement) should be clearly stated.

A clause should be included stating that the agreement could be terminated, if either party breaches its terms.

http://www.medicalprotection.org/uk/sessional-gp/issue-1/top-ten-risks-for-locum-gps

The practice should list:

- Fees
- Timetable of work
- Definition of core work

- Additional and enhanced services
- Definition of contractor responsibilities
- Definition of locum responsibilities
- Arrangements for termination of the agreement
- The basic fee for each session (standard sessions, based on the model contract for salaried GPs, comprises 4hrs and 10 min of work. The length of a 'session' should be clarified and agreed in advance together with the expected consultation rate).
- An hourly rate, for shortened sessions and sessions that overrun.
- An extended hours rate. A rate for additional work – i.e. work carried out in addition to that which is defined within the agreement as being expected within a session.
- Details of fee arrangements for private work – for example, whether it will be done in lieu of standard appointments and visits, or in addition to the agreed work (in which case a fee will need to be agreed and set out in the agreement) or not done at all.
- A fee for on-call work
- Arrangements for travel reimbursement
- A cancellation charge where a session is cancelled by the practice at short notice (see below sections on 'Contractor's Responsibilities' and 'Arrangements for the termination of the agreement').

There are some areas that frequently prove contentious and should be addressed explicitly (either inclusion or exclusion):

- Dealing with nurse queries
- Telephone triage outside of agreed surgeries
- Signing repeat and non-repeat prescriptions
- Signing prescriptions on behalf of other practitioners such as nurses
- Defining what the on-call duties are
- Whether any private work etc. will be undertaken and what proportion of payment will be retained?
- What happens to fees incidental to seeing patients?

GPs in the main have to perform to meet clinical skills needed for the jobs and if they are not good at:

- Following procedures
- Treating patients as an individual and with respect
- Operating as a team with other GPs and nurses
- Sharing of a good practice
- Assisting and training others
- Clinical leadership
- Communicate clearly
- Expressing their concerns
- Developing quality

Then the partners should take immediate remedial action with the said GP, lest complaints from the patients lead to action by PCT against the surgery.

15.4 Triage

Triage is part of a modern surgery practice in order to filter or prioritise, or even save GPs time by providing a very valuable service in advising and directing the patient for the best possible service at that time for his/her needs. The nurse is there to help the patient and is not a barrier to seeing the GP.

A specially trained nurse usually carries out triage and special times may be allocated for the triage service. When a patient calls the surgery, receptionists will have to ascertain the reason for the call and except for emergencies, should be able to direct the call to the triage nurse during the appropriate times. All GPs should not only supervise the nurses but also be available for consultation by the nurse in special circumstances.

The triage nurse may direct the patient to the most appropriate health professional such as a doctor, pharmacist, health visitor or even self-help. The patient may not always need to see a doctor.

If the triage nurse feels it would be more appropriate to see the doctor an appointment will be booked in to see the duty doctor. She will be able to advise on:

- Babies under 2 – triage nurse can only see for nappy rash/sticky eye/oral thrush;
- Boils;
- Chesty (ages 18-50 only). Patients with chronic chest problems should still see a doctor;

- Diarrhoea & vomiting;

- Ear pain (but not blocked ears);

- Eye infections/styes/conjunctivitis/red eye (but not anyone with blurred vision or visual disturbance – patient should see a doctor). Foreign bodies in eye – patient should go directly to eye casualty at nearest General Hospital;

- Flu;

- Head lice – patients do not need to be seen but will be advised on how to treat their family's hair – prescriptions will not be given for this;

- Impetigo & scabies (but if recurring will need to see a doctor);

- Skin rashes (but if you have had for longer than a week you should see the doctor)

- Sore throat/tonsillitis;

- Urinary Infections – female patients over 16 years old. All male patients should see a doctor;

- Worms – patients do not need to be seen but could request a prescription for the whole family from the receptionist for this.

After the new contract, when GP Partners were made a type of 'entrepreneur', some have misused the system e.g.

- They have stopped doing some clinics, leaving this to other salaried GPs;

- They also stopped doing evening clinics and employ locum or salaried doctors for the service;

- They glibly state that they are available for triage during the afternoons and evenings and feel it is better to pat with some income but reduce stress levels;

- At least one GP partner, who usually looks after the surgery management, tries to do jobs that are in the areas of responsibility of the PMgr. It is like **'having a dog and barking yourself'**. His skill and specialty is not put to use and PCTs can do nothing about it as long as QOF targets are met and there are very little complaints about the surgery and the particular GP.

In other industries it used to be said that a manager has to take decisions and if he/she does not take any, then the manager cannot be held responsible! Also in several cases the nurse doing the triage may not be specially trained.

15.5 Clinics

GP surgeries vary in size and can have a wide range of staff including nurses, health visitors, district nurses, counsellors, podiatrists and community psychiatric nurses. See Section 14.7.

Depending on the number of GPs in the surgery, the type and number of clinics offered would vary but usually the following clinics would be provided and patients seen by the GPs and nurses in the practice:

- Asthma
- Cervical Smears
- Child Health Surveillance
- Diabetes
- Hypertension

Maternity – Ante and Postnatal

- Minor surgery

In some special cases they may provide:

- Contraception and sexuality/Family Planning
- Travel appointments may be during normal surgery hours with the nurse.
- Dieticians, podiatrists on special occasions

Mental Health might be opted out by the surgery.

External staff might do some clinics including PCT Nurses, midwives, dieticians, podiatrists, health visitors, district nurses, counsellors, and community psychiatric nurses etc.

15.6 Do's and Don'ts

Do's

GPs in the main have to perform to meet clinical skills needed for the jobs and they should be good at:

- Doing work to improve quality of their work.
- Ensuring continued professional development by attending weekly lectures.
- Undertaking specific clinical procedures/assessments.
- Keeping up to date.
- Systematic self-assessment procedures for controls in place to identify and manage clinical risks.
- Being an effective team player.
- Supporting principle of standards.
- Respecting their team.
- Making sure changing the practice occurs in the light of audits, research, complaints and risk management.
- Developing more formal links with health and social care, primary and secondary care, social services etc.
- Implementing evidence-based practice.
- Supporting the development of IT infrastructure, IT training of all staff and continual assessment to check progress and improvements.
- Developing relationships with other GP practices in the area.
- Developing relationships with community staff – health visitors, community nurses, and allied health professionals.
- Constantly striving to improve relationship with the general public, patients, local acute hospital units, and local education and research specialists.

Don'ts

GPs in the main have to perform to meet clinical skills needed for the jobs and if they are not good at:

- Following procedures
- Treating patients as an individual and with respect
- Operating as a team with other GPs and nurses
- Sharing of a good practice
- Assisting and training others
- Clinical leadership
- Communicate clearly
- Expressing their concerns
- Developing quality

GPs need to be trained, as necessary, till they achieve a level of understanding and proficiency in the above skills.

15.7 Home Visits

If the patient is too unwell to come to the surgery, the patient may request a home visit. Please ring before 11am and give the receptionist as much information as possible. Please ensure to leave a contact number as it is likely the doctor will ring you before visiting to confirm if a home visit is necessary.

All visits are done after the morning surgery and administration tasks, which mean that the doctor may only be in a position to leave the surgery from 1pm-3pm. If the patient feels the condition needs emergency attention then please call for an ambulance.

A home visit is at the doctor's discretion and will only be performed for medical, not social needs.

15.8 Risk Management

Ensure all clinical procedures are evidence-based.

Clinical risk reduction procedures should be in place.

Adverse events are detected and complaints investigated; lessons learnt applied forthwith.

Ensure internal audits of clinical and organisational operations and improvements to have high quality data and performance

Poor clinical performances are detected early and dealt with quickly.

Continuing professional development programmes should be in place for all clinical, professional, and administrative staff.

16. Partners

GP Partnerships

Legally, a partnership is an agreement between two or more individuals. It means one is always in control but within the framework of PCT/CCGs and other regulations, everything depends on the profitability of the GP practice and the relationship with the other partners, as set out in the Partnership Agreement – Deed of Partnership – where the relationships with other partners, including share of profits and losses, are usually set out and witnessed by a solicitor. Partnerships are particularly common in professional services e.g. accountants, solicitors, vets, GPs, dentists.

16.1 Advantages

- Part own the business and have a say in how it is run
- Share the profits and losses of the practice with the other partners.
- Stability of employment. Taxed on profits, not on income
- Use salaried staff to build the profits that will fund your lifestyle

16.2 Disadvantages

- Personally liable for any losses. In fact any partner in isolation can be made responsible for the debts of the entire business.

- Taxed on profits and not on your income. If profits not drawn then have to pay tax on any undrawn profits.

- Management, accounting and other non-clinical considerations take up a lot of time.

- Unless one joins a GP Partnership in its infancy, joining a partnership later can be a costly business.

- Responsible for hiring, firing and monitoring staff. Being personally legally and financially responsible for the actions of others can be a daunting prospect.

- No employment rights. No sick pay, no holiday pay, no paid maternity. Being ill, pregnant or going on holiday simply means that less work gets down and therefore less income is taken. This in turns reduces profits and therefore your share.

16.3 Costs

It depends on a lot of factors and each has to be weighed carefully.

- Building costs – rent or lease, loans, interest rates, valuation etc. need careful assessment
- Share of contribution to the surgery working capital – bank accounts, purchase of stock, fittings and furniture etc.

16.4 Parity

- Time taken to achieve parity – 100% – if 4 years then, full costs paid after 4 years and also share of full profits after 4 years only. A partnership may only offer one 80% of normally expected full share in year 1, 85% in year 2, 90% in year 3, and 100% thereafter.
- Some may consider the new partner a full partner from day one.

16.5 Earnings

- Depends on the make-up of the local population and its needs and how the business is developed.
- As per one survey, on average, a GP partner takes home approximately £110,000. The lowest figure is in the South West (approx. £100,000) and the highest is

in the East of England (£120,000).

- Also, partners in practices where there are 6 partners or more earn approximately £20,000 less than partners in small practices.

16.6 Contract

An ordinary partnership can have between two and twenty partners. However, the Partnership Act of 2002 has made it legal for some forms of partnership, e.g. big accountancy firms, to have more partners who also enjoy limited liability.

People in business partnerships can share skills and the workload, and it may be easier to raise the capital needed. For example, a group of doctors are able to pool knowledge about different diseases, and two or three doctors working together may be able to operate a 24/7 service. When one of the doctors is ill or goes on holiday, the business can still cope.

There are forms available for free for setting up a Partnership Agreement and it is advised that one such form is chosen as a draft for filling in the relevant details, and then handed over to the solicitor to formalise the agreement between partners in the GP Practice.

Candidate Briefing Pack for the post of GP Partner – Monkfield Medical Practice – 2011-12 – a wonderful example of laying out the details for an incoming Partner.

16.7 Management Miscellaneous

This refers to all types of GP surgeries – single-handed practices, partners with 2 or more GPs, GMS, PMS, PCTMS, APMS or any other that may come in future changes.

For a surgery to move into modern times and to provide holistic care, the GP partners have to be very open to changes and not dwell on how things were done.

They must know the difference between high aspiration and its good, but far from perfect, results.

- Be alert and aware of instances, which are clearly avoidable as they inflict patient harm. Consider these as system failures, not just accidents or bad luck.

- Learning from the achievements of other surgeries from various meetings attended.

- Define and focus on strategic challenges clearly.

- Look beyond improving individual issues e.g. registration or prescription and focus on improving the entire surgery.

- GPs are known for handling complex medical cases; they should aim to give its highest quality of care to all patients while reducing costs.

- The practices should be prepared for strategic transformation while preserving the successful ones. Fundamental changes are needed to surgery's approach toward customers, workforce, operations, and information and knowledge management.

- Make improvement and transformation to the surgery a priority. The approach of patient-centred care is more important than a win for financial outcomes.

- Quality should be the vision and mission of the surgery, not simply continuous improvement; make the staff provide excellence in all they do.

- GP partners should request all sections to report good performance data along with reporting an imperfect situation. Even if events had no patient impact, there was still significant room for improvement. "Are we as good as we can be?" should be the buzzword.

- Change, especially transformational change, is daunting for any organisation. Practices face all daunting challenges inherent with endemic changes in NHS – cultural sensitivities, technological upgrades, and a vast organisation to shift to 'new thinking'. Self-examination and critical assessment should identify what caused barriers between desired outcomes and what actually happened on a day-to-day basis. There should be a bottom-up approach, the idea that real quality care must characterise the frontline relationship between receptionists and patient. Only then would the practices achieve consistent, good results.

- Every staff member should be encouraged to report anything that does not seem quite right, without fear of reprisal. This culture emphasises respect for the talents, knowledge, and experience of each team member. Transitioning to a workplace environment of greater equality can be tricky in a medical culture where physicians, by education and tradition, are considered the ultimate authority.

- Standardising Hand Hygiene – compliance should reach 100%

- It is generally believed that clinicians, doctors, nurses, and therapists are lax in hand sanitation. The standard practice of preceding every patient contact with hand washing or germicide is not widely complied with. Through employee awareness, patient education, installation of additional sanitizer dispensers, reminder signs, the presence of monitors, and other means, compliance should increase to nearly 100%. After this increase, initial monitoring should be eventually reduced to sampling, and the change should be well ingrained in all staff.

Measurement and Reporting

Transformation is only possible with transparent reporting to all staff. One of the first steps is to make data accessible and form a transparency group. This communicates a high level of trust in personnel and allows for better decision-making.

Transparency means disseminating good and bad results in a clear, concise, and regular manner.

Change management succeeds when there is an innate understanding that people want to do good work. Access to the right data enables personnel to achieve and make informed decisions. Change management requires a culture transformation – not an easy change for any entity.

Initially, focus on core measures on patient satisfaction, infection prevention, control protocols, and mortality. Also collect data for some existing financial and operational measures.

Sustained transformation requires an ongoing understanding that the collection of data for better patient outcomes is clearly mandated. If there are improved patient outcomes it becomes a business strategy.

Surgeries must concentrate on patient and quality outcomes, patient safety, and the patient experience. Surgeries must firmly believe that cost and the benefits of quality compete. Partners must make the cost of quality virtually a non-issue.

Information Systems

Each employee should perceive that they have two jobs: one in providing care or service, and the other in assisting in quality improvement. Surgeries must develop their own knowledge management system.

All information, from helping patient situations, to decision support tools, to contact information for subject-matter experts, should be stored in the computer system.

Surgeries should form a transparency group to measure and publish results across a spectrum of key benchmarks: safety, infection prevention and control, patient satisfaction, and complaints. Results should be published widely in print and through email to all staff.

'**Are we as good as we could be**?' should always be asked.

Even if one does nothing else, get people's minds around the fact that no matter how good the practice is, '**there are ways to be better**'.

Surgery management has to shift their thinking to treat patients as customers. Good customer service is not an option; in today's environment it is crucial to survive.

17. Outside Contacts

17.1 PCT

This is a crucial document to read, not just for the receptionists but also for the PMgr, as this embodies all the good practice to follow in GP surgeries. These areas are covered in several sections but only a few listed below:

- Policy and guidance
- Organisation policy
- Patient choice
- Freedom of Information
- Performance
- Social services
- Information policy – the development and ongoing implementation of the department's IT strategy.
- Health advice for travellers

The surgery should have details of all the crucial people it may have to contact from time to time.

For a PMgr to perform well, he should have a sound relationship with the PCT. The following key people could help or even sink the surgery and we should treat them with care.

1. Prescription Advisor

One of the very few clinical people in the administrative set of PCT.

The PMgr should seek his advice often and follow the yearly targets set by him. Failure to do so would mean a bad reputation for the surgery as it fails to understand that costs should be reduced and generics prescribed instead of branded medicines.

Financially reaching the target may get the surgery only few thousand pounds compared to QOF in several cases but consequential effects of non-achieving would be disastrous for the surgery. The motto is –

RESPECT THE PRESCRIPTION ADVISOR at all times.

2. Complaints Officer (CO)

The Complaints Officer is crucial to the surgery, if the surgery aims to have a good name in PCT, the CO's help is usually invaluable and COs try to help with minimising complaints, and advise the best way to deal with certain difficult situations.

It is better to go to him first, before even a patient complains, explaining the situation and put it in writing to him, should a patient say that he would write to him.

Meet him/her often and have brief sessions on certain complaints and how you dealt with it and seek his comments and approval for future guidance. Sometimes some GP partners might not like this way, but the PMgr has to convince the Partners about the merit of the approach.

3. Finance Officer

So crucial for any payments to the surgery, and when an issue arises about a shortfall in payment, then a good rapport would work wonders. Never argue with him and play the role of **'village idiot'** – it gives others a sense of superiority and the PMgr will get what he wants for the surgery.

4. IT Officer

Without his help surgery would not get spare computers, immediate service, training in time etc. Always develop good relationship with the person.

There are other semi-gods in the PCT; never deal with them with any attitude. Remember that, even if the surgery should be provided with equipment, it should not be construed as surgery's right. These people are helping the surgery and the kudos and glory is theirs. Be generous and compliment them always.

5. CEO

The super god is the CEO of the PCT and the PMgr may rarely come in contact with the CEO. Never pass an opinion on him or his team – good or bad – all will be relayed back to them to the surgery's detriment. A PMgr should never be judgmental.

CEOs have certain strengths and they are where they are, due to those strengths. PCT staff, in general are extremely helpful and in a sense they want all surgeries to do well as they also get graded up.

Denouncing a few surgeries under their management does not give them credit in the long term. Respect them as they are also under pressure and want to do a good job and it is to no one's credit to antagonise them, even if the PMgr feels passionately that they are wrong.

Usually the PMgr might have perception problems, and should not let those affect the surgery relationship with the PCT.

There are a number of other officers in the PCT who have to be contacted on issues pertaining to their specialities, and the PMgr should get a copy of a PCT telephone list for surgery use.

17.2 HMRC, NHS Pensions

– Section 10.0

17.3 Hospitals, Walk-in Centres, Carers, District and Community Nurses, Social Services

Every surgery should have the contact list of all the local hospitals with names and details of consultants and hospital staff whom GPs and Nurses may wish to contact regularly. The list of telephone numbers should be given to receptionists and other staff if need arises to contact them (Table 2.2.1 in Section 2.2).

The same applies to Walk-in Centres, Carers, District and Community Nurses, Social Services etc.

17.4 Banks

PMgr should have details of the banks the surgery has accounts with. He would be required deal with them for drawing cash for GP Partners' salaries, petty cash, paying in cheques (received for insurance, travel immunisations, private patients etc.).

17.5 ACAS

It is the Advisory, Conciliation and Arbitration Service for the UK. It is a non-departmental government body (NGO), which is largely funded by the Government Department for Business Innovation. It is governed by an independent council, which means that it could operate in an independent, impartial and confidential manner.

It offers three types of services to employers; these are Advice, Conciliation and Arbitration. The companies and organisations in the UK frequently used these services. HR professionals might seek ACAS help on complex employment laws, in the day-to-day operational and management environment of the workplace.

Many of the services offered by ACAS are free at the point of demand and some must be paid for.

Their website is a crucial tool for all staff in the surgery to consult and clear doubts frequently on HR issues.

17.6 Sales Representatives

The PMgr should always involve, when dealing with the contractors, SR with pharmaceutical reps, who have a special relationship with the GPs to discuss medicine research, current status of developments, and to promote 'branded' drugs. They do give sweeteners to GPs in way of 'treats' – free medicine samples, small gadgets, pens etc.

It is not unusual for the SR to arrange through the reps, lunch treats like pizza etc. on staff birthdays. For the pharmaceutical companies these expenses are meagre compared to thousands that would be spend on 'branded' drugs. It is better not to dwell on ethics, as these would be unenforceable and should be left to the surgeries to have their own policies on such special occasions.

17.7 Others – Professional, Utilities and Service Personnel

Details for the accountant, lawyers, estate agents, Job Centre, recruitment agencies for staff, nurses and GPs, loan companies, architects, etc., should be available for the PMgr to contact them, when need arises.

The surgery should also have details of contact persons for issues relating to: building, heating, alarm system, electricity, gas, and telephones, etc.

18. Accounts

Generally a surgery will have an accountant, who may visit the surgery for one day or part of a day a week, as agreed with the partners, to maintain the accounts and advise staff and GPs on various financial, tax and related issues that may arise. Only in some practices, if a Practice Manager (PMgr) were suitably experienced in accounting, would they be involved by the Partners in dealing with certain issues, playing second fiddle to the accountant.

Practice Payments

The general principles of payments in earlier years are given below. Lots of changes have occurred in recent years and the statement would elucidate current payment headings.

Most payments to practices are made via the Exeter Payments system, which is a national system, used by PCTs and Payments Agencies.

After the close of the registration quarter, the Exeter system calculates the Global Sum payments due to the GMS practices. The amounts calculated are paid for the three months of the quarter and then run again the following quarter.

PMS Practices are paid a monthly contract value which is agreed with their PCT. GMS Practices are paid quarterly.

Most practices participate in the Quality and Outcomes Framework (QOF). Essentially there are 2 types of payments made in relation to QOF: Aspiration payments, which are paid monthly, and Achievement payments, which are paid annually. These payments are made via the Exeter system from data received from QMAS.

Each month the PCTs advise the Agency of any Enhanced Service payments to be paid and these are paid with the GMS and PMS monthly payments.

From the above payments, employee, employer and AVC superannuation is deducted on the basis of the estimated pensionable pay of the GPs, non-GP partners and salaried GPs notified to the Agency each year. The contributions are subsequently paid over to the Pensions Agency each month.

When we receive the GPs annual certificates of pensionable profits, the contributions due for the year are reconciled to the deductions made on account and the underpayments/overpayments are actioned in the next monthly GMS/PMS payment due to be paid.

Levies are then deducted (paid to the LMC) and courier charges for the collection of medical records etc.

Seniority and Age 2 and Age 5 Target payments are paid on a quarterly basis.

Seniority payments are paid to GP Providers (not salaried GPs) and they reward experience, based on years of Reckonable Service. The payments become payable once a GP has been in an eligible post for 2 years and has 7 years' Reckonable Service, and take into account the GP's Superannuable Income Fraction.

Each month details are received from the PPD via NHS Connecting for Health of the dispensing and prescribing drugs payments due to the practices.

The prescribing payments are paid with the monthly Global Sum payments and are paid two months in arrears i.e. March prescriptions paid in May and the dispensing payments are paid on the first working day of the month, with March prescriptions paid on the first working day of June.

Within the monthly Global Sum payments and PMS payments we include payments for locums covering maternity, paternity, adoption leave and sickness, and also Retainer Scheme payments.

Rent and Rates payments including Notional Rents, Actual Rents and Cost Rents are paid to practices on a monthly basis with the Global Sum and PMS payments.

GP premises are reviewed on a three yearly basis, and when a new rent has been assessed by the District Valuer and approved by the PCT, we pay the new rent to the practice and pay any rent arrears that may be due.

Direct payments for Non-Domestic Rates and water charges to the Council and water companies on behalf of the practices.

These payments are made on the Integra payments system.

Statements giving details of these payments are sent to practices on an annual basis for inclusion in the practice accounts.

Reimbursements are also made to training practices in respect of their GP Registrars. The Deanery advises the Agency of the GP Registrars working in our areas and advises the practices of the salary to pay their GP Registrar. Changes are afoot regarding stopping such payments.

Medical Practitioner Fee payments including Mental Health Assessments, adoption reports/examinations etc. are paid normally on a weekly basis via the Integra payments system.

Statements to practices where payments have been made are available on Open Exeter.

Currently, around half of all GPs work as independent contractors under contract to provide core primary health care services and additional services as negotiated within the GP contract.

As such, these GPs are self-employed, running small businesses or practices. They have management responsibilities for staff, premises and equipment. Since most of these GPs receive a profit share, the amount each GP is paid depends not only on income to the practice but also on expenditure.

Income comes from NHS work under the GP contract and private work, such as insurance examinations, private medical examinations and certificates and outside appointments (for example industrial appointments or clinical assistant posts).

Expenditure includes the running costs of the practice – staff salaries, cost of the premises (rent, taxes, repairs, maintenance and insurance), service costs (heating, water, electricity, gas, telephone, stationery and postage), training costs and other expenses – and the capital costs of medical and office equipment.

Currently, there are two forms of contract that GP practices may have with their local Primary Care Organisations (PCOs), the General Medical Services (GMS) contract, or Personal Medical Services (PMS) contract.

The contract defines the services that they will provide, standards to achieve, and the payment that they will receive.

The GMS contract is a contract made between an individual practice and a PCO. All the partners of the practice, at least one of whom must be a GP, have to sign the contract. It includes national terms applicable to all practices (the 'Practice Contract').

A description of which services will be provided by that practice, i.e.:

- Essential services
- Additional services if not opted out
- Out-of-hours cover if not opted out
- Enhanced services, if opted in
- A level of quality of essential and additional services that the practice 'aspires' to
- Support arrangements, for example for information technology, and premises
- A summary of the total financial resources

Essential services:

Essential services are the services that all practices must undertake. These services include the day-to-day medical care of the practice population such as health promotion, management of minor and self-limiting illness and referral to secondary care services and other agencies as appropriate, the general management of patients who are terminally ill and chronic disease management.

Additional services:

Services that the practice will usually undertake but may 'opt out' of. If the practice opts out, the PCO takes responsibility for providing the service instead. The practice then receives a reduced global sum payment.

The services included are:

Cervical screening – opting out results in a 1.1% decrease in global sum contraceptive services – opting out results in a 2.4% reduction in global sum.

Vaccinations and immunisations – opting out of vaccinations and immunisations results in a 2% drop in global sum; opting out of childhood immunisations leads to a 1% reduction in global sum child health surveillance (excluding the neonatal check) – opting out leads to a 0.7% decrease in global sum.

Maternity services excluding intra-partum care (which is an enhanced service) – opting out causes a 2.1% drop in global sum.

Certain minor surgery procedures: curettage, cautery, cryocautery of warts/verrucae and other skin lesions – opting out results in a 0.6% reduction in global sum.

Enhanced services:

Enhanced services are commissioned by the PCO and paid for in addition to the global sum payment.

There are three types:

Directed enhanced services:

These are enhanced services under national direction with national specifications and benchmark pricing that all PCOs must commission to cover their population. These services change from year to year and include access targets, payment targets for childhood immunisations, influenza vaccinations, and more complex minor surgery, such as joint injections, and incisions or excisions

National enhanced services:

These services have national minimum standards and benchmark pricing but are not directed (that is PCOs do not have to provide these services). Examples include anticoagulation monitoring, treatment of drug or alcohol abuse and minor injury services.

Local enhanced services:

These services are developed locally to meet local needs. For example special services for refugees. Out-of-hours care practices can 'opt out' of providing an out-of-hours service. The decision must be made for the whole practice – individual doctors within a practice cannot 'opt out' alone.

The cost of opting out for a practice is 7% of the global sum. There is nothing to stop practices that have opted out from offering surgeries or consultations within the time periods specified as out-of-hours. These services could be paid for through the practice global sum or might be paid for as an enhanced service.

Currently, enhanced services providing out-of-hours surgeries can be negotiated at a local level with PCOs, but in future are likely to be part of a Directed Enhanced Service for enhanced access.

Payment to practices comprises the following components:

The global sum + quality payments + enhanced services payments + payment for premises + information technology payments + dispensing payments (if applicable).

The global sum: this is the major part of the money paid to practices. It is paid monthly and intended to cover practice-running costs. It includes provision for delivery of essential services and additional and out-of-hours services (if not opted out), staff costs, career development and locum reimbursement (for example for appraisal, career development and protected time).

Quality payments The Quality and Outcomes Framework was developed specifically for the new GMS contract but similar arrangements are in place for those GPs working within PMS contracts. Financial incentives are used to encourage high-quality care.

The GMS quality framework is divided into four domains: Clinical, Organisational, Additional Services, and Patient Experience.

Every domain has a set of 'indicators' that relate to quality standards or guidelines that can be achieved within that domain.

The indicators are developed by an expert group based on the best available evidence at the time and are updated regularly. All data should be obtainable from practice clinical systems.

18.1 General Principles

Basic principles of accounts can be studied by referring to standard accounting books. Only the special circumstances pertaining to GP surgery practice will be highlighted here.

The typical headings for income and expenses for a GP practice are indicated. These are input on the left column. The next set of columns is for the 12 months followed by the total. The next column is monthly actual (total divided by the number of months e.g. after 3rd month Total/3; after 7 months Total/7). The final column is the original budget for the year averaged monthly (omitted in the attachment as figures would vary from one surgery to another).

See 18.1a for Surgery Yearly Income Expenses account layout.

18.1.1 Income

Would include the following:

- Contract value
- MPIG Correction value
- Aspiration
- Aspiration uplift
- Total seniority
- Water payments
- LTNC payments
- Choose & Book
- Childhood Immunisation targets
- Rent/Rates – monthly
- PBC Des component two – ad hoc
- Minor surgery – monthly
- ACH pay on account – ad hoc
- Sickness/locum cover – ad hoc
- IM&T payments
- Flu payments (influenza)
- Pneumo Immun. – monthly & ad hoc
- Des C&B component 2 RWD – ad hoc
- IUCD – monthly & ad hoc

- Gonadrelin – monthly & ad hoc
- NPT – monthly & ad hoc
- Child pneumo. – ad hoc
- Access Des Award – ad hoc
- Superann. repayment GPs
- Hibs, Admin LHRH, Intra-partum etc.

Total Inflows

Less:

- Employee Superannuation 6%
- Employers Superannution 14%
- AVC contributions
- Statutory Levy
- Voluntary Levy
- Total Net Payment

Other Incomes:

- Prescribing drugs
- Insurance
- P/Cash
- Transfers etc.
- Bank Interest/deposit a/c
- Other Incomes

Total Turnover

The Carr-Hill allocation formula

Geographical and social factors result in differing workload for GPs. When the new GMS contract was introduced in 2004, the Carr-Hill formula (developed by Professor Roy Carr-Hill of York University) was also introduced to adjust payment to individual practices to allow for these factors. It allocates global sum payments and quality payments to practices on the basis of the practice population, weighted for factors that influence relative needs and costs in order to reflect the differences in workload these factors generate. The Carr-Hill formula replaced a previous system of weighting payments to practices according to social factors that was called the Jarman Index. Introduction of the Carr-Hill allocation formula has been controversial and there are likely to be some adjustments to the factors used for weighting in the near future.

Minimum practice income guarantee

The minimum practice income guarantee protects those practices that lost out under the redistribution effect when the Carr-Hill resource allocation formula was introduced in place of the Jarman Index. It is calculated by subtracting the global sum allocation (GSA) under the new GMS contract from the global sum equivalent (GSE) – the amount the practice would have earned for providing the same service under the old GMS contract (The Red Book). If the GSA is less than the GSE, a correction factor (CF) will be applied as long as necessary to make up the difference.

18.1.2 Expenses

- Staff salaries – Gross pay
- HMRC – Employee NI, Tax, Pens.
- HMRC – Employer NI, Pension
- GP Locums etc.
- OOH service – Mastercall SVC Ltd
- Premises – Rent, Rates & Insurance
- Premises – Zurich Assurance
- Premises – Axa Sunlife
- Premises – Tesco etc.
- Insurance Premises – Guardian Financial Services
- Premises – Siemens Fin. Service
- Doc. Medical Insurance/Testing
- Premises – Gas, Elec., utilities

- Premises, repairs & maintenance
- Drugs & Medical supplies
- Motor Expenses
- Shell UK Ltd
- Telephone, Fax, Mobiles etc.
- Architect/solicitors
- Postage, Printing & Stationery
- Loan account
- Capital Bank
- Subscription e.g. MDU, RCGP, GMCBMA, GMC, RCGP
- Accountancy Fees
- Depreciation: Fixtures/Fittings – est.
- Depreciation: Motor Vehicles – est.
- Sundries (incl. petty cash)
- H3G+ CMP Inform. Group
- Group Seniority + others
- GPs Bank charges & interest
- Dr A salary
- Dr B salary
- Dr C salary
- Dr D salary
- S/OPCT Deductions
- Motor

Total Expenses

- Surplus/Deficit
- Credit/Debit not income/expenses
- Bank o/b
- Bank c/b – calculated

Bank monthly closing balance-actual

18.1.3 Budget (Setting Methodology)

Every year, the PCT sets a prescribing budget for each practice, using a formula that contains a number of factors including:

- Population profile and list size of the practice using a weighted capitation unit known as the ASTRO PU prescribing unit;
- An average spend per patient for the PCT, calculated for cardiovascular, respiratory and diabetes drugs, using QOF prevalence data. This figure is then applied to each practice appropriately;
- Consideration of historic spend of the practice;
- High cost drug spent by the practice;
- Adjustments made for deprivation and care home patients, for each practice;
- Recent NICE guidance and other national clinical treatment guidance;
- New medicines.

Each practice is reviewed regularly by the PCT's medicines management team using the database of prescription information provided by the NHS Business Services Authority, known as ePACT. The medicines management pharmacists will also provide support and expertise to the practice to help manage their budgets.

The practice will usually set a review programme for key target areas within current prescribing. Some practices have created their own practice formularies to ensure clinical and cost effective prescribing policies are maintained.

All budgets must be based on realistic projections of activity levels, pay, inflation, and priorities and known cost pressures. All available information about future changes and developments must also be considered.

18.1.4 Budget Computations

The PMgr should prepare the budget 1-2 months before the end of the accounting year. The income and costs should be estimated on a realistic and conservative basis.

Aim should be to:

- Increase practice income.
- Decrease costs.
- Minimise wastage.
- If staff costs need to be increased due to extra staff for the benefit of the practice, then have a realistic figure for increase of income to support an increase in staff. Without that increase in income, the request would be turned down. It is better not to raise the issue than earn a bad opinion from the GP Partners that the PMgr is unrealistic and even out of his depth when it comes to accounts.
- Always ensure that when aiming for staff increase, the increase cost does not exceed more than 60% of the increased income forecast. 50% would be a safer bet.
- Prepare a list of all staff, including GPs.
- Prepare total staff costs, inputting hours worked for each, hourly rates and annual salary.
- Compute the NI and pensions – a lot of receptionists at low income cannot afford to pay for a pension in formative years of their careers in NHS.
- The % of GP salary to total income should be around 40%; this would be adequate to have two partners earning £120000 each.
- The % of staff costs to total income should not exceed 30%; preferably 27.5%.
- The present day youngsters are very good at computing and more effort should be taken to use them for work relating to reports, audits etc. Plan for a PT receptionist for 12 hours a week – 3 days @ 4hrs per day in afternoon, may reduce backlogs and may not cost an arm and leg to the surgery (£7 x 12 x 52 = £4368).
- Specify where the increase in income would come from.
- Specify where the reduction in expenses would accrue and what efforts would be taken to achieve that – rearranging staff duties, improving performance.
- If a Locum GP has to be discontinued due to their high costs, especially if they come appointed via an agency, then go for a salaried GP. Even if it is not the right way for the long-term good of the surgery. Always aim for a GP partner, preferably 100% after 4 years of service.
- Aim for more clinics and budget for an increase employ another nurse to provide a better service. A surgery with two nurses for 5 GPs and 2.5 for 8 GPs would be perceived as a good surgery to register.
- Always aim to provide extra service than last year and the first areas to focus would be 'pull up the socks' on those areas where the surgery is underperforming.

Sample Budget:

The figures are all 'doctored in' – it does not represent any particular surgery. It shows the basics.

The PMgr should prepare such a budget, plan for any increase in staff and reduction in costs.

See 18.1.4a and 18.1.4b – typical staff budget formats are below.

Ensure the realistic reduction costs and any extra income to be received would support any increase in staff costs.

If not, do not make an issue for staff increase, because at the end of the day, 'bottom line – profit' is the key factor.

If the present PMgr does not understand and appreciate this key principle, there are many in the queue to join the practice.

Always **'help the Partners to help yourself'**.

18.1.4a Staff Budget

Re	Details	Time	Rate/Hour	Hours/Week	Weeks/year	Total per year	No	Grand Total per year	Monthly	Employer NI 11% >£87/wk >£4524/yr	Employee Pension 8%
1	Practice Manager	FT	12.00	32	52	19968	1	19968	1664.00	183.04	133.12
2	GP Secretary	PT	10.00	20	52	10400	1	10400	866.67	95.33	0
3	Snr Receptionist	PT		37	52	0	1	0	0.00	0.00	0.00
4	Receptionists (3+3)+1										
4.1	R1		8	20	52	8320	1	8320	693.33	76.27	0.00
4.2	R2		8	10	52	4160	1	3380	281.6667	0.00	0.00
4.3	R3		8	20	52	8320	1	6448	537.3333	59.11	0.00
4.4	R4		8	10	52	4160	1	3380	281.67	0.00	0.00
4.5	R5		7	15	52	5460	1	4836	403.00	44.33	0.00
4.6	R6		6.5	15	52	5070	1	5070	422.50	46.48	0.00
4.7	R7 for holiday cover		6.5	20	52	6760	1	6240	520.00	57.20	
5	Practice Nurse 1	FT	16.00	16	52	13312	1	13312	1109.33	122.03	0.00
6	Practice Nurse 2	PT	16.00	12	52	9984	1	9984	832.00	91.52	116.48
7	Healthcare Assistant	PT	10.00	16	52	8320	1	8320	693.33	76.27	0.00
8	IT Specialist	PT	9.00	25	52	11700	1	11700	975.00	107.25	136.50
9	Support Staff	PT	6.50	8	52	2704	1	2704	225.33	0.00	0.00
10	Total						15	114062	9505.17	958.82	386.10
11	ErNI							11505.78			
12	ErPen							4633.20			
13	ADMIN EXPENSES							28000.00	2500.00		
14	Total Expense							158200.98	12005.17		
15	NET INCOME							520000.00	27000.00		
15	Balance							361799.02			
							7.5% pension				
16	GP1						7.5%	90000	7500.00		
17	GP2						7.5%	45000	3333.00		
18	GP3						7.5%	53333	4111.11		
					float			21,000			

Comments:

Pension employee 6% employer 8% – Total 14%

NI employer 11% with limits mentioned.

For a budget, try to look at all expenses – admin, GPs, super ann., staff costs etc.

Do not do a business plan without a breakdown of each and every element of expenses and income.

18.1.4b Staff Budget – Format 2

18.1.4b	staff and budget format 2		Present Accounting Year				Next Accounting Year	
surgery		Surgery actuals				staff		
partners		6		hr/wk	rate	yr		
list size		10200				x52		
Staff total number		20	A	24	10.5	13104		
staff hr/wk		471	B	20	7	7280		
			C	15	6.12	4774		
salary		206221	D	10	6.12	3182		
NI	20301		E	20	6.12	6365		
Pension	6226		F	5	6	1560		
NI+Pen	26527	26527	G	5	6.12	1591		
Total		232748	H	32	14.08	23429		
			Nurse	13.2	25	17160		
			HCA	10	15	7800		
Income		960650	cleaner	6	12	3744		
% staff		24.23	Total	160.2		89989		
Expenses			NI			12011		
			Pension			3000		
GP Salary		285000						
before profit			grand tot			105000		105000
% GP salary to Income		29.67						
2 Partners			increase	32.8				20060
xtra income		120000	NI & Pen. Est					3000
total	42.28	405000	Grand tot	193				128060
						to aim for	09-10.	
staff			income		425000	increase	flu vacc.	7000
receptionists		13					rent/rates	3000
Nurses FT		2					chld. Imm	4000
HCA		1					pbc	3000
IT - FT		1					prescribin	5000
Med. Secretary FT		1					hibs (A25)	8000
PMgr		1						
Cleaner P/T		1					total	30000
staff role and hours suggested			expenses	250000				
reception	5x3+4x2	23				reduce	repair	-15000
telephone	,,	23					arch/sol.	-3500
registration	,,	23					GP locum	-15000
Filing	,,	23				increase	staff	20060
IT (Moeena)	(+claims)	15				,,	GP 1 xtra	40000
Med. Sec*	5X3	15					(£3333x12)	
Pr. Mgr		32						
HCM		10					total	26560
Nurse		23	net profit		175000			
cleaner		6	% staff		30.13	(128060x100/425000)		
						hr/wk	rate	yr
Total		193	increase					x52
			staff	nurse p/t		9.8	25	12740
*train a receptionist to do				(13.2+9.8=	23 hr			
the job with courses					1 FT			
on				(5x3+4x2)	Nurse			
med. Sec in PCT.			increase	reception		23	6.12	7320
						(5x3+4x2h)		
						total for the year		20060

Comments:

i. Be brutal about reducing expenses but realistic.

ii. Be very realistic/conservative about Income.

iii. If a staff is promising, develop the person for other roles like IT specialist, Med. Secretary - do not worry about.

18.1.5 Auto-preparation of Accounts

The Excel-based account below is developed for one surgery and it can be set up for any surgery, if they so wish. Please note none of the totals would tally in the attachment as they have been modified. The integrity of the auto-account preparation is not affected in any way. If any one row were deleted in Income or Expenses, the output would be seriously affected. So leave the row blank for the moment.

The first page is for Income. The appropriate figures need to be input into the respective columns when payment advisements are received.

The second page is for Expenses. With all the invoices, bank cheque books, the current bank statements, and the monthly details to be input – preferably end of 2nd week in each month.

Both these operations should not take more than 30 min. per month. First time operation may take an hour.

Page 3 is the accounts for the surgery – computed for each month.

This is only an indication of how the surgery is doing so far.

Caution needs to be exercised if the surgery has surplus funds, say, after 5 months – these are not for immediate spending as PCT give higher amounts in the first quarter but it gets reduced in the 2nd quarter.

The advantage of this system is that the final accounts should be ready for the accountant once the closing period month details are input – by mid-April of the closing accounting period.

For records purposes Fixed Assets, depreciation, capital allowances, GPs income (not monthly drawings) and profit sharing, staff salary with coding and deductions.

Superannuation monthly deductions for each GP partner have to be completed by the Accountant. However, if the PMgr is adept with accounts, he should be able to prepare these data well before the end of the year.

The monthly averaged total figures should be compared with the budget figures and raise alarm during the year and not at the end.

This simple layout would help surgeries immensely, and one need not be an account specialist to operate the system.

The objective for the surgery should be to send all records to the accountant by June/July of each year (if the annual accounting period ends March 31) for checking and filing with HMRC.

18.1.5a GMS Practice Accounts

	GMS Practice	01-May	30-May	01-Jul	01-Aug	01-Sep	01-Oct	31-Oct	01-Dec	31-Dec	30-Jan	27-Feb	01-Apr	Total	year-year
Re:	List Size	3620	start dt. wt. 3688		3750 wt. 3915			4200 wt. 4100							
A	Inflows:														
A1	Contract value	16211.98	16211.98	16211.98	16427.20	16427.20	16427.20	17195.11	17177.65	17177.65	17262.19	17262.19	17262.19	201255	196339
A2	MPIG Correction value	1126.95	1126.95	1126.95	1126.95	1126.95	1126.95	690.87	690.87	690.87	690.87	690.87	690.87	10907	13523
A3	Aspiration	3906.82	3906.82	3906.82	3906.82	3906.82	3906.82	3906.82	3906.82	3906.82	3906.82	3906.82	3906.82	46882	46694
A4	Aspiration uplift													7814 (Aspirat.>)	11718
A5	Total Seniority			1966.50			1210.92		7813.64	1233.75			1233.75	5645	3132
A6	Water payments										561.72			562	0
A7	LTNC Payments						250.00							250	0
A8	Choose & Book						468.36			472.56				1873	2853
A9	Childhood Immunisation targets	1500.00		931.68			2502.96	105.14		2587.50		127.67	2488.86	11368	9938
A10	Rent/Rates	2062.50	2062.50	2055.40	2062.50	2062.50	2062.50	2062.50	2062.50	2062.50	2062.50	2062.50	2062.50	24750	29750
A11	PBC Des component two - monthly		2989.14											2989	4402
A12	Minor Surgery - monthly	1108.12			511.44			298.34				852.40		2770	5066
A13	ACH pay on account - adhoc	31442.09												31442	17578
A14	Sickness / Locum cover - adhoc													0	16348
A15	IM&T Payments - adhoc													0	0
A16	Flu Payments (influenza)	112.65									3755.00			3868	10062
A17	Pneumo Immun. - monthly & adhoc	22.53						193.55				225.30		441	199
A18	Des C&B component 2 RWD-adhoc		737.58											738	2577
A19	IUCD - monthly & adhoc	1912.65			969.65			442.20				649.92		3974	1817
A20	Gonadrein - monthly & adhoc	270.97			387.10							193.55		852	930
A21	NPT - monthly & Adhoc	396.72			3079.38			2445.39				3169.95		9091	1686
A22	Child pneuomo - adhoc													0	98
A23	Access Des Award - adhoc			5085.42										5085	5248
A24	Superann. repayment Drs JC,SJ												1234.38	1234	2629
A25	Hibs, Admin LHRH, Intra Partum etc					87.59						150.20		218	10486
	Total Inflows	60073.98	27034.97	33347.25	28538.63	23523.47	27955.71	27339.92	31651.48	28131.65	24484.10	33046.37	28879.37	374007	393073
A26	Less: Employee Superannuation 6% (A26-A30 shown in expenses)	913.55											64.82	10614	6926
A27	Employers Superannution 14%	1752.02	1752.02	1752.02	1752.02	1752.02	1752.02	1752.02	1752.02	1752.02	1752.02	1752.02	-345.16	18927	16161
A28	AVC contributions	0.00	0.00	0.00	0.00	0.00	0.00	0.00	0.00	0.00	0.00	0.00	0.00	0	0
A29	Statutory Levy	449.66	0.00	0.00	463.48	0.00	0.00	467.64	0.00	0.00	469.42	0.00	0.00	1850	1796
A30	Voluntary Levy	0.00	0.00	0.00	0.00	0.00	0.00	0.00	0.00	0.00	0.00	0.00	-280.34	31392	0
	Total	3115.23	2715.63	2715.63	3179.11	2715.63	2715.63	3183.27	2715.63	2715.63	3185.05	2715.63			24883
	Total Net Payment	56958.75	24319.34	30631.62	25359.52	20807.84	25240.08	24156.66	28935.85	25416.02	21299.05	30330.74	29159.71	342615	368190
	Other Incomes:														
A31	Prescribing Drugs		2940.89			1974.64		950.98	754.06	1497.72	5315.52		1499.11	14933	19972
A32	Insurance														1102
A33	P/Cash, transfers etc		3386.96							25.15		4780.56		8193	0
A34	Bank Interest/ deposit a/c	2.54	2.67	2.80	2.29	2.29	22.01	2.17	1.80		331.32	0.06	0.05	368	0
A35	Other Incomes - Total	2.54	6330.52	2.80	2.29	1974.64	22.01	953.15	755.86	1522.87	5646.84	4780.62	1499.16	23493	21074
B	Turnover	60121.98	33365.49	33350.05	28540.92	25498.11	27977.72	28293.07	32407.34	29654.52	30130.94	37826.99	30378.53	397546	414148

DR. V. SUBRAMANIAN

18.1.5a GMS Practice

Re:	B	Turnover	01-May start dt. 60121.98	30-May 33365.49	04-Jul 33350.05	01-Aug 28540.92	01-Sep 25498.11	01-Oct 27977.72	31-Oct 28293.07	01-Dec BACS 32407.34	31-Dec 29654.52	30-Jan 30130.94	27-Feb 37826.99	01-Apr 30378.53	Total 397546	year-year (% claim made)
C		Expenses:														
C1		Staff salaries - Gross pay	4168.77	5599.56	5155.33	5348.02	5544.38	5127.62	5124.19	7357.30	6032.73	6020.35	5836.55	6141.46	67476.26	yes 100
"		HMRC - Employee NI, Tax, Pens.			287.43		501.15		11.50	9.20	1440.58	11.50	898.73	1949.04	5109.13	yes 100
"		HMRC - Employer NI, Pension	316.34		504.62		523.78		261.89		785.67		261.89	523.78	3117.97	yes 100
C3		GP Locums etc				1530.00	8200.00	6000.00	3000.00	6000.00	2000.00				26730.00	yes 100
"		OOH service - Mastercall SVC Ltd	284.51			281.80	284.51	346.83	281.80	287.22	346.83	281.80	398.31	284.51	3357.21	yes 100
C4		Premises - Rent, Rates & Insurance		279.09	655.75			395.43					72.00		1123.18	yes 100
"		Premises -Contents insurance					26.68	13.34	13.34	13.34	13.34	13.34		26.68	120.06	yes 100
"		Premises -Building insurance										509.28	254.64	254.64	1018.56	yes 100
"		Premises - Insurance													0.00	yes 100
"		Premises - Financial Serv													0.00	yes 100
"		Premises - Fin. Service	218.70		47.85	218.70		71.35	242.20		47.21	214.48		47.21	1107.70	yes 100
C5		Doc. Medical Insurance/Testing												259.61	259.61	yes 100
C6		Premises - Gas, Elec. utilities	334.97	145.00	238.85	279.85	243.85	281.27	1120.91	263.65	490.31	334.06	231.80	470.92	4435.44	yes 100
C7		Premises, repairs & maintenance	2620.00	1230.00	2500.00	1000.00	9257.07	62.32	578.00		244.50	2464.50	1216.28	789.31	21961.98	yes 100
C8		Drugs & Medical supplies	583.98	500.65	1043.06	1325.64	2087.89	741.66	1392.10	886.07	779.29	1169.44	6905.34	1729.02	19144.14	yes 100
C9		Motor Expenses			247.50	117.35		210.00	468.58		55.72		162.82	315.26	1099.15	yes 100
"		Petrol	283.83	488.78	301.27	384.34	535.30	44.38	331.43	289.31	181.34	244.82	607.02	534.80	3562.88	yes 100
C10		Telephone, Fax, Mobiles etc		903.70		88.12	535.67	50.80	47.07	744.91	191.09	49.40			3752.58	yes 100
C11		Architect / solicitors				3615.01									3615.01	yes 100
C12		Postage, Printing & Staionery				293.13		10.28			20.46	16.28			340.15	yes 100
"		Loan account			245.00						-2509.49	2509.49	5018.98	2509.49	7773.47	yes 100
		Capital Bank													0.00	yes 100
C13		Subscription e.g. MDU, RCGP, GMC	1061.42				1093.30	546.65	90.00	1093.30		546.65	546.65	1093.30	6071.27	yes 100
		BMA, GMC, RCGP	338.00												338.00	yes 100
C14		Accountancy Fees											2000.00		2000.00	yes 100
C15		Depreciation: Fixtures / Fittings - est													0.00	
		Depreciation: Motor Vehicles - est.													0.00	
C16		Sundries (incl. petty cash)	96.00	200.00	296.00		1478.41	400.00	250.00	425.00	467.25	402.02	358.55	232.00	4605.23	yes 100
		H3G+ CMP In form Group													0.00	yes 100
c19		Seniority + others to GPs													0.00	yes 100
C17		Bank charges & interest				22.71	-22.71	48.45			7.00		3.25	225.00	433.70	yes 100
C18		Dr A		3333.00			7327.33			6666.66	3333.33	3333.33		6666.66	38176.31	on profit 0
"		Dr B	3333.00	3333.00	3333.00	3334.00	4013.33	6666.66		6666.66	3333.33	3333.33		6666.66	44012.97	on profit 0
"		DR C		6000.00	13000.00	6000.00	12756.76	12756.76				15000.00	7000.00		72513.52	on profit 0
C19		DR D	2550.00	2550.00	2550.00	2550.00	2550.00	2550.00						15300.00	15300	50
C2		PCT Deductions (see A26-A30)	3115.23	2715.63	2715.63	3179.11	2715.63	2715.63	3183.27	2715.63	2715.63	3185.05	2715.63	-280.34	31391.73	yes 100
C9		Motor-	1300.91												1300.91	7355 50
		Total Expenses	20625.66	27278.41	40787.29	29567.78	59652.33	39039.43	16396.28	33418.25	19976.12	39639.12	27488.44	37439.01	391308.1	unclaimed 8300
		Surplus / Deficit	39496.3	6087.08	-7437.24	-1026.86	-34154.2	-11061.7	11896.79	-1010.91	9678.40	-9508.18	10338.55	-7060.48	-83895.1	(dad's a/c)
		cr/ dt amounts not income/ expenses	-76366.7								-7528.5					deduct from
		Bank o/b	111276.5	58816.47	64903.55	57466.31	56439.45	22281.35	11219.64	23116.43	22105.52	24257.19	14749.01	25087.56		final bank c/b =
		Bank c/b calculated	74406.20	64903.55	57466.31	56439.45	22285.23	11219.64	23116.43	22105.52	24255.45	14749.01	25087.56	18027.08	24277	(110407 8-86131.1)
		Bank monthly closing balance-actual	58816.47	64903.55	57466.31	56439.45	22281.35	11219.64	23116.43	22105.52	24257.19	14749.01	25087.56	18027.08		

258

18.1.5a GMS Practice

Income & Expenditure Account

P84652 BACS A/C 1000 7090

Income:	Cell	year to year ACTUAL	year to year ACTUAL	<....Draft......>	year to year ACTUAL	year to year (15 months) <....Draft......>
Turnover	053	397546	421133	414148	524806	524806
Expenditure:		add unpres. cheques				
Practice: Medicines + Levies	070	19144				
Practice: Locums, Emergency serv	059,060	30087 49231	112677	90362	132149	23076 109073 132149
Premises: Rent, rates, Insurance	061,o56	10793				5160
Premises - use of home, heat/light	est	750				750
Premises: Utilities	068	4435				3269
Premises - repairs, maintenance	069	21962 37940	71093	51834	55825	21675 30854
Staff, Salary, Ee/Er- NI, Tax, Pension	056,57,58	75763 77 75840	54577	56913	70172	69300 69300
Admin: Telephone, Comm, Comp.	073,74	7368				6536
Admin: Post, stationery, printing	075	340				3189
Admin: MPS, GMC, BMA, RCGP	078,79	6409				11783
Admin: Accountancy Fees	080	2000				4373
Admin: Motor	071,72,92	5312				11971
Admin: Superannuation & Seniority	010,91,85	37037				29386
Admin: Miscellaneous						4088
Admin: Sundries	083,84	4605 63071 200 63271	45263	56922	76583	1359 74685
Financial: Bank loans + interest	076,77,90	15857 15857	5439	30345	12625	16723 16723
Financial: Hire purchase + interest	est	0				0
Depreciation: Fixtures / Fittings - est	est	550				590
Depreciation: Motor Vehicles - est	est	3700				3961
Depreciation: Computer equipment	est	250 4500 4500	3860	4500	4828	277 4828
Finance Costs: Bank charges	086	434 434 434	317	296	145-12	145 145
Total Expenditure		246797 0 277 247074	293126	298845	352327	326684 328684
Net Profit (Partners Income)		150472	128028	115303	172491	196122 12 196134

Fixed (Tangible) Assets:	F/hold Property	Fixture/ Fittings	Motor Vehicles	Total
2007 - cost				
Depreciation				
2008 Book value				

Current Accounts:	as at 1.1.07	Net Income	Capital Input	less: drawing	Add: unp. Chq	Total Drawing
Dr A				38176	0	38176
Dr B				20000	0	20000
Dr C				24013	917	24930
Dr B				72514	7000	59514
				154703	7917	162620

18.1.5a GMS Practice

Long Term Liabilities: Amount term interest with
- Business term loan
- Surgery loan
- Car loan
- Hire purchases

Superannuation details

	Dr A 7%	Dr A 14%	Dr B 9%/14%	Dr C 9%/14%	Dr D 9%/14%	Total 6%	Total 14%		
Apr 08.	325.37	1051.21				325.37	1051.21	C	
May	325.37	700.80				325.37	700.80	H	
Jun	325.37	700.80				325.37	700.80	E	
Jul	325.37	700.80				325.37	700.80	C	
Aug	325.37	700.80				325.37	700.80	K	
Sep	325.37	700.80				325.37	700.80		
Oct	325.37	700.80				325.37	700.80	L	
Nov	325.37	700.80				325.37	700.80	I	
Dec 08.	325.37	700.80				325.37	700.80	S	
Jan 09.	325.37	700.80				325.37	700.80	T	
Feb	325.37	700.80				325.37	700.80		
Mar 09.	325.37	700.80				325.37	700.80	D	
Total	3904.44	8760.01	0.00	0.00	0.00			E	
EDY adjustment 4.09					-898.79			T	
Grand Total					-898.79	2097.18		A	
								I	
								L	
								S	

Seniority
Jun-08	1000.00	
Sep-08	1100.00	
Dec-08	1200.00	
Mar-09	1300.00	
Total	4600.00	0.00

P60 and staff pay details for 12 mo to 31.3.09

	Pay	Tax	code
Jane			503L
Rachel	update		503L
	staff list		503L
	pay, tax		503L
	tax code		503L
	from P60		
			503L
			503L
			405L
			518L
			503L
			518L
Sandra			508L
Total	0.00	0.00	

Pensions Paid (not as separate cheques but in main payment to HMRC/IR)

Total 0.00

Unpresented cheques as of 31.3.09

1 petty cash	200.00	
4 staff locum	29.00	
6	48.00	
8 void	0.00	
11 JC	917.00	
16 SJ	7000.00	
Total	8194.00	

1402

18.1.5b Template Financial Summary

Category	Amount
Liquid Assets	
Personal Checking - BofA	8,000
Personal Savings - M&T	18,000
Persnal Emergency Fund	-
Business Checking - BofA	17,000
Liquid Asset Total	**43,000**
Investments	
Investment Account	-
Tax Bonds	34,000
Investment Total	**34,000**
Retirement	
Retirement Account	-
Retirement Total	**-**
Properties	
Condo	225,000
Rental Property	290,000
Property Total	**515,000**
Total Assets	**592,000**
Properties	
Student Loan	26,000
Condo Mortgage	200,000
Rental Property Mortgage	300,000
Total Liabilities	**526,000**
Net Worth	**66,000**

19. QOF

The Quality and Outcomes Framework (QOF)

QOF is the annual reward and incentive programme detailing GP practice achievement results.

QOF is a voluntary process for all surgeries in England and was introduced as part of the GP contract in 2004.

QOF awards surgeries achievement points for:

- Managing some of the most common chronic diseases, e.g. asthma, diabetes;
- Implementing preventative measures, e.g. regular blood pressure checks;
- The extra services offered such as child health care and maternity services;
- The quality and productivity of the service, including the avoidance of emergency admissions to hospital;
- Compliance with the minimum time a GP should spend with each patient at each appointment.

When QOF was first introduced as part of the GMS contract in 2004, the following principles were agreed on where QOF standards should apply:

- Responsibility for ongoing management of the patient rests primarily with the GP and the primary care team;
- There is evidence of health benefits resulting from improved primary care;
- The disease is a priority in a number of the four nations.

19.1 QOF Domains and Indicators

The QOF has a range of national quality standards, based on the best available research-based evidence covering four domains. Each domain has measures of achievement, known as indicators, against which practices score points according to their level of achievement. Practice payments are calculated on the points achieved and prevalence (see prevalence below).

The four domains are:

Clinical

The above domain has indicators across different clinical areas e.g. coronary heart disease, heart failure, and hypertension.

Organisational

The above has indicators across the five areas of records and information, information for patients, education and training, practice management, medicines' management and quality and productivity. It requires practices to hold policy information and have processes in place that actively demonstrate sound practice and understanding amongst their practice team.

Patient experience

The above has an indicator on the length of patient consultations.

Additional services

The above has indicators across the four service areas of cervical screening, child health surveillance, maternity services and contraceptive services.

However, the Ministers have tinkered with QOF domains, indicators and payments continually and they are a shadow of what they were originally.

As part of the 2014/15 GMS contract changes, NHS Employers and the General Practitioners Committee (GPC) of the BMA agreed a number of changes to QOF effective from 1 April 2014.

The key changes were:

- The retirement of 24 indicators from the clinical domain, releasing 185 points (three points released from retirement of LD002 will transfer to the learning disability enhanced service funding);

- The retirement of six indicators from the public health domain, releasing 33 points;

- The retirement of the patient experience indictor PE001, releasing 33 points;

- The retirement of nine indictors from the quality and productivity domain, releasing 100 points.

Of the above retirements, the resource from 238 points will be transferred in to global sum. This funding will not be subject to the six per cent out-of-hours deduction (if applicable).

The resources released from the remaining 103 points will see 100 points used to fund a new enhanced service aimed at avoiding unplanned admissions and delivering proactive case management for vulnerable peoples and 3 points transferred to the learning disabilities enhanced service.

http://bma.org.uk – tabulation of indicators with description and points are well elucidated on this website.

QOF for 2015-16 – changes proposed was being under negotiation (see NICE website).

Background:

For 2012/13, there was a maximum of 1,000 points available to practices across QOF, which in turn determines payments. The key payment dates for each year:

- By 31 March – practices are paid retrospectively for points achieved in the previous year. The pounds per point for 2012/13 for England – £133.76. The value of a QOF point differs across Wales, Scotland and Northern Ireland.

- By the end of June – payments should be completed, although they can be made earlier when they have been agreed by the practice and the primary care organisation.

Payments are subject to certain thresholds (targets) and take account of the national prevalence of diseases, by applying a standard calculation to all practices.

Prevalence

A practice's achievement payments are based on the number of patients on each disease register, known as 'recorded disease prevalence'. In certain cases, practices can exclude patients – known as 'exception reporting'. Strict criteria are used for this process and practices may be required to provide evidence of any patient that is 'exception reported'.

19.2 QOF Clinical Indicators 2012/13: Summary Lists

The quality and outcomes framework of the GMS contract 2012/13 came into effect on 1 April 2012. The details can be accessed via the websites of BMA, NHS, NICE, etc. The clinical domain covers the following areas:

- Asthma – 45 points
- Atrial fibrillation (AF) – 27
- Cancer – 11
- Cardiovascular Disease (primary prevention(PP)) – 11
- Coronary Heart Disease (secondary prevention) (CHD) – 69
- Chronic kidney Disease (CKD) – 36
- Chronic Obstructive Pulmonary Disease (COPD) – 30
- Contraception (SH) – 10
- Dementia (DEM) – 26
- Depression (DEP) – 31
- Diabetes Mellitus (DM) – 88
- Epilepsy – 14
- Heart Failure (HF) – 29
- Hypertension (BP) – 69
- Hypothyroidism (THYROID) – 7
- Learning Disabilities (LD) – 7
- Mental Health (MH) – 40

- Obesity (OB) – 8
- Osteoporosis (secondary prevention of fragility fractures) – (OST) – 9
- Palliative care (PC) – 6
- Peripheral arterial disease (PAD) – 9
- Smoking – 73
- Stroke and transient ischaemic attack (Stroke) – 22
- Medicines Management (Medicines) – 36
- Quality and Productivity (QP) – 5

Total Points

Each disease area has a series of evidence-based indicators.
Points are attached to each indicator and determine the sum paid to each practice.
The tables would indicate the following:

Amendments due to:

- Increased threshold
- Replacing previous indicator
- Reducing points
- New indicator

QOF has seen evidence based indicators achieved by almost every GP practice in the UK to a very high level. The QOF has delivered benefits to patients through the improved monitoring and treatment of acute and chronic health problems. The coordinated and comprehensive care patterns supported by the QOF have also helped to reduce inequalities across the UK.

Through the QOF, general practices are rewarded financially for aspects of the quality of care they provide. QMAS ensures consistency in the calculation of quality achievement and disease prevalence, and is linked to payment systems.

The payment rules underpin the new GMS contract are implemented consistently across all systems and all practices in England.

For 2009/10, practices were paid, on average, £126.77 for each point they achieved.

The value in pounds per point for 2012/13 for England is £133.76.

Current Indicators for 2014-15:

19.2a QOF Indicators for 2014-15

Each year indicators, points, and awarded achievement levels are changed and the above list has details for 2014-15.

The original table details have been edited to show just the point details only.

Changes are proposed for 2015-16 and discussions are proceeding.

The practices will have all the changes and guidance through CCGs, and publications like PULSE.

19.3 DES

Directed enhanced services

Directed enhanced services (DESs) are special services or activities provided by GP practices that have been negotiated nationally. Practices can choose whether or not to provide these services.

Directed enhanced services 2012/13

In 2012/13 the Extended Hours DES was extended by one year, in England, to 31 March 2013. The Patient Participation DES, which was introduced in April 2011 for two years and will continue in 2012/13.

The following existing DESs are to be re-commissioned by PCTs, in England, for the twelve-month period ending on 31 March 2013:

The alcohol reduction scheme, and the learning disabilities health check scheme.

The requirements for these clinical DESs remain the same and the payment scheme will mirror the payment scheme at the same rate that applied for the period 1 April 2011 to 31 March 2012.

19.4 2015-16 QOF Changes

How QOF works – QOF domains and indicators

The QOF has a range of national quality standards, based on the best available, research-based evidence covering four domains. Each domain has measures of achievement, known as indicators, against which practices score points according to their level of achievement. Practice payments are calculated on the points achieved and prevalence (see prevalence below).

The two domains are:

Clinical – this domain has indicators across different clinical areas, e.g. coronary heart disease, heart failure, and hypertension.

Public health (PH) – this domain has indicators across clinical and health improvement areas, e.g. smoking and obesity.

PH including additional services sub-domain – this sub-domain has indicators across the two service areas of cervical screening and contraceptive services.

QOF points

For 2014/15, there are a maximum of 559 points available to practices across QOF, which in turn determine payments. The key payment dates each year are:

By 31 March – practices are paid retrospectively for points achieved in the previous year. The pound per point for 2014/15 will be confirmed later in the year. The value of a QOF point differs across Wales, Scotland, and Northern Ireland.

By the end of June – payments should be completed, although they can be made earlier when the practice and commissioner have agreed them.

Payments are subject to certain thresholds (targets) and take account of the national prevalence of diseases, by applying a standard calculation to all practices.

Prevalence

A practice's achievement payments are based on the number of patients on each disease register, known as 'recorded disease prevalence'. In certain cases, practices can exclude patients, who are known as 'exception reporting' – more details are available in the Statement of Financial Entitlements. Strict criteria are used for this process and practices may be required to provide evidence of any patient that is 'exception reported'.

19.5 Sites to Check

www.nhsemployers.org

www.bma.org.uk for QOF guidance

From the above sites, changes and guidance for 2015-16 can be downloaded.

19.6 Target Indicators

For meeting targets

There are ample publications and details in websites about the indicators and meeting targets and the steps used in the past in the surgeries worked are mentioned for a few diseases.

19.6.1 Coronary Heart Disease (CHD)

Indicators, including those outside the QOF framework, which are continually reviewed for better patient management are listed below:

- Call and recall of patients.
- Yearly patient reviews.
- Past history of myocardial infarction and CHD.
- Angina is clinical diagnosis – should have 12 ECG performed.
- A normal ECG does not exclude coronary artery disease.
- Newly diagnosed angina patients to be referred to exercise tolerance testing (ETT) myocardial perfusion testing.
- Patients not to be referred to ETT if:

They are on maximal medical treatment and still have angina symptoms;

The diagnosis of CHD is unlikely (refer to cardiologist);
They are physically incapable of performing the test;

- They have clinical features suggestive of aortic stenosis or cardiomyopathy;
The results of stress testing would not affect management.

- Alternative to ETT – cardiologist, general physician or GP with special interest.

- BP to be measured annually; 150/90 or less is the guideline for control.

- Cholesterol annually 5.0 mmol/l or less; for over this value patients should be offered lipid lowering therapy.

- Aspirin 75-150 mg/day for CHD. Clopidogrel 75 mg/day for contraindications to aspirin or intolerant of aspirin. Avoid aspirin in patients who are anti-coagulated.

- Beta blockers (unless a contraindication or side effects are recorded) and ACE inhibitors or A2 antagonist (unless contraindicated) to be recorded.

19.6.2 Hypertension (BP)

Hypertension (BP) – 'MUST DO' CRITERIA These are the absolute minimum criteria that practices need to audit as they have an important impact on outcome and there is firm research evidence to justify their inclusion. Every practice must include these criteria in the audit.	
1	Patients who have been diagnosed as hypertensive have been recorded in a practice hypertension register.
2	The records show that in patients without target organ damage, the blood pressure has been measured at least twice on each of at least three separate occasions prior to commencement of drug therapy.
3	The records show that at diagnosis, the following symptoms and signs of target organ damage have been sought: retinopathy, left ventricular hypertrophy, angina, stroke, heart failure, peripheral vascular disease and renal disease.
4	The records show that an assessment has been made of the risk factors for cardiovascular and cerebrovascular disease and that if necessary, appropriate advice and treatment has been given: smoking habit, body mass index, diabetes mellitus, serum cholesterol (if additional risk factors present), excessive alcohol intake, physical inactivity and family history of premature coronary artery disease.
5	The records show that the mean pre-treatment blood pressure level was at least a diastolic of 95mmHg or greater and/or a systolic of 160mmHg or greater, or a diastolic of 90-95mmHg in the presence of other cardiovascular risk factors, and/or target organ damage.
6	The records show that the patient has been reviewed at regular intervals not

	exceeding 6 months.
7	The records show that the hypertension is well controlled, the average of the last three recorded diastolic blood pressure readings being 90mmHg (diastolic) or below, and 160mmHg (systolic) or below.
8	The records show that a patient with refractory hypertension and/or suspected secondary hypertension has been referred for specialist advice.
'SHOULD DO' CRITERIA – These are additional criteria for which there is some research evidence of their importance.	
9	The records show that at least annually there is an assessment of side effects caused by antihypertensive drugs that the patient is taking.
10	The records show that at least annually the patient has been given advice about dietary salt restriction.

The British Heart Foundation
Tel: 08450 708070
http://www.bhf.org.uk

19.6.3 Diabetes

Indicators, including those outside the QOF framework, which are continually reviewed for better patient management are listed below:

- Call and recall of patients.
- Yearly patient reviews.
- Avoid undiagnosed patients with diabetes.
- Diagnose diabetes as per WHO 1999 criteria:

Random glucose test – glucose >11.1 mmol/l – 2 occasions;
Fasting glucose test – >7.0 mmol/l; 12 hr. fasting; 2 occasions;
Glucose tolerance test – >11.1 mmol/l diabetes;
<7.8 mmol/l normal.

- Register to exclude:

Children age 16 and under with diabetes and under specialist care;
Patients with gestational diabetes.

- Because of vascular risks, regular reminders to patients about smoking.

- Smoking cessation services help diabetic smokers to quit; referral to clinics should be discussed with patients.

- Fructosamine instead of HbA1C – patients with haemoglobinopathies.

- HbA1C – stable patients test every 6 months, others more frequently.

- HbA1C target between 6.5% and 7.5% based on the risk of macrovascular and microvascular complications.

- Systematic annual screening of all people with diabetes.

- Annual review to highlight need for referral for vasculopathy and neuropathy to detect problems with feet.

- Record presence or absence of peripheral pulses annually.

- Foot sensation abnormal if monofilament and or vibration sensation impaired – record neuropathy test results.

- BP – aim for 140/80.

- Diabetic nephropathy greater than 300 mg/day; urine albumin concentration and serum creatinine to be measured at diagnosis and at regular intervals.

- Patients with microalbuminuria or proteinuria to be commenced on ACE inhibitor or considered for angiotensin II antagonist therapy.

- Cholesterol less than 5.0 mmol/l; for greater value start on statin therapy.

Diabetes – clinics' requirements for surgeries

1 Initially, the estimated time to see each diabetic patient is about 20 min. Consequently, a maximum of 6 patients need to be booked for the clinics. PCT Nurse to notify any increases in number to receptionists and practice nurse.

2 PCT Nurses – H Grade nurses are able to do the clinic with no involvement of the GPs except for any discussions pertaining to fine-tuning off medication, it is imperative that their time is utilised more effectively and the preparatory and finishing work is done in-house by the practice nurses and receptionists.

3 The protocols for the clinic have been provided by Torex and can be accessed by using Premier, then the patients record, then clicking icon 'ISIS' and selecting GMS Diabetes mellitus. The various screens will appear one after another once the details for each screen is input.

4 The PCT Nurse will see all diabetic patients in the clinics. The details of insulin dependent patients, who are seen by hospitals and under their monitoring, will be entered in the computer. GPs' roles are to utilise hospital services and follow hospital consultants' recommendations. (New contract stipulates what factors to be assessed and reported and does not expect GPs to do it.)

5 Blood test results needed prior to giving appointments to PCT Nurse:

The details required to be determined, and recorded are:

LFT
HbAIC
Fasting Lipid Profile
Urea
Creatinine

If the details are not available, then a blood test has to be done and results obtained prior to giving clinic appointment with PCT Nurse.

Patients are invited to come and pick up the blood test forms to be taken to the hospital. Practice nurse has to identify such patients and the receptionists have to telephone/contact them to come to surgery and pick up the blood test forms.

Once the results are obtained, then practice nurse has to put the data in the computer 'ASAP'.

1 Urine sample – all patients to give sample for urine test – to be done on the day (prior to clinic appointment) with a PCT Nurse.

2 Nurse's Folder for any referral as required:

The following need to be provided in a folder for the PCT Nurse:

- Referral form for Dietician
- Referral form for Chiropodist
- Referral form for Retinopathy evaluation
- Nearest Optician
- Diabetic Protocol – PCT Nurse will assist with proving such a protocol.

Essential equipment and test units:

- Micro-albumin Test strips – need to be available in the consulting room
- Tuning fork

- Electronic BP equipment

Inviting patients – steps to follow by practice nurse:

- Initially patients not seen for over 1 year
- Check whether the patient has had blood test results with all the relevant details listed in '5' above.

If yes – then make appointment for the PCT Nurse.

If no, then arrange for blood test as stated in '5' above.

- Make a list of patients with name, surname, DoB and telephone number and give to the senior receptionist to arrange for appointments with the PCT Nurse on the appropriate dates for the clinic.
- Initially max. 6 patients per clinic (see 1 above).
- Once patients not seen over 1 year have been called, then patients not seen over 6 months need to be called.
- Practice Nurse with GPs will have to assess the monthly performance for the diabetic clinic and make recommendations on improvements so as to meet the set targets and reach quality points predicted.

19.6.4 Mental Health Patient Policy

1 Register should be in the folder.

2 Patient should be called 3 times at least to attend clinic and this should be documented in the notes and on the computer.

3 Copy of calling/recalling letter should be filed in the note and documented on computer.

4 If they do not attend clinic/surgery appointment despite requesting to attend, they should be referred to the Psychiatric Service, informing them that we are concerned and need help – all should be documented in notes and on the computer.

The new GPs' contract includes mental health among ten clinical areas attracting payment for the achievement of clinical indicators. Studies have shown that one in six people of working age have a mental health problem and that most of these are managed in primary care, only about nine per cent are referred to specialist services for assessment and treatment.

Following this development is the disease registers. The Mental Illness Register is a vital resource for all GP practices. In addition to keeping records of patients identify as having mental health problems, care is better organised around three reviews: medication, physical checks and coordination with secondary care. These can be monitored and audited from computer systems to improve the management of depression, anxiety, schizophrenia, and postnatal depression in both primary and secondary care. In particular lithium toxicity often attributed to drug interactions can be greatly reduced through regular blood test and medication reviews.

In general the register is useful in mapping out care pathways, asking for more resources to manage patients better and to make sure they do not fall through the net.

The Primary Care Mental Health Worker will support the practice to achieve all the points allocated for the management of patients and all the work will be rewarded through the QOF and QMAS.

19.7 Support with Clinical Audit

The Medical Audits Advisory Group (MAAG) recorder is normally used to determine a sample size for clinical audits that represents the patient population and reflects the clinical activities that took place in the practice/surgery for which an audit is required, particularly audits under the prescribing incentive scheme for antidepressant/antipsychotic drugs, Z drugs etc. PCT will help the surgeries with what the prescribing advisor requires of the surgery and, if necessary, can redesign forms to serve other purposes as well.

19.8 Patient Information

GUIDANCE ON THE CALDICOTT REPORT FOR THE PROTECTION AND USE OF PATIENT INFORMATION – 2001

Recommendations and Principles:

Principle 1 –
Justify the purpose.

Principle 2 –
Don't use patient-identifiable information unless it is absolutely necessary.

Principle 3 –

Use the minimum necessary patient-identifiable information.

Principle 4 –

Access to patient-identifiable information should be on a strict need-to-know basis.

Principle 5 –

Everyone with access to patient-identifiable information should be aware of their responsibilities.

Principle 6 –

Understand and comply with the law. Every use of patient-identifiable information must be lawful.

19.9 Access

All practices should be aware that the specifications for LES 1, 2 and 3 required practices to be open at reception for both telephone and face to face access for 45 hours a week by the end of May 20.

20. New Set-Ups

The following were formed to change and improve quality of performance, monitoring of all services under the NHS, GP services forming part of the functions:

Clinical Commissioning Groups (CCGs) – Section 20.1

The Care Quality Commission (CQC) – Section 20.2

GPES (General Practice Extraction Service) and CQRS (Calculating Quality Reporting Service) – Section 20.3.

20.1 Clinical Commissioning Group (CCG)

CCGs are a core part of the government's reforms to the health and social care system. In April 2013, they replaced primary care trusts as the commissioners of most services funded by the NHS in England. They now control around two-thirds of the NHS budget and have a legal duty to support quality improvement in general practice.

CCGs are clinically led groups that include all of the GP groups in their geographical area. The aim of this is to give GPs and other clinicians the power to influence commissioning decisions for their patients.

Each CCG has a constitution and is run by its governing body.

Clinical commissioning groups work with patients and healthcare professionals and in partnership with local communities and local authorities. On their governing body, Groups will have, in addition to GPs, at least one registered nurse and a doctor who is a secondary care specialist. Each CCG has boundaries that are coterminous with those of local authorities, though one authority may have several CCGs. Clinical commissioning groups are responsible for arranging emergency and urgent care services within their boundaries, and for commissioning services for any unregistered patients who live in their area. All GP practices must belong to a clinical commissioning group.

The announcement that GPs will take over this commissioning role was made in the 2010 White Paper, 'Equity and Excellence: Liberating the NHS'. This is part of the Government's wider desire to create a clinically driven commissioning system that is more sensitive to the needs of patients. The 2010 White Paper became law under the Health and Social Care Act 2012 in March 2012.

In June 2014 there were 211 CCGs in NHS.

Commissioning involves planning and buying services by assessing the needs of the population; prioritising outcomes; purchasing medicines, equipment and services; managing service providers; measuring impacts and planning next steps.

Regardless of the organisational structures used to plan and purchase services, key priorities are similar. The focus is on offering high-quality healthcare to meet the needs of local people as effectively and efficiently as possible. There is a shift away from focusing on outputs towards delivering optimum health outcomes.

CCGs commission most of the hospital and community NHS services in the local areas for which they are responsible. Commissioning involves deciding what services are needed, and ensuring that they are provided. CCGs are overseen by NHS England, which retains responsibility for commissioning primary care services such as GP and dental services, as well as some specialised hospital services. All GP practices now belong to a CCG, but groups also include other health professionals, such as nurses.

Services CCGs commission include:

- Most planned hospital care
- Rehabilitative care
- Urgent and emergency care (including out-of-hours)
- Most community health services
- Mental health and learning disability services

A set of performance indicators:

These will help measure how well an individual CCG is tackling theses health issues:

- Preventing people from dying prematurely
- Enhancing the quality of life for people with long-term conditions
- Helping people to recover from episodes of ill health or following injury
- Ensuring that people have a positive experience of care

There are various publications on CCGs' roles, performance and ratings, and these can be seen via Google on sites like NHS UK, Kings Fund, and Wikipedia.

20.2 Care Quality Commission (CQC)

CQC is an executive non-departmental public body of the Department of Health. It was established in 2009 to regulate and inspect health and social care services in England.

It was formed from three predecessor organisations:

- The Healthcare Commission
- The Commission for Social Care Inspection (CSCI)
- The Mental Health Act Commission (MHAC)

The commission was established as a single, integrated regulator for England's health and adult social care services by the Health and Social Care Act 2008 to replace these three bodies. The Commission began operating on 1 April 2009.

In October 2014 the Government announced that the Commission was going to begin inspecting health systems across whole geographical areas from 2015, including social care and NHS.

GP Practices' Compliance

Running a primary care business is now more complex than it has ever been before. In the case of general practitioners this is in part due to the need to achieve CQC registration and meet ongoing compliance requirements.

The QCS (Quality Compliance System) is to manage the CQC for GP practices' compliance obligations of registration and inspection in simple and effective fashion.

Purpose

Health and social care services are provided to ensure people with safe, effective, compassionate, high-quality care and to improve continually.

Role and Inspections

To monitor, inspect and regulate services to make sure they meet fundamental standards of quality and safety, and publish findings, including performance ratings. Our job is to check whether hospitals, care homes, GPs, dentists and services are meeting national standards.

We currently inspect most hospitals, care homes and home care services at least once a year, and we inspect dental services at least once every two years.

Types of inspections

Scheduled:

These are unannounced inspections that focus on a minimum of five of the national standards, and they're also tailored to the type of care that is provided at the service.

Responsive:

These are unannounced inspections that are carried out where there are concerns about poor care.

Themed:

These inspections focus on specific standards of care or care services.

Home care inspections:

Inspect home care agencies differently from other types of services. Find out more about how they inspect home care agencies from the websites.

CQC work in partnership with organisations such as Monitor, Ofsted, and Health Watch England, NHS England and more.

GP services:

These services include your typical GP surgery but also a range of other services such as out-of-hours or mobile doctor services, walk-in centres, minor injury units, and urgent care centres

Doctors/GPs and Clinics:

Specialisms/services.
Diagnostic and screening procedures.

Family planning services.

Maternity and midwifery services.

Services for everyone.

Surgical procedures.

Treatment of disease, disorder or injury.

Part of the commission's remit is protecting the interests of people whose rights have been restricted under the Mental Health Act.

Rights under the Mental Health Act Categories:

Public, mental health community services, mental health hospital services.

Monitor the use of the Mental Health Act and protect the interests of people whose rights are restricted under that Act.

Most people receiving mental health care do not have their rights restricted. However, in some instances this happens to protect the person receiving treatment or others.

The CQC recently released guidance setting out how its new inspection and regulation regime will work in general practice. The new approach will see practices rated as either outstanding, good, requires improvement, or inadequate.

Medeconomics has distilled the guidance into a useful three-part series that looks at different aspects of the inspection process, with links to key sections of the guidance.

What will the CQC assess?

How will inspections work?

How will the CQC rate practices?

The CQC has said that all 8,000 English practices will be inspected using the new ratings system by April 2016.

20.3 GPES and CQRS

The General Practice Extraction Service (GPES) is a primary care data extraction service managed by the Health and Social Care Information Centre (HSCIC). GPES will extract information from general practice IT systems for a range of purposes.

From April 2013, GPES forms part of the new process to provide payments to GPs and clinical commissioning groups (CCGs). GPES will extract data from GP clinical systems and pass this to the Calculating Quality Reporting Service (CQRS). CQRS is the system responsible for making payments to contractors.

The first major deliverable for GPES will be the data for the Quality and Outcomes Framework (QOF). With QMAS being replaced by CQRS, GPES will in future become the primary means for extracting data to support the QOF. GPES will extract data, including year-end data, direct from general practice clinical systems and pass this to CQRS to calculate payments. Payments will continue to be made via the Exeter system.

Potential patient benefits include:

- Improving the screening of patients for serious conditions like cancer, so that treatment is given as quickly as possible.
- Improving the provision of health care for vulnerable and disadvantaged people.

Helping the NHS to understand major public health issues like flu epidemics so that services can be delivered to those who need them most.

21. Healthcare Professionals

Healthcare assistant

Healthcare assistants (HCAs) work in hospital or community settings, such as GP surgeries, under the guidance of a qualified healthcare professional. The role can be varied depending upon the healthcare setting.

Most commonly, HCAs work alongside nurses and are sometimes known as nursing auxiliaries or auxiliary nurses. HCAs also work alongside qualified midwives in maternity services.

The role of Healthcare Assistant and specialists have been dealt with in Sections

Their specialties and status in PCT and GP surgeries have also been briefly mentioned.

Healthcare specialists in GP surgeries may include:

- Healthcare assistant to do the health checking of patients and in some cases for registration purposes to approve the patients. They do continual monitoring of patients. They may be full-time or part-time employees of the practice.

- Midwives may be employed part-time to do antenatal and postnatal work with a GP proving the lead.

- PCTs may provide dieticians to visit GP surgeries to enable patients to be advised on their diets and health issues. Normally there is no charge for their visits to the surgeries.

- Surgeries may also arrange visits by Community and District Nurses as required and usually there is no charge for such visits.

- GPs will usually refer patients to consultants in the hospitals who may send the patients to healthcare specialists e.g. physiotherapists, audiology, mental health, foot care; and in special circumstances to practitioners of alternative medicines like ayurvedic, acupuncture, homeopathy etc.

District Nurses, Health Visitors, Midwives and Counsellors

The details of the District Nurses under the PCT should be displayed in notice board in the reception area or entrance hall.

If one of the doctors advises that a patient's problem could be helped by psychological therapy and, if the patient agrees, referral will be made to the specialist. The patient will be sent all information and an assessment form to complete. Until the patient returns the completed form, the patient will not be given an appointment. There are a number of treatment options, including CBT, group therapy, and individual counselling available for a GP to prescribe.

These members of staff may be attached to the surgery to care for our patients, but employed by other NHS agencies. Surgery staff work closely with these members and share patient information to provide good continuity of care.

District Nurse Team

The details of the District Nurse Team under the PCT should be displayed on a notice board in the reception area or entrance hall. The name of the Lead Sister and where they are based should be clearly indicated, with contact details. The team provides care in the home for those patients not able to attend surgery. Services include:

- Wound management and dressings
- Injections
- Blood tests
- Leg ulcer care
- Incontinence assessment
- Provision of appliances
- Post-operative care
- Catheter care
- Terminal care

They do not provide social care such as bathing and home care (see useful numbers page).

Their location in the same building means they liaise with our Practice Nurses and the GPs over patient care and have access to the computer system and staff to facilitate excellent communication.

The District Nurses are available seven days a week from 0830 to 1700hrs, including Bank Holidays. There is an evening District Nursing Service available from 1800 to 2230hrs.

Referrals to the District Nurse can be made directly by patients Monday-Friday and at weekends.

To contact the District Nurses outside normal hours i.e. evenings and Bank Holidays, a contact number should be provided.

Baby Clinics and Child Health Surveillance

1. Baby Clinics

The baby clinic dates and times should be clearly stated and unfortunately these may not be a walk-in service.

PCT Health staff – Health Visitor and Nursery Nurse may run these clinics. No doctor is usually present in the clinic. The surgery should indicate the telephone number to make appointments.

2. Child Health Surveillance

8-week baby checks and other child development assessments are performed. These clinics run on certain dates, morning or afternoons and are usually by appointment.

When a baby is registered with the practice, the parent is advised to book the 8-week check and immunisation appointments.

The surgery coordinates the development checks with the Health Visitors who record the weight and length of babies in the red book.

The surgery nurse normally does baby immunisations on given dates and times, indicating morning or afternoon. Refer to any schedule displayed.

The surgery finds this a convenient time as it coincides with the walk-in baby clinic run by the Health Visitors and developmental checks. A parent is free to book at other times for maximum flexibility but please inform the receptionist that the appointment is for baby immunisation. See Section 2.5 for details of immunisations needed.

GP involvement in the care of pregnant women has declined significantly over the past 30 years and midwives are now the main health care providers for 'low risk' pregnancies. The role of GPs in maternity care could disappear completely, unless valid future responsibilities can be defined and clarified.

Midwives care for and support pregnant women, their partners and babies, before, during, and after the birth. Some midwives give advice before a baby is conceived, but most will support the mother after pregnancy has been confirmed.

The work of a midwife includes:

- Monitoring the health of the mother and baby with physical examinations and ultrasound scans.
- Counselling the expectant mother on issues such as healthy eating, giving up smoking, giving up drinking, domestic abuse, exercise.
- Exploring the mother's options for the birth, for example natural childbirth, pain controlling drugs, hospital or home delivery.
- Looking after the mother and baby during labour and birth, and for up to a month after the birth.
- Advice on method of feeding baby, in particular encouraging and supporting women to choose breastfeeding. However, please support the mother if she chooses to bottle-feed her baby.
- Midwives run antenatal and parenting classes, which involves teaching.

In the current cost-conscious climate, the most effective solution would be for a pregnant woman to book in with a midwife, for the midwife to have her medical records on her first visit, and the midwife then informing the GP of the pregnancy of one of their patients. Where there are pre-existing medical problems, the woman should be referred by the midwife to the appropriate service, which may be the GP or may be other services.

Women in England currently have a choice to receive their care from their GP or a midwife. The midwife will explain this choice to them when they book their first GP involvement in the care of pregnant women has declined significantly over the past 30 years and midwives are now the main health care providers for 'low risk' pregnancies.

The role of GPs in maternity care could disappear completely, unless valid future responsibilities can be defined and clarified.

GP knowledge on maternity issues has fallen behind current evidence and a considerable amount of retraining will be required to enable them to fulfil their role in pregnancy in relation to the health of the woman and the baby who have medical needs. Even more training would be required if GPs are expected to deal with the pregnancy and birth and the post-partum period, as a midwife would.

GP

GP involvement in the care of pregnant women has declined significantly over the past 30 years and midwives are now the main health care providers for 'low risk' pregnancies.

As soon as the patient finds out that she is pregnant she should make an appointment with a doctor. At this initial appointment patient will be expected to provide the date of her last menstrual period. The doctor will take a history and examine the patient including her blood pressure (no internal examination is required) then help her choose where she would like to have her baby. She could calculate her due date and gestation using the pregnancy dates calculator available with the GP in the surgery. It is possible these days using Choose and BOOK system to book directly with the hospital using their on-line booking.

The patient will be informed about booking appointments and ultrasound scans.

A midwife from the hospital (http://www.kingstonmaternity.org.uk/), runs antenatal clinics every week at set times and dates. Antenatal care is shared between the doctors and the midwife. Surgery GPs do not perform home deliveries. The midwife would be happy to discuss home delivery and other preferences.

Postnatal checks

Postnatal – Following the birth of your baby, all mothers should have a check-up at 6 weeks. All of GPs can undertake postnatal checks. This is a good opportunity to ask the doctor any questions the patient may have about her progress. The GP will discuss many aspects about the postnatal period, take blood pressure, perform any necessary examinations and discuss contraception.

GPs like to allow more time (20 minutes) for these appointments. Please ensure that receptionists are advised about the nature of appointment when booking.

The baby development checks are not part of the postnatal check. These are performed at the developmental clinic by appointment.

Dietician

Allied Health Professions

A number of the professionals included below would be working more in hospitals but some specialists do come to visit the surgeries by prior arrangement.

The Allied Health Professions cover a variety of roles; these are the six roles in most demand:

Occupational Health Therapists,
Operating Department Practitioners,
Physiotherapists,

Podiatrists,

Radiographers,

Speech and Language Therapists.

The allied health professions (AHPs) offer a wide range of opportunities. As key members of today's healthcare team, AHPs provide treatment that helps transform people's lives. There are many roles within the allied health professions.

These range from treating a broken toe to assessing someone's diet. Whether one is interested in science, the arts, or physical movement, one will always find something suitable.

Health and social care today is about teamwork, so AHPs will also be part of a team and may even lead one. This might mean working with other AHPs or other professionals such GPs, hospital doctors, teachers, or social workers for example.

AHPs often see patients and clients in different surroundings. You will find AHPs working in hospitals, clinics, housing services, people's homes, schools and colleges to name but few. Not surprisingly, the academic requirements and training demands are high, but then so are the rewards, both in terms of job satisfaction and career prospects.

Professions regulated by the Health and Care Professions Council:

Arts therapists

Biomedical scientists

Chiropodists/Podiatrists

Clinical scientists

Dieticians

Hearing aid dispensers

Occupational therapists

Operating department practitioners

Orthoptists

Paramedics

Physiotherapists

Practitioner psychologists

Prosthetists/Orthotists

Radiographers

Social workers

Speech and language therapists

Health professionals in the UK are expected to be '**Fit to Practice**'. They are expected to meet certain requirements, but also to know their own limitations.

22. Health & Safety

Health & Safety at Work, etc.

The 1974 Act requires employers to provide whatever information, instruction, training and supervision as is necessary to ensure, so far as reasonably practicable, the health & safety of their employees. This is further expanded by the Management of Health & Safety at Work Regulation 1999, which identifies situations where health & safety training is particularly important, e.g., when people start work or are exposed to new or increased risks.

The lack of a systematic health & safety induction may result in the following difficulties:

- Rise in accidents and occupational health issues, due to poor or limited communication of hazards and risks contained within their workplace.

- Building evacuations will take longer with the potential for people to get trapped during a fire due to no information given about escape routes/emergency exits and assembly points.

- Decline in accident/incident reporting due to people not knowing or understanding the need for reporting.

- Delay in first aid attention with the possibility of accident conditions worsening.

- Prosecution by the HSE for breach of duties contained within the Health & Safety at Work Act and the Management of Health & Safety at Work Regulations.

This policy applies to those members of staff that are directly employed by the NHS Commissioning Board (NHS CB) and for whom the NHS CB has legal responsibility. For those staff covered by a letter of authority/honorary contract or work experience, the organisation's policies are also applicable whilst undertaking duties for or on behalf of the NHS CB. Furthermore, this policy applies to all third parties and others authorised to undertake work on behalf of the NHS CB.

Purpose:

- Ensure, as far as is reasonably practicable, the health, safety, and welfare of NHS CB staff;
- Ensure, as far as is reasonably practicable, the health, safety and welfare of other people, for example contractors, visitors, general public who may be affected by NHS CB's activities;
- Satisfy the requirements of the relevant regulations.

Specific responsibilities of staff are:

- To comply with local fire procedures;
- To comply with local first aid procedures;
- Not to attempt to repair any item of electrical equipment (unless properly authorised to do so) but to report it to their PMgr;
- Not to bring personal mains electrical equipment into work;
- To report to the PMgr any obstructions to any walkways, entrances and exit areas and avoid creating such obstacles;
- Not to move any equipment without relevant training;
- To report any building and/or equipment defects and/or shortfalls in cleanliness to the PMgr;
- To set a good personal example with respect to health and safety.

The act also covers areas of:

- Violence/bullying and harassment;
- Third party contractors – people undertaking work, for example, building maintenance;
- Control of substances hazardous to health (COSHH);
- Work-station assessment;
- Disabled persons;
- Information & training;
- Record keeping;

- Incident reporting.

22.1 Legal Issues

All practices must follow the legal requirements of:

- Practice Safety Policy.
- If you have five or more employees, you must have a written policy.
- Health and Safety Poster or leaflets available in the reception area.
- Employers' liability Insurance certificate displayed.
- Recording and notifying accidents.
- First aid arrangements and instructions listed and displayed.
- Consultation with employees frequently with the aim of redesigning or improving their workplace.
- Identifying the persons responsible for the procedures.
- Holding regular fire drills.
- Safeguarding the personal safety of the staff e.g. issuing emergency or personal alarms etc.

There are a number of additions to H&S Acts and these have to be checked continually at the website to be updated.

23. Remedial Issues

23.1 Causes

These arise mostly due to PCTs not being satisfied with a GP practice, and finally it resorts to taking remedial actions. The life of the practice GPs and staff would be 'hell' from the beginning to the end of resolution of the issues.

The causes for all these actions may be due to 'actual incidences', major complaints of a very serious nature, fraud, or similar issues of inaction by the GPs of the practice.

However, in most cases, it may be due to issues based on perceptions only and once PCT takes a stand then it is like an uncontrollable 'juggernaut' rolling down the practice way.

PCT has well qualified admin staff and in some cases create a 'storm over a tea cup', churning out by writing phenomenally worded documents of 200-300 pages, explaining the same issues from several different angles and a legal follow-up costing both the PCT and the practice a lot of money, time, and wasted efforts.

23.2 NCAS Role

The practitioners are aware of the role of NCAS (National Clinical Assessment Service) – in general terms, covering local procedures for an investigation into a practitioner's performance. The practices are usually referred to NCAS for a formal assessment in two main cases:

- When the practice has an incidence(s) of malpractice and serious untoward incidents.

- When the practice has not had any procedures or protocols and record keeping, despite no malpractice being found.

The manager should have the general conception that anything relating to records,

CDM procedures, protocols, recruitment, health and safety, etc. are issues which could be dealt with internally without NCAS involvement. These could be resolved, some informally and some formally with the PCT.

The manager should also be aware that in cases of malpractice, referral to NCAS might be made by the PCT and in extreme cases of malpractice, where a patient has come to serious harm or death or in cases of fraud the referral to GMC may take place. Police may be called in by the PCT or GMC as they deem fit.

23.3 Investigations

The list below gives just an outline of what would be investigated for remedial issues.

The Practice Manager should have in the practice files the following:

- Key elements of the investigation process with probable queries arising from such an investigation. The written notes are to be handed to all practitioners involved in the inquiry.

- The key statements on professional standards made by the GMC; Good Medical practice for GPs as per RCGP procedures.

- Alcohol and drugs/substance misuse and when the management should act in the best interests of the individual family and the practice.

- Disciplinary procedures pertaining to work/suspension and all actions that need to be taken prior to enforcing suspension.

- Harassment, bullying and victimisation policy and procedures.

- General terms about local procedures for an investigation into a practitioner's performance and the role of NCAS.

- Mental Health policy and the facilities available.

- Root cause analysis policy. Application of this policy will be in cases of serious untoward incidents, mental health issues, etc.

23.4 PAG (Performance Assessment Group) Assessment

The Clinical Advisor is responsible for overseeing practice assessments.

A practice assessment can take place on any practitioner if the PCT believes that the practitioner is underperforming to such an extent that a formal assessment is necessary.

Having discussed the matter first with the PCT, and received the formal assessment request form, the Clinical Advisor will instruct the PAG Manager to commission two assessors from the PAG's panel of trained assessors.

The terms of reference will be agreed with the PCT and given to the assessors. The assessors will then carry out the assessment and prepare a report to go to the PCT.

A variety of assessment tools are used to assess the practitioner. These tools are set out in the respective PAG Assessment Toolkits, of which there is currently one for GPs and one for Dentists. The PAG may have developed a pharmaceutical toolkit.

The various elements of the toolkit include an appraisal questionnaire for staff, a patient questionnaire, a clinical notes review and a number of case based assessments.

The assessors are experienced senior practitioners and are appointed from outside the locality of the practitioner who is being assessed. They would have attended PAG training courses.

The recommendations of the assessors and any further recommendations made by the PAG, if appropriate, will be passed to the PCT for consideration and transmitted onward to the practitioner, who will be asked to implement the recommendations agreed to by the PCT.

It is generally good practice for there to be feedback about the implementation of the recommendations, to the PAG.

The practitioner being assessed is informed when the assessors have been commissioned that there is to be an assessment of his practice; he is advised to contact his Defence Organisation and they are invited to co-operate with the process.

The broad objective of the assessment procedure is to establish what deficiencies exist in a practice and to remedy those deficiencies in the interests of all concerned, being the patients, the practitioner, the PCT and the service generally.

23.5 Complaints Procedures

NHS staff aim to give the best possible care to patients, but sometimes things do go wrong and the NHS Complaints Procedure was set up to use if one wants to complain about the services or treatment one gets from the NHS.

It is crucial to want to feedback positive comments on the care and services the surgery has received. These comments are just as important as they tell the NHS organisation what factors are contributing to a good experience for patients.

If patients are unhappy with the treatment or service they have received from the NHS surgery they are entitled to make a complaint, have it considered, and receive a response from the NHS organisation or primary care practitioner concerned.

The NHS complaints procedure described below covers complaints made by a person about any matter connected with the provision of NHS services by NHS organisations or primary care practitioners in England (for instance doctors, dentists, opticians, and pharmacists). The procedure also covers services provided overseas or by the independent sector where the NHS has paid for them. There may be different arrangements in place for the internal handling of complaints in Foundation Trusts.

Who can complain?

http://www.nhs.uk/england/aboutTheNHS/complainCompliment.cmsx#whocancomplain%23whocancomplain

What is the time limit for making a complaint?

http://www.nhs.uk/england/aboutTheNHS/complainCompliment.cmsx#timelimit%23timelimit

To whom should I complain initially?

http://www.nhs.uk/england/aboutTheNHS/complainCompliment.cmsx#initialcomplaint%23initialcomplaint

What if I'm still unhappy after local resolution?

http://www.nhs.uk/england/aboutTheNHS/complainCompliment.cmsx#stillunhappy%23stillunhappy

NHS Foundation Trusts

http://www.nhs.uk/england/aboutTheNHS/complainCompliment.cmsx#foundationtrusts%23foundationtrusts

Independent Review

http://www.nhs.uk/england/aboutTheNHS/complainCompliment.cmsx#IndependentReview%23IndependentReview

The Health Service Ombudsman

http://www.nhs.uk/england/aboutTheNHS/complainCompliment.cmsx#HealthServiceOmbudsman%23HealthServiceOmbudsman

Where can I get further advice and help?

http://www.nhs.uk/england/aboutTheNHS/complainCompliment.cmsx#furtherhelp%23furtherhelp

23.6 Disciplinary Procedures

General Principles

Employers use disciplinary procedures to tell employees that their performance or conduct isn't up to the expected standard and to encourage improvement. Please see Section 9.7.

The Practice Manager (PMgr) should have the following checklists on file and staff should be shown the details and where files are located for reference.

23.6.1 Investigating Checklist

- The details of the key elements of the investigation process have been listed with probable queries arising from such investigation. The written notes have been handed to the practitioners.

- Familiar with key statements on professional standards made by the GMC. They are also familiar with Good Medical Practice for GPs. Both publications are on file.

- There are policies in file for alcohol and drugs/substance misuse and when the management should act in the best interests of the individual family and the practice.

- The practice has a policy in file on disciplinary procedures pertaining to work/suspension and all actions that needs to be taken prior to enforcing suspension.

- The practice has in files harassment, bullying and victimisation policy and procedures. Practitioners are aware of the procedures.

- The practitioners are aware in general terms about local procedures for an investigation into a practitioner's performance and the role of NCAS. The case are usually referred to NCAS for a formal assessment in two main cases:

- When the practice has an incidence(s) of malpractice and serious untoward incident(s);

- When the practice has not had any procedures or protocols and record keeping, even though no malpractice has been found.

- Manager has the general conception that anything relating to records, CDM procedures, protocols, recruitment, health and safety, etc. are issues which can be dealt with internally without NCAS involvement. These could be resolved, some informally and some formally.

The PMgr should be aware that in cases of malpractice, referral to NCAS might be made by PCT and in extreme cases, where a patient has come to serious harm or death or in cases of fraud, referral to GMC may take place. Police may be called in by PCT or GMC as they deem fit.

- There is a policy in file. The facility is available.

- Root cause analysis policy is in file and everyone is aware. Application of this policy will be applied in cases of serious untoward incidents, mental health issues, etc.

23.6.2 Managing Checklist

a. The Partners, in particular the Clinical Lead, should be quite confident in his/her ability to manage the doctors in the following areas:

- Clinical skills
- Clinical Governance
- GPs and nurses
- Issues
- Financial management
- QOF and CDM management

b. The PMgr should be able to manage the:

- Reception staff
- Medical secretary

- IT manager
- GPs and nurses in so far as admin issues are concerned

Disciplining Checklist

1. Disciplinary procedures and protocols should be in place and kept in the Practice Manager's office for reference. There is a 6 monthly review of the procedures with a view to tightening them or upgrading them.

2. The Practice Manager and Clinical Lead have appropriate work experience and the Practice Manager usually attends HTPCT courses when they are being conducted.

3. List of training courses available externally are in hand and will be utilised as the need arises.

4. Lawyers will provide supporting or managing role as need arises.

5. Clinical Lead and Practice Manager work in tandem, aiming for the same goal of doing things right for the good of the practice.

6. Templates for conduct, capability and probationary issues are available with various letters to use at various stages.

7. Managers are aware of the distinction between investigative interviews wherein the cause of the issues are discussed, and disciplinary interviews wherein the issue of disciplinary actions are discussed and decided.

8. Occupational health service protocols are in place and would be issued when a situation arises

Documenting Checklist

1. The practice is very transparent about its policies, procedures and finance.

2. All appraisal reports are kept. Performance related issues when discussed are kept in their personal files.

3. Data protection Act plays a crucial role in terms of confidentiality and the manager is not only aware but takes care to implement it. The confidentiality of each staff member's details is of paramount importance.

4. At monthly meetings, the complaints received for each practitioner and for the practice are discussed and recorded. Also, when complaints are received on the same day it is discussed with the practitioner and the Clinical Lead and they are kept abreast of actions taken.

5. Both Clinical Lead and the manager are aware of the procedures, which are in files, to follow should an investigation were to be conducted. Regularly consulted

ACAS and BMA for advice on such occasions to ensure that the current practices are followed.

6. Locum files have similar information.

7. Separation of information as ethnicity and other details are well known to all members of staff.

8. If the complaint is about the practitioner, then a record is kept in the practitioner's file in addition to complaints file for the year.

Untoward incidents, if it pertains to the practitioner, are also copied in the practitioner's file (summary only), in addition to the practice file.

All records pertaining to the practitioner and correspondence with him are kept in his file. Suitable references would be kept in the practitioner's, if the main information is bulky and in practice files.

Alerting Checklists

1. There is a policy to let the manager know of any area of concern – not so much as 'whistle-blowing' policy but as constructive comments for the improvement of the practice and individuals. The guidance for Public Concern at Work and two other documents on Do's and Don'ts are in practice files for reference.

2. All members of staff have been told and shown about the whistle-blowing policy and shown where it's kept for reference. It is part of continual training programme and discussed in monthly meetings as issues arise.

3. Posters are not displayed but procedures are available for reference in the office.

4. GPs express any shortage of skills directly to the Clinical Lead, who then informs practice manager. Nurses and admin staff inform PMgr first, who then informs the Clinical Lead.

5. Team working is crucial part of the training and practice development programme for all staff. Staff are encouraged to see it this way only.

6. Without team work the practice cannot function effectively. Emphasis is laid on meetings where all staff are present and issues aired for general discussions and suggestions.

7. As far as GPs are concerned the performance problems are highlighted when the Clinical Lead does an appraisal, clinical supervision and both informal and formal meetings with the GP. Should the GP raise issues about trust in the process the issue is discussed and in relevant cases it is modified. The aim is to have a working policy won, in which GPs have total trust.

8. No special benchmark is used other than informal discussions with the neighbouring practices; comparing their policies with ours; suggestions raised in their practices would be incorporated if considered relevant.

9. All discussions with GPs are shared with them informally, formally when they meet and also in monthly meetings as the main focus are to improve practice performance.

10. The practice manager does exit interviews in case of GPs in general. However, in some cases the Clinical Lead does the interview in presence of other partners. Lessons learnt documented for future.

Developing Checklist

1. Clinical Lead is primarily responsible for the development of the practitioners. He is also responsible for their continual clinical supervision and appraisals.

2. The admin. The Practice Manager deals with systems associated with the above development.

3. The practitioners also attend courses in HTPCT on every Tuesdays. Courses are also offered for their study leave period to upgrade their skills. Any additional courses, relevant to the practice and to their skill levels, are also attended.

4. The induction processes for the new GPs involve other existing GPs in so far as clinical issues are concerned. The practice manager deals with the admin issues.

Similar procedures apply for the nurses.

For all admin staff there is an induction programme, which is rigidly followed and the Practice Manager takes the lead role in their continued development.

The following issues are dealt with: **(Mandatory for all staff.)**

Health and Safety policies; fire safety; housekeeping; accidents and abnormal occurrences; smoking; personal hygiene; risk assessments; safety advisers and committee; occupational health; Health and Safety training requirements; clothing; use of computers; electrical equipment; chemical hazards; spillages; disposal; consulting rooms/kitchens; use of other equipment; any other hazards; patients and supplier visits; basic communications; absenteeism and lateness; other locations; grievance procedures; discipline procedures; security, etc.

5. Development delivery is reviewed for clinical effectiveness e.g. from informal discussions and formal discussions on specific case studies and how best to handle it in the future. Lessons learnt are recorded in the GPs file for review during the annual appraisal.

Development delivery is reviewed for admin. Issues as below:

Exit interviews (when a candidate leaves); feedback from staff; suggestions; pre-course briefing; interim validation as programme proceeds; end of programme assessment; short test/questionnaire for admin. Staff on reception duties; review meeting to discuss further action plans; final implementation of review meeting; and modifications to training programme from lessons learnt from staff/GP/manager.

6. Staff selection process involves a close match to practice requirement – costs and objectives.

7. The training costs do not have a pre-set amount. No restraint is placed on training because of the costs. The underlying principle being – training saves money in the long run and time in terms of avoiding new recruitment due to staff leaving.

8. The partners have a system by which each one covers when the other is absent or on holidays. The Practice Manager trains one member of staff as replacement Practice Manager during any absence.

9. Courses arranged by HTPCT or neighbouring colleges are used to develop communication skills for the nurses and practice manager. Admin staff skill improvement is through HTPCT courses.

10. The Practice Manager is skilful in dealing with irate patients, conflict situations.

11. The PMgr does not lose his/her cool and focus is on the interests of the practice bearing in mind the staff development plans.

12. The practice stands primarily for patient care and it is always kept in focus. No compromise to that mission objective will be made. Decision-making and conflict resolution always tends to reflect that. However, no compromise should be made, by sacrificing guidelines or legal procedures.

It is better that Partners, GPs and PMgr are aware of these procedures and checklists (Check via Google for updates).

1. The Clinical Lead does have overall responsibility for all GPs, nurses and practice staff and all aspects of management.

2. All concerns are raised with the PMgr in the initial instance and for clinical issues depending on seriousness with the Clinical Lead.

3. The PMgr should inform the Clinical Lead when the surgery is over and the Clinical Lead decides on actions to be taken. This procedure has been followed and found to be a robust system.

4. The action points are relayed to all staff, including the one who raised the issue; lessons learnt are minuted and avoidance in the future is clearly stated.

5. The GPs, nurses and admin staff were given job descriptions and Contracts of Employment with standard terms as per guidelines.

6. The responsibilities, clinical skills and clinical governance issues are stated clearly at the outset. All supportive documents are held in the main office for the staff/nurses/GPs to refer to from time to time. GPs, nurses and all admin staff should go through a yearly appraisal and personal development plans reviewed. Any issues raised by the staff are discussed in full to their satisfaction and record of interview and appraisal kept in their files.

7. All the GPs in the surgery should have been involved in the past with interviewing. However, prior to interview details are discussed in detail about the candidate after giving them the CV and details of the candidate. Equal Opportunities procedures are stressed and are sensitive to all cultural issues at the time of interview.

8. All GPs are selected by interview only.

9. The emphasis, when a new GP joins or for an existing GP, is placed on the assessment process – Clinical aspects and Clinical Governance.

10. All GPs who join will have an induction programme and appraisal in 3 months' time followed by annual review after that. Also, the Clinical Lead does Clinical supervision in formal way once in 3 months and informal way, almost every other day, when cases are discussed after the morning surgery and after clinics in the afternoons.

11. Procedures and protocols are in place for local policies e.g. child protection, mental health etc. Continual discussions on these issues take place in monthly meetings.

12. Quick reference guides for local policies and procedures are also in place.

13. List of all staff, including those who work part-time:

14. All GPs, nurses and admin staff have annual appraisals. No one is excluded.

15. Health Visitors, CPN, Link worker, District Nurses, Counsellors, Secondary Care Team etc.

16. PCT personnel e.g. Prescription Advisor, Complaints Manager, Clinical Governance Lead etc. also advice on our performance and management on various issues. Their details to be kept on file.

17. Local information: List of all doctors, dentists, pharmacists, opticians, hospitals and their departments with consultants' names, Social Services, authorities and trusts etc. is given at the time of joining the practice.

List of Policy and Guidance A-Z:

Child protection;

Confidentiality etc.;

Emergency planning;

Equality and human rights;

Freedom of information;

Health advice for travellers;

Health and social care topics;

Human resources and training;

Information policy;

International;

Medicines, pharmacy and industry;

Organisation policy;

Patient choice;

Performance;

Research and development;

Social services inspectorate;

Social services performance assessment;

Please see the websites for further studies in addition to the policies, which should be kept in the Practice Manager's office for reference.

23.7 Gender Issues

STANDARDS of CARE GUIDELINES for GPs on the TREATMENT OF CHILDREN & YOUNG PEOPLE with GENDER DEVELOPMENT ISSUES.

A child or young person who is experiencing unusual gender development may or may not continue to experience the condition of gender dysphoria in adulthood. However, it is vital that the individual concerned is shown understanding and respect for his or her current gender experience.

Treatment should be flexible and meet the needs of the individual as far as are consistent with clinically safe practice. Decisions about the nature and the extent of treatment may be taken by a young person if deemed to be Gillick competent by the practitioner. From 16 onwards the young person is automatically deemed Gillick competent (see below) Any young person deemed Gillick competent may, effectively, exclude a relevant adult (one with Parental Responsibility – see below) from the decision making process, but this would be *extremely* unusual and, in most cases, undesirable.

The General Practitioner may have to be aware of:

- Gender development disorders are rare in children and adolescents. They are sometimes associated with emotional and behavioural difficulties.

- Gender disorders in young people can be manifested in different ways: cross-gender play and interests, sometimes accompanied by an expressly stated wish to belong to the opposite gender to that assigned, or even a claim to actually be a member of the opposite gender.

- Associated with these symptoms may be a dislike of the sexual appearance of the body. This may be more marked if pubertal changes have started.

- Children and adolescents should be referred to a specialist team, where there is expertise in caring for younger individuals who are experiencing gender development issues.

- Initially, it is likely to fall to the GP to ensure that the young person and (bearing in mind the constraints of confidentiality) the young person's family are fully informed of all the possible treatments and their outcomes, positive and negative. A young person who is deemed Gillick competent may refuse family involvement. Any information given to a child must be age appropriate. Educational literature and ongoing support of the family should be provided. If, whilst under the care of a specialist clinic, an adolescent is prescribed hormone-blocking therapy at any time during puberty, the GP may be involved in ongoing treatment.

The GP should continue to liaise with the Endocrinologist at the clinic, to ensure that the necessary preliminary health checks are achieved and that responsibility for continuing monitoring is agreed.

It is an essential requirement, prior to embarking on any reversible or partially reversible treatments, that a young person be Gillick competent. An INFORMED CONSENT form (Annex B[4][5]) must be provided to the individual and (for those under sixteen) the person with Parental Responsibility, at least six weeks in advance of the treatment starting. The clinic will usually be responsible for providing the form and will have had the necessary discussions with the individual and relevant adult. The GP should also check that this protocol has been covered and should provide a further opportunity for discussion with the patient and his/her family.

- It is important to make the young person feel that help and support is available and that, under certain circumstances, the effects of puberty can be delayed by medication.

- A young person who is faced with the prospect of pubertal changes, or who is already experiencing them, could experience depression and even suicidal feelings. Much reassurance will be needed to make individuals feel that their condition is experienced by others, that although rare, it is not unique and can be treated.

- It is particularly important that where possible and appropriate, when a young person of male phenotype identifies as female, that beard growth is blocked, and that where a young person of female phenotype identifies as male, breast growth is blocked.

- If the GP is to provide ongoing prescriptions for any hormone blocking treatment, then liaison with the relevant Endocrinologist is important. Referral to, and liaison with, local psychological support systems should continue for the child/adolescent concerned and his/her family. Liaison with a school or college may be required, with the consent of the young person, and relevant literature provided.

- Sometimes these manifestations gradually disappear altogether, especially if the child presents before puberty, sometimes they resolve into a gay or lesbian sexual preference, sometimes the cross gender symptoms will persist into adulthood and the individual may then seek further treatment.

- At this stage, referral to adult services will be necessary. (See below) It is vital that there is good communication between those who have been caring for the young person up to that date, and those who will be taking over the future care. The GP has a vital role in liaising with these other agencies and ensuring that they liaise adequately with each other.

- It is especially important with young people, to encourage them to consider whether they may wish, in the future, to have a family. Specific information should be provided about local, private or NHS facilities suitable for storage of gametes.

- N.B. It is inappropriate and may be considered misconduct for any medical specialist to assume that a patient, who opts for gamete storage, or has already done so, is in any way equivocal about, or not committed to, the transition process.

23.8 Tidy-up Tasks

GP Partners should be ever alert once the Remedial procedures start. Much as it may cause a great deal of aggrievement and loss of focus on day-to-day issues of patient welfare, it is imperative the Partners 'wake up' and tighten the procedures in the practice with no room for slip-up from then on.

They should:

- Look at the issues, which prompted such strong actions by the PCT,
- Analyse with the colleagues as to where it could have gone wrong,
- How they could have played the part differently,
- The discussions should be recorded and copied to everyone to deliberate,
- Report back on any additions or corrections and,

- Record those as well.

GP Partners should review the procedures of dealing with the patients – verbal, non-verbal communications, prescriptions, registrations, home visits, emergency appointments, medications, relationship with the pharmacists, PCT, Healthcare Professionals, Community Nurses etc. and make a sweeping 'root and branch' improvement.

Computer inputs, recording of data and results etc., are to be frequently checked for correctness and accuracy.

Employment procedures, document lists the surgery should have for reference etc. should be tightened.

PCT should not be perceived as the aggressor and the Partners should aim to calm the situation and see how relationship could be restored to normality.

Respond to all memos from PCT and other parties to the Remedial procedures with:

- Simple answers without innuendos etc.
- Be to the point and succinct.
- Never resort to lengthy answers, which may result in misrepresentation.
- Follow the 'KISS' principle (keep it simple stupid) when it comes to dealing with PCT.
- Improve medicine management, infection control and health & safety issues.

23.9 Look Back Exercises

'**Look back**' exercises on patients seen by the GP(s) during a certain period may be requested.

A '**look-back exercise**' is "a retrospective review of the care provided to patients to determine if advice or treatment given was correct and safe, and whether further advice, investigation or treatment is required in response to any shortcomings identified during an investigation."

The PCT advisor may suggest ways of how to review patients seen by the GP(s). He may devise a form and suggest the surgery to invite all patients and do a review on each of them and record on the form. If any patient has moved to another practice, then the surgery must notify both the patient and new GP so that they can look into the note and see the patient and take appropriate action.

23.10 Practice Manager Role

The Practice Manager should deal with the remedial issues cleverly by not playing a leading role for the GPs – it is the GP's call to deliberate and answer.

He should try to mediate by seeking non-legal and less formal approaches to avoid legal actions.

MDS or MPS would be involved resulting in yet lengthy and worded correspondences, preventing focused care to the patients by the GPs.

'Do not bite the hand that feeds' is a good motto to follow. Make peace with the PCT ASAP.

The Practice Manager should also be aware that unless in cases of fraud, the GP's income would not be in any way curtailed or diverted; even if the GP or Partners are suspended, the income has to flow through the practice account with Partners' full responsibility and apart from mental anguish and loss of public credibility, during the period of investigation, their financial status would not be affected in any way.

In some cases the Partners may end up earning more! This will usually happen, if older GPs are made to retire early, thereby, there are fewer Partners to share the profit.

23.11 General Outcome

There are several outcomes depending on the severity of malpractice.

- Fraud – GP or GP Partners may be struck off practice via GMC's 'Fitness to Practice' procedures.

- Death – it would be difficult to prove unless the GP had prescribed a very high dosage of medication or failed to check an error by a receptionist who usually prepares repeat prescriptions. The other parties involved may be the pharmacist, who had supplied the medicine; and these days they want to play a bigger role in prescribing, and along with that results culpability for not checking before handing the medicine to the patient. They should have alerted the practice on such 'blunders'. Still, the GP is the easiest target for the PCT to deal with. Rarely a GP may be removed from practice. If the error is a rare one for that GP, he may be referred to the Deanery for a period of retraining and some supervision.

- For others, the PCT may decide to ask the Partner or GP to retire gracefully or face legal procedures and, if they are of over retirement age and still practicing, they may leave the practice without any referral to the issues in their career. For younger GPs, below the retirement age, the PCT may refer them to the Deanery for a period of retraining and some supervision.

- Even if the PCT ends up not having a robust case, they would salvage their prestige by appointing an outside GP to supervise the practice for a short period of 6-8 months and the PCT may have to pay for that exercise from their limited budget.

Generally, the PCT can inflict executive sanctions and procedural hardships, but have very limited scope for financial sanctions as this can be legally contested and won, with the PCT paying penalties.

24. Health Issues

Healthy living

Health issues involves a range of issues for the well-being of the individual, like:

- Eating well – information on what one needs to have a healthy, balanced diet, healthy weight – check body mass index (BMI).
- Sensible drinking – guide to alcohol levels.
- Sexual health – information on taking care of one's sexual health.
- Protection from the sun.
- Smoking – reasons to give up smoking, how to quit, and where you can get information and support.
- The importance of hand hygiene – simple steps on effective hand washing to help prevent the spread of infections and illnesses.

Despite incredible improvements in health, there are still a number of challenges, which should have been easy to solve, but not so:

- Lack of timely access to health care systems.
- Non-communicable diseases, such as cardiovascular disease, cancer, diabetes and chronic lung diseases.
- AIDS/HIV
- Tuberculosis with new cases each year.
- Pneumococcal diseases every year, making it the number one vaccine-preventable cause of death.
- These and other diseases kill more people each year than conflict alone.

24.1 BMI

BMI

Body Mass Index (BMI) is a number calculated from a person's weight and height. BMI provides a reliable indicator of body fatness for most people and is used to screen for weight categories that may lead to health problems.

Calculate for adults – over 20 years – and children & teens 2-19 years separately.

BMI gives you an idea of whether you're underweight, overweight or an ideal weight for your height. It's useful to know because when your weight increases (or decreases) outside of the ideal range, health risks may also increase.

Find your height at the top or bottom of the chart. Follow the column up or down until you reach your weight to get your BMI rating. Click on the relevant box below to see what your rating means.

The body mass index is a calculation of body fat that takes into accounts your age, weight and height. The result is given as a number. For adults the BMI categories are:

Under 18.5: Underweight

18.5-25: Normal weight

25-30: Overweight

30-35: Obese

35 and over: Morbidly Obese

The BMI is a useful measurement for most people over 18. But there are limitations to this system. For instance:

- Adults with a very athletic build (e.g., professional athletes) could show as overweight. This is because muscle weighs more than fat and the BMI does not take this into account.
- If you're pregnant, the BMI does not apply. You should seek advice from your doctor or midwife on what a healthy weight is.
- View special charts for children and young people under 18.

In children and teenagers (below the age of 18), weight is compared with other people of their age, height and gender. BMI is then given as a percentage or 'centile' of this group.

Some people think that BMI is not a good way of deciding if a person is overweight or obese. It is especially difficult to say if a child or young person is overweight or obese because they are still growing, and each child grows at a different rate. Most people felt unhappy about the words used with the BMI and didn't like to think of being **'obese'**.

See your nurse/GP if you require a more precise reading.

24.2 BP

When a heart beats, it pumps blood round the body to give it the energy and oxygen it needs. As the blood moves, it pushes against the sides of the blood vessels. The strength of this pushing is blood pressure. If blood pressure is too high, it puts extra strain on the arteries (and heart) and this may lead to heart attacks and strokes.

Having high blood pressure (hypertension) is not usually something that one feels or notices. It does not tend to produce obvious signs or symptoms. The only way to know the blood pressure is to have it measured.

Blood pressure is measured in 'millimetres of mercury' (mmHg) and is written as two numbers. For example, if the reading is 120/80mmHg, the blood pressure is '120 over 80'.

Even if one does not have high blood pressure at the moment, it is important to keep the blood pressure as low as one can. The higher the blood pressure, the higher the risk of health problems.

For example, a blood pressure of 135 over 85 may be 'normal' but someone with this reading is twice as likely to have a heart attack or stroke as someone with a reading of 115 over 75.

a. Blood pressure chart

Use the blood pressure chart below to see what your blood pressure means. The blood pressure chart is suitable for adults of any age. (The level for high blood pressure does not change with age.)

24.2a BP Chart – Typical Values

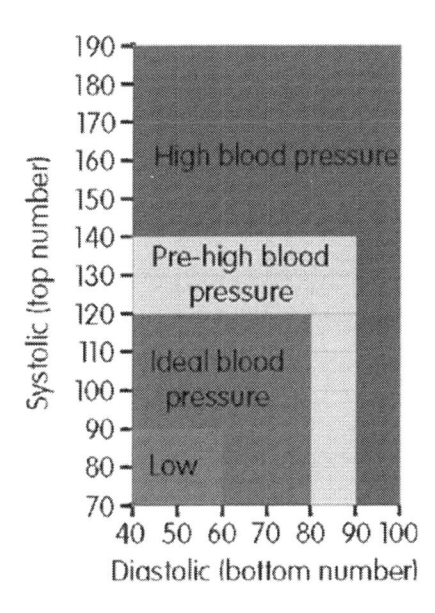

[Chart: Systolic (top number) on y-axis from 70 to 190, Diastolic (bottom number) on x-axis from 40 to 100, showing zones: High blood pressure, Pre-high blood pressure, Ideal blood pressure, Low]

Blood pressure readings have two numbers, for example 140/90.

The top number is your **systolic** blood pressure. (The highest pressure when your heart beats and pushes the blood round your body.) The bottom one is your **diastolic** blood pressure. (The lowest pressure when your heart relaxes between beats.)

The blood pressure chart below shows ranges of high, low and healthy blood pressure readings.

b. Blood pressure chart for adults

Using this blood pressure chart:

To work out what your blood pressure readings mean, just find your top number (systolic) on the left side of the blood pressure chart and read across, and your bottom number (diastolic) on the bottom of the blood pressure chart. Where the two meet is your blood pressure.

c. What blood pressure readings mean

As one can see from the blood pressure chart, only one of the numbers has to be higher or lower than it should be to count as either high blood pressure or low blood pressure:

- **90 over 60 (90/60) or less:** You may have low blood pressure. More on low blood pressure.

- **More than 90 over 60 (90/60) and less than 120 over 80 (120/80):** Your blood pressure reading is ideal and healthy. Follow a healthy lifestyle to keep it at this level.

- **More than 120 over 80 and less than 140 over 90 (120/80-140/90):** You have a normal blood pressure reading but it is a little higher than it should be, and you should try to lower it. Make healthy changes to your lifestyle.

- **140 over 90 (140/90) or higher (over a number of weeks):** You may have high blood pressure (hypertension). Change your lifestyle – see your doctor or nurse and take any medicines they may give you. So:

- **If your top number is 140 or more** – then you may have high blood pressure, regardless of your bottom number.

- **If your bottom number is 90 or more** – then you may have high blood pressure, regardless of your top number.

- **If your top number is 90 or less** – then you may have low blood pressure, regardless of your bottom number.

- **If your bottom number is 60 or less** – then you may have low blood pressure, regardless of your top number.

24.3 GI Values

The Glycaemic Index (GI) is a ranking of carbohydrate-containing foods based on the overall effect on blood glucose levels. Slowly absorbed foods have a low GI rating, while foods that are more quickly absorbed have a higher rating. This is important because choosing slowly absorbed carbohydrates, instead of quickly absorbed carbohydrates, can help even out blood glucose levels when you have diabetes.

Foods are given a GI number according to their effect on blood glucose levels. Glucose is used as a standard reference (GI 100) and other foods are measured against this.

The websites given below give the GI values of foods.

The number listed next to each food is its glycaemic index. This is a value obtained by monitoring a person's blood sugar after eating the food. The value can vary slightly from person to person and from one type or brand of food and another. A noticeable difference is the GI rating of Special-K, which produced considerably different results in tests in the US and Australia, most likely resulting from different ingredients in each location. Despite this slight variation, the index provides a good guide to which foods you should be eating and which foods to avoid.

The glycaemic index range is as follows:

Low GI = 55 or less
Medium GI = 56-69
High GI = 70 or more

The glycaemic index (GI) is a numerical system of measuring how much of a rise in circulating blood sugar a carbohydrate triggers – the higher the number, the greater the blood sugar response. So a low GI food will cause a small rise, while a high GI food will trigger a dramatic spike. A list of carbohydrates with their glycaemic values is shown below. A GI of 70 or more is high, a GI of 56 to 69 inclusive is medium, and a GI of 55 or less is low.

a. High, Medium and Low GI Foods

One of the Internet's most comprehensive lists of foods with their glycaemic index. If you are following the GI or certain diet you should aim to include more foods with a low glycaemic index in your diet. Your body will digest these foods slowly leaving you feeling full for longer and allowing you to eat less calories without feeling hungry. Adding a low GI food to a meal will lower the glycaemic index of the whole meal.

Factors that may affect the GI of a food include:
Cooking methods: frying, boiling, and baking.

- Processing and the ripeness of fruit and certain vegetables.
- Wholegrain and high fibre foods act as a physical barrier to slow down absorption of carbohydrate. This is not the same as 'wholemeal', where, even though the whole of the grain is included, it has been ground up instead of left whole. So some mixed grain breads that include wholegrain have a lower GI than either wholemeal or white bread.
- Fat lowers the GI of a food. For example, chocolate has a medium GI because of its fat content and crisps will actually have a lower GI than potato cooked without fat.
- Protein lowers the GI of food.
- Milk and other dairy products have a low GI because of their high protein content, and because they contain fat.

- **Note:** If you were to restrict yourself to eating only low GI foods, your diet is likely to be unbalanced and may be high in fat and calories, leading to weight gain and increasing your risk of heart disease. It is important not to focus exclusively on GI and to think about the balance of your meals, which should be low in fat, salt and sugar and contain plenty of fruit and vegetables.

The GI value relates to the food eaten on its own and in practice we usually eat foods in combination as meals.

Bread, for example, is usually eaten with butter or margarine, and potatoes could be eaten with meat and vegetables.

An additional problem is that GI compares the glycaemic effect of an amount of food containing 50g of carbohydrate but in real life we eat different amounts of food containing different amounts of carbohydrate.

Note: The amount of carbohydrate one eats has a bigger effect on blood glucose levels than GI alone.

24.4 GL Values

GL stands for Glycaemic Load. It's a unit of measurement that tells you exactly what a particular food will do to your blood sugar. Foods with a high GL have a greater effect on your blood sugar, which isn't desirable. Foods with a low GL encourage the body to burn fat, which is what we're aiming for.

Keeping your blood sugar balanced is the concept at the heart of the low GL diet – sustainable weight loss will follow.

When your blood sugar level increases, the hormone insulin is released into the bloodstream to remove the glucose (sugar). Some glucose goes to the brain and muscles where it's used as an energy fuel, but any excess goes to the liver where it's turned into fat and stored, causing you to gain weight. Insulin is known as the fat-storing hormone.

The glycaemic load (GL) is based on the glycaemic index (GI). Put simply, the glycaemic index of a food tells you whether the carbohydrate in a food is fast or slow releasing (fast is bad, slow is good). What it doesn't tell you are exactly how much of the food is carbohydrate. Glycaemic load on the other hand tells you both the type and amount of carbohydrate in the food and what that particular carbohydrate does to your blood sugar. It doesn't tell you how much of that carbohydrate is in a serving of a particular food. You need to know both things to understand a food's effect on blood sugar. That is where glycaemic load comes in. The carbohydrate in watermelon, for example, has a high GI. But there isn't a lot of it, so watermelon's glycaemic load is relatively low. A GL of 20 or more is high, a GL of 11 to 19 inclusive is medium, and a

GL of 10 or less is low.

Foods that have a low GL almost always have a low GI. Foods with an intermediate or high GL range from very low to very high GI.

Both GI and GL are listed here (See 24.4a). See also 24.4b for typical food values.

24.4a Glycaemic Index and Glycaemic Load Chart

FOOD	Glycaemic index (glucose = 100)	Serving size (grams)	Glycaemic load per serving
BAKERY PRODUCTS AND BREADS			
Banana cake, made with sugar	47	60	14
Banana cake, made without sugar	55	60	12
Sponge cake, plain	46	63	17
Vanilla cake made from packet mix with vanilla frosting (Betty Crocker)	42	111	24
Apple, made with sugar	44	60	13
Apple, made without sugar	48	60	9
Waffles, Aunt Jemima (Quaker Oats)	76	35	10
Bagel, white, frozen	72	70	25
Baguette, white, plain	95	30	15
Coarse barley bread, 75-80% kernels, average	34	30	7
Hamburger bun	61	30	9
Kaiser roll	73	30	12
Pumpernickel bread	56	30	7
50% cracked wheat kernel bread	58	30	12
White wheat flour bread	71	30	10
Wonder™ bread, average	73	30	10
Whole wheat bread, average	71	30	9
100% Whole Grain™ bread (Natural Ovens)	51	30	7
Pita bread, white	68	30	10

Corn tortilla	52	50	12
Wheat tortilla	30	50	8
BEVERAGES			
Coca Cola®, average	63	250 mL	16
Fanta®, orange soft drink	68	250 mL	23
Lucozade®, original (sparkling glucose drink)	95±10	250 mL	40
Apple juice, unsweetened, average	44	250 mL	30
Cranberry juice cocktail (Ocean Spray®)	68	250 mL	24
Gatorade	78	250 mL	12
Orange juice, unsweetened	50	250 mL	12
Tomato juice, canned	38	250 mL	4
BREAKFAST CEREALS AND RELATED			
PRODUCTS			
All-Bran™, average	55	30	12
Coco Pops™, average	77	30	20
Cornflakes™, average	93	30	23
Cream of Wheat™ (Nabisco)	66	250	17
Cream of Wheat™, Instant (Nabisco)	74	250	22
Grapenuts™, average	75	30	16

Glycaemic index and glycaemic load

FOOD	Glycaemic index	Serving size	Glycaemic load
	(glucose = 100)	(grams)	per serving
BREAKFAST CEREALS AND RELATED			
PRODUCTS			
Muesli, average	66	30	16
Oatmeal, average	55	250	13
Instant oatmeal, average	83	250	30

Puffed wheat, average	80	30	17
Raisin Bran™ (Kellogg's)	61	30	12
Special K™ (Kellogg's)	69	30	14
GRAINS			
Pearled barley, average	28	150	12
Sweet corn on the cob, average	60	150	20
Couscous, average	65	150	9
Quinoa	53	150	13
White rice, average	89	150	43
Quick cooking white basmati	67	150	28
Brown rice, average	50	150	16
Converted, white rice (Uncle Ben's®)	38	150	14
Whole wheat kernels, average	30	50	11
Bulgur, average	48	150	12
COOKIES AND CRACKERS			
Graham crackers	74	25	14
Vanilla wafers	77	25	14
Shortbread	64	25	10
Rice cakes, average	82	25	17
Rye crisps, average	64	25	11
Soda crackers	74	25	12
DAIRY PRODUCTS AND ALTERNATIVES			
Ice cream, regular	57	50	6
Ice cream, premium	38	50	3
Milk, full fat	41	250mL	5
Milk, skim	32	250 mL	4
Reduced-fat yogurt with fruit, average	33	200	11
FRUITS			
Apple, average	39	120	6
Banana, ripe	62	120	16
Dates, dried	42	60	18
Grapefruit	25	120	3

Grapes, average	59	120	11
Orange, average	40	120	4
Peach, average	42	120	5
Peach, canned in light syrup	40	120	5

Glycaemic index and glycaemic load

FOOD	Glycaemic index (glucose = 100)	Serving size (grams)	Glycaemic load per serving
FRUITS			
Pear, average	38	120	4
Pear, canned in pear juice	43	120	5
Prunes, pitted	29	60	10
Raisins	64	60	28
Watermelon	72	120	4
BEANS AND NUTS			
Baked beans, average	40	150	6
Black eyed peas, average	33	150	10
Black beans	30	150	7
Chickpeas, average	10	150	3
Chickpeas, canned in brine	38	150	9
Navy beans, average	31	150	9
Kidney beans, average	29	150	7
Lentils, average	29	150	5
Soy beans, average	15	150	1
Cashews, salted	27	50	3
Peanuts, average	7	50	0
PASTA and NOODLES			
Fettuccini, average	32	180	15
Macaroni, average	47	180	23
Macaroni and Cheese (Kraft)	64	180	32

Spaghetti, white, boiled, average	46	180	22
Spaghetti, white, boiled 20 min, average	58	180	26
Spaghetti, wholemeal, boiled, average	42	180	17
SNACK FOODS			
Corn chips, plain, salted, average	42	50	11
Fruit Roll-Ups®	99	30	24
M & M's®, peanut	33	30	6
Microwave popcorn, plain, average	55	20	6
Potato chips, average	51	50	12
Pretzels, oven-baked	83	30	16
Snickers Bar®	51	60	18
VEGETABLES			
Green peas, average	51	80	4
Carrots, average	35	80	2
Parsnips	52	80	4
Baked russet potato, average	111	150	33
Boiled white potato, average	82	150	21
Instant mashed potato, average	87	150	17
Sweet potato, average	70	150	22

Glycaemic index and glycaemic load

FOOD	Glycaemic index	Serving size	Glycaemic load
	(glucose = 100)	(grams)	per serving
VEGETABLES			
Yam, average	54	150	20
MISCELLANEOUS			
Hummus (chickpea salad dip)	6	30	0
Chicken nuggets, frozen, reheated in microwave oven 5 min	46	100	7

Pizza, plain baked dough, served with parmesan cheese and tomato sauce	80	100	22
Pizza, Super Supreme (Pizza Hut)	36	100	9
Honey, average	61	25	12

24.4b Food Values

FOOD	SERVING SIZE	TOTAL CALORIES	FAT GMS	PROTEIN GMS	CARBS GMS	FIBER GMS	CHOL MGS	SODIUM MGS	PCR value	FCR value	GI Index
Almond, blanched	1 oz.	165	14.3	6.2	5.6	2.9	0	8	1.1	2.6	
Apple, raw	1 med.	81	0.5	0.3	21	3.7	0	0	0.0	0.0	
Apricot, raw halves	1 cup	79	0.6	2.3	18.3	3.9	0	2	0.1	0.0	
Artichoke Hearts, raw	1 medium	60	0.2	4.2	13.4	6.9	0	120	0.3	0.0	
Asparagus, fresh	5 spears	18	0	2	2	2	0	1.6	1.0	0.0	
Avocado, California, pureed 1 cup	1 cup	407	39.8	4.8	15.9	11.3	0	27.8	0.3	2.5	
Baked Beans, vegetarian (Van Camp's)	1 cup	206	0.6	10	42	trace	0	950	0.2	0.0	
Banana, fresh, raw	1 medium	120	1	1	28	3	0	1	0.0	0.0	
Barley, pearled, cooked	1 cup	193	0.7	3.5	44.3	6	0	5	0.1	0.0	
Bean Sprouts, canned (LaChoy)	2 oz.	6	0.1	0.7	1.4	0.7	0	17	0.5	0.1	
Biscuit Mix, regular (Bisquick)	1/3 cup	160	6	3	24.7	trace	0	467	avoid	avoid	
Black Bean, canned (Green Giant)	1/2 cup	90	0	7	21	6	0	580	avoid	avoid	
Blackberry, raw	1/2 cup	37	0.3	0.5	9.2	3.6	0	0	0.1	0.0	
Black-eyed Peas, canned	1/2 cup	90	1	7	18	4	0	300	0.4	0.1	
Black-eyed Peas, dried, boiled	1/2 cup	100	0.5	6.7	17.9	8.3	0	3	0.4	0.0	
Black-eyed Peas, frozen, boiled	1/2 cup	112	0.6	7.2	20.2	1.3	0	5	0.4	0.0	
Blueberry, fresh	1/2 cup	41	0.3	0.5	10.2	1.7	0	5	0.0	0.0	
Bok Choy, raw, shredded	1/2 cup	5	0.1	0.5	0.8	0.4	0	23	0.6	0.1	
Brazil Nut, shelled, unblanched	1 cup	919	92.7	20.1	17.9	8	0	2	1.1	5.2	
Bread, 7-Grain (Pepperidge Farm)	2 slices	180	2	5	36	2	0	340	0.1	0.1	
Bread, Oat (Rainbow Split Top)	1 oz. (slice)	70	1	3	13	na	0	140	0.2	0.1	
Bread, Oat Bran (Roman Meal)	1 slice	68	0.9	2.9	13.2	1.1	0	140	0.2	0.1	
Bread, Pita, white	1 oz.	78	0.3	2.6	15.8	0.5	0	152	0.2	0.0	
Bread, Wheat, (Wonder)	1 slice	70	1	3	13	0.8	na	180	0.2	0.1	
Bread, White, plain (Wonder)	1 slice	70	1	3	13	0.7	na	140	0.2	0.1	
Broccoli, florets, raw, chopped	1/2 cup	12	0.2	1.3	2.3	0.5	0	12	0.6	0.1	
Brussels Sprouts, raw	1/2 cup	19	0.1	1.5	3.9	1.9	0	11	0.4	0.1	
Brussels Sprouts, frozen	3.3 oz.	35	0	3	7	3	0	15	0.4	0.0	
Butter, salted	1 tbsp.	100	11.4	0.1	0	0	31	115	0.0	0.0	
Butter, unsalted	1 tbsp.	100	11.4	0.1	0	0	31	1	0.0	0.0	
Buttermilk, cultured	1 cup	99	2.2	8.1	11.7	0	9	257	0.7	0.2	
Carrot, raw	1 medium	31	0.1	0.7	7.3	2.3	0	25	0.1	0.0	
Cashew dry	1 oz.	163	13.2	4.3	9.3	0.9	0	0	0.5	1.4	
Cereal, Oat Bran	1 oz.	110	1	6	17	5.1	0	1	0.4	0.1	
Cheese, Cheddar, lite	1 oz.	80	5	9	1	0	20	220	9.0	5.0	
Cheese, Cottage, nonfat	1/2 cup	90	0	14	7	0	10	400	2.0	0.0	

323

FOOD	SERVING SIZE	TOTAL CALORIES	FAT GMS	PROTEIN GMS	CARBS GMS	FIBER GMS	CHOL MGS	SODIUM MGS	PCR value	PCR value	GI Index
Coconut, Raw, shredded	1 cup	283	26.8	2.7	12.2	7.2	0	16	0.2	0.2	2.2
Coconut Dried sweetened flaked	1 cup	351	23.8	2.4	35.2	3.2	0	189	0.1	0.1	0.7
Cornmeal	1 cup	605	7.9	15.6	123.3	4.8	0	58	avoid	avoid	avoid
Couscous, cooked	1/2 cup	101	0.1	3.4	20.8	1.3	0	4.5	0.2	0.2	0.0
Croissant, plain, 2.5 oz.	1 croissant	310	19	7	27	2	0	240	0.3	0.3	0.7
Egg, Chicken, raw	1 large	75	5	6.3	0.6	0	213	63	10.5	10.5	8.3
Egg White, Chicken, raw	1 large	17	0	3.5	0.3	0	0	55	11.7	11.7	0.0
Egg Yolk, Chicken, raw	1 large	60	5.1	2.8	0.3	0	214	7	9.3	9.3	17.0
Eggplant, cooked	1 cup	27	0.2	0.8	6.4	2.4	0	3	0.1	0.1	0.0
English Muffin, plain	1 muffin	130	1	5	26	1	0	410	0.2	0.2	0.0
English Muffin, with raisins	1 muffin	160	2	5	33	1	0	300	0.2	0.2	0.1
Grapefruit, Ruby Red, fresh	1 cup	85	0.2	1.1	22.3	0.4	0	2	0.0	0.0	0.0
Grapefruit, White, fresh	1 cup	85	0.2	2	20.9	0.4	0	0	0.1	0.1	0.0
Kidney Bean, canned	1/2 cup	90	0.9	7	20	5	0	330	0.4	0.4	0.0
Lentil, boiled	1/2 cup	115	0.4	8.9	19.9	4	0	2	0.4	0.4	0.0
Mango, fresh, cubed	1 cup	107	0.5	0.8	28.1	3	0	3	0.0	0.0	0.4
Milk, Cow, 2%	1 cup	121	4.7	8.1	11.7	0	18	10	0.7	0.7	0.4
Millet Flour	4 oz.	370	4	12	84	7.4	0	2	0.1	0.1	0.0
Oat Flour	1 cup	390	3	14	81	4	0	0	0.2	0.2	0.0
Pasta all 100% durum wheat semolina	2 oz.	210	0	7	42	0	0	0	0.2	0.2	0.0
Peas, Green, frozen	1/2 cup	62	0.2	4.1	11.4	1.6	0	70	0.4	0.4	0.0
Potato, raw, peeled, diced	1/2 cup	59	0.1	1.5	13.5	1.2	0	5	0.1	0.1	0.1
Prune, dried	1 cup	385	0.8	4.2	101	11.6	0	6	avoid	avoid	avoid
Radish, raw, sliced	1/2 cup	11.6	0.3	0.3	2	0.9	0	0	0.2	0.2	0.2
Radish, White, raw, sliced	1/2 cup	7	-0.1	0.6	1.3	0.7	14	0	0.5	0.5	0.0
Raisin, seedless, dark	1 cup	435	0.7	4.7	114.7	7.7	8	0	avoid	avoid	avoid
Raisin, seedless, golden	1 cup	438	0.7	4.9	115.3	2	17	0	avoid	avoid	avoid
Red Bean, canned (Green Giant)	1/2 cup	90	1	6	19	5	17	0	0.3	0.3	0.1
Rice, Brown, long grain, cooked	1/2 cup	109	0.9	2.5	22.5	1.8	340	0	0.1	0.1	0.0
Rice, White, long grain, cooked	1/2 cup	194	5.6	13.7	52.3	0.3	5	0	0.3	0.3	0.1
Rice Flour, brown	1/2 cup	287	2.2	5.7	60.4	3.6	3	0	0.1	0.1	0.0
Rice Flour, white	1/2 cup	289	1.1	4.7	63.3	1.9	6	0	0.1	0.1	0.0
Salt, iodized	1 tsp	0	0	0	0	0	0	2300	0.0	0.0	0.0
Spinach, frozen, not cooked	1 cup	37	0.5	4.6	6.2	4.7	0	115	0.7	0.7	0.1
Sweet Potato, approx. 4 oz.	1 potato	117	0.1	2	27.5	3.4	0	11	0.1	0.1	0.0
Turnip, raw, cubed	1/2 cup	18	0.1	0.6	4.1	1.2	0	44	0.1	0.1	0.0
Walnut, English, dried	1 oz.	182	17.6	4.1	5.2	1.4	0	3	0.8	0.8	3.4
Wheat Flour, White	1 cup	400	1	11	87	3.4	0	0	0.1	0.1	0.0
Yogurt, Plain, lowfat	8 oz.	140	4	10	16	0	15	2	0.6	0.6	0.3
typical food	28.3.09										

GENERAL PRACTICE MANAGEMENT

FOOD	SERVING SIZE	TOTAL CALORIES	FAT GMS	PROTEIN GMS	CARBS GMS	FIBER GMS	CHOL MGS	SODIUM MGS	PCR value	FCR value	GI Index	Sugar GMS
Breakfast:												
Quaker oats 1/2 cup	40g	150	3.0	5.0	27.0	4.0	0.0	0.0				1
Rasam	20g	30	1.0	0.0	0.0	0.0	0.0	30.0				0
vegetables	50g	20	0.0	1.9	8.0	2.1	0.0	20.0				2
Filter coffee	1 cup		0	0	2.4	0	0	0	0	0	10	1
10.30m:												
Milk 2%	1	120	4.8	8.0	11.0	0.0	18.0	10.0	0.4	0.2	32	5
Cashew dry 1/8 cup 14g	14g	85	6.5	2.0	5.0	0.0	0.0	0.0	0.4	1.3	22	0.5
Almonds 6 no without skin	10g	58	5.0	2.0	1.2	2.1	0.0	0.0				0.6
Lunch:												
Egg boiled	1 large	75	5.0	6.3	0.6	0.0	10.0	63.0	10.5	8.3		
Soup, vegetarian vegetable	100g	40	1.8	2.0	8.0	1.3	0.3	50.0	0.3	0.2	38	0.4
Salad with sprouted Methi seeds, hemp seeds	10.75 oz.	207	4.7	5.0	8.0	1.2	0.0	20.0	0.6	0.6	38	3.8
Fruit	1 med.	81	0.5	0.3	5.0	3.7	0.0	0.0	0.1	0.1	38	11
Cottage cheese, no fat, low salt	1/4 cup	45	0.0	7.0	3.5	0.0	5.0	50.0				0
Tea:												
Filter coffee	1 cup	8	0.0	0.0	2.4	0.0	0.0	0.0	0	0	10	1
1 1/2 inch Cucumber, 1 tomato, 1 carrot	100g	16	1.0	0.5	1.5	0.0	0.0	0.0				1.5
Dinner:												
no rice, no wheat, substitute cauliflower rice	50g	70	5.5	1.4	4.0	1.4	15.0	10.0	0.4	1.4	38	0
Vegetables - stir fry, spinach, beans	1/2 cup	109	0.9	2.5	10.0	1.8	5.0	50.0	0.3	0.1	58	0
etc little peas)	100g	50	0.4	2.4	5.0	2.0	0.0		0.2	0.1	30	2.1
cooked	01-Feb	50	1.0	1.2	8.0	2.0	0.0	60.0				0
Rasam, sambar	8 oz.	50	2.0	2.0	5.0	0.0	15.0	30.0	0.4	0.4	14	0
Yogurt, Plain, homemade	125g	80	4.5	4.3	5.8	0.0	3.4	10.0	0.0	0.0		5.75
Total Food Value		1344	47.6	53.8	121.4	21.6	71.7	403.0	0.4	0.4		35.7
% daily values		2500	<70	56	375	30	<300	6000				90
Net Carbs (Total Carbs - Fiber)						99.8						

Recipe: cauliflower or Broccoli cut to rice size pieces,......, stirfry with olive oil, coriander, jeera seeds, samf for ,,,, 4

Breakfast - substitute quakwr oats with Cauliflower rice

The above takes into account Carbs abd GI index values in selecting menu for self. Others should treat this with caution and not follow if a. they are not diabetic; and b. if not type 2

10 mins and treat this instead of Rice.

325

The GI is of foods based on the glucose index – where glucose is set to equal 100. The other is the glycaemic load, which is the glycaemic index divided by 100 multiplied by its available carbohydrate content (i.e. carbohydrates minus fibre) in grams. (The 'Serve size (g)' column is the serving size in grams for calculating the glycaemic load; for simplicity of presentation I have left out an intermediate column that shows the available carbohydrates in the stated serving sizes.) Take watermelon as an example of calculating glycaemic load. Its glycaemic index is pretty high, about 72.

According to the calculations by the people at the University of Sydney's Human Nutrition Unit, in a serving of 120 grams it has 6 grams of available carbohydrate per serving, so its glycaemic load is pretty low, 72/100*6=4.32, rounded to 4.

24.5 5-a-Day Concept

Fruit and vegetables are part of a balanced diet and can help us stay healthy. That's why it's so important that we get enough of them.

The 5 A DAY message highlights the health benefits of getting five 80g portions of fruit and vegetables every day. That's five portions of fruit and veg in total. 5 A DAY is based on advice from the World Health Organisation, which recommends eating a minimum of 400g of fruit and vegetables a day to lower the risk of serious health problems, such as heart disease, stroke, type 2 diabetes and obesity.

It's a simple and popular device that the powers that be have been using to get us to eat more of the things that will keep us healthy: so a handful of dried mango pieces is, say, one of your five-a-day, where a salad – full of freshly sprouted mung beans (one point), tomatoes (another point) and lettuce (one point) might be three. The idea is that if you take care to accumulate five of your five-a-day in any one-day you'll stand a chance of maintaining a good state of physical health long-term.

The following reasons are given as justification for recommending 5 portions:

A bad diet MIGHT contribute to severe illnesses.

An increase in the consumption of fruit and vegetables is important to help manage illnesses like asthma, heart problems, diabetes, and various forms of cancer.

The reason why fruit and vegetables are so beneficial is because of their array of compounds: vitamins, minerals, phytochemicals (including flavonoids, glucosinilates and phyto-oestrogens).

Some vitamins and phytochemicals are antioxidants, which destroy cancer-causing free radicals in the body.

The suggested quantities are meant to be consistent with dietary recommendations around the world, including those from the World Health Organisation.

Eating produce is better than taking supplements. It's great to see this acknowledged –

in fact we'll quote the source – "It appears that the benefits of fruit and vegetables stem not only from the individual components, but also from the interactions between these components. Dietary supplements containing isolated vitamins or minerals do not appear to have the same beneficial effects as fruit and vegetables themselves. Indeed, in some studies, supplements caused more harm than good."

It is also worth noting that the 5 portions is a recommended minimum amount, and that the importance of variety is emphasised.

The above are general guidelines for the adults and for children different standards apply. There are also cautionary notes about fructose and juices. So causation has to be exercised and one is advised to see more articles in websites on this topic.

25. Patient Information

This involves a variety of things and the sites given in References would be most helpful for staff and patients to go through.

Official gateway sites include information about NHS organisations, local NHS services, what the NHS does, how it works, and how to use it. You can search for details of doctors, dentists, opticians, pharmacies, walk-in centres, hospitals, etc. You can look at performance indicators to see how your local services are doing, waiting times, etc.

NHS 111 England – Call 111 (24 hours) if you urgently need medical help or advice but it's not a life-threatening situation.

25.1 Rights

Rights and Responsibilities

Patients should be treated with respect and as a customer in a GP's care. Being a customer means a patient has responsibilities too.

GPs will:

- Ensure patients have 24-hour access to medical advice

- Aim for patients to have access to a suitably qualified medical professional within 48 hours of one's initial contact during surgery hours, or in an urgent case, the same day

- Work in partnership with patients to achieve the best medical care possible. Involve the patient and listen to his/her opinions and views in all aspects of medical care.

The patients are requested that they:

- Let the practice know if they intend to cancel an appointment or are running late

- Treat staff with courtesy and respect. Reception staff may have to ask some personal questions to assist GPs in providing the patients with the best service.

- Inform the practice staff of any alterations in their circumstances, such as change of surname, address, telephone number, marital status etc. Please ensure that the practice have their correct telephone number, even if it's ex-directory.

The prevention of disease, illness and injury is a primary concern. The medical staff will advise and inform the patients of the steps to take to promote good health and a healthy lifestyle. Patients are responsible for their own health and that of any dependents. It is important that patients adhere to information and advice given to by health professionals, and co-operate with the practice in endeavouring to keep the patients healthy.

Zero Tolerance Policy

The practice considers aggressive behaviour to be any personal, abusive and/or aggressive comments, cursing and/or swearing, physical contact and/or aggressive gestures.

The practice will request the removal of any patient from the practice list who is aggressive or abusive towards a doctor, member of staff, other patient, or who damages property. All instances of actual physical abuse will be reported to the police as an assault.

25.2 Confidentiality

Confidentiality/Data Protection

Doctors and staff use a computer to hold patient information to enable them to provide good continuity of care. Patient's data are always kept securely. Some of it may be used by other authorised agencies e.g. district nurses and hospital consultants.

The surgery is registered under the Data Protection Act.

Please read:

- Confidentiality leaflet – A Patient Guide:

  http://www.giggshillsurgery.co.uk/docs/Confidentuality%20Issues%20-

%20A%20Patients%20Guide.pdf

- Freedom of Information Act details:
http://www.giggshillsurgery.co.uk/docs/Freedom%20of%20Information%20Act%20v07.pdf

Comments and Suggestions

GP surgeries should always be happy to accept comments and suggestions from their patients. These should be discussed regularly in monthly Practice Meetings.

25.2.1 Confidentiality

Data Protection Act

The Data Protection Act 1998 came into force in March 2000. Its purpose is to protect the right of the individual to privacy with respect to the processing of personal data. The Act laid down eight data protection principles:

- Data must be processed fairly and lawfully.
- Personal data shall be obtained only for one or more specific and lawful purposes.
- Personal data shall be adequate, relevant and not excessive in relation to the purpose(s) for which they are processed.
- Personal data shall be accurate and where necessary kept up to date.
- Personal data processed for any purpose(s) shall not be kept for longer than is necessary for that purpose.
- Personal data shall be processed in accordance with the rights of data subjects under the 1998 Data Protection Act.
- Appropriate technical and organisational measures shall be taken against unauthorised or unlawful processing of personal data and against accidental loss or destruction of, or damage to, personal data.
- Personal data shall not be transferred to a country outside the EEA, unless that country or territory ensures an adequate level of protection for the rights and freedoms of data subjects in relation to the processing of personal data.
-

25.3 Whistleblowing

If staff bring information about a wrongdoing to the attention of their employers or a relevant organisation, they are protected in certain circumstances under the Public Interest Disclosure Act 1998. This is commonly referred to as 'blowing the whistle'. The law that protects whistle-blowers is for the public interest. So people are encouraged to speak out if they find malpractice in an organisation. Blowing the whistle is more formally known as 'making a disclosure in the public interest'.

Qualifying disclosures are disclosures of information where the worker reasonably believes one or more of the following matters is either happening, has taken place, or is likely to happen in the future:

- A criminal offence
- The breach of a legal obligation
- A miscarriage of justice
- A danger to the health and safety of any individual
- Damage to the environment
- Deliberate attempt to conceal any of the above

If a staff member is going to make a disclosure it should be made to the PMgr or GP Partner, so that employment rights are protected.

Staff, who **'blow the whistle'** on wrongdoing in the workplace, can complain to an employment tribunal, if they are dismissed or victimised for doing so. An employee's dismissal (or selection for redundancy) is automatically considered 'unfair', if it is wholly or mainly for making a protected disclosure.

25.3.1 How to 'blow the whistle'

The way a worker can 'blow the whistle' on wrongdoing depends on whether they feel they can tell their employer.

The worker should check their employment contract or ask human resources/personnel if their company has a whistleblowing procedure.

If they feel they can, they should contact their employer about the issue they want to report

If they can't tell their employer, they should contact a 'prescribed person or body'. A worker can only tell the prescribed person or body, if they think their employer:

- Will cover it up
- Would treat them unfairly if they complained
- Hasn't sorted it out and they've already told them

25.3.2 Dismissals and whistleblowing

Staff can't be dismissed because of whistleblowing. If they are, they can claim unfair dismissal – they'll be protected by law as long as **certain criteria** are met.

Types of whistleblowing eligible for protection. These are called '**qualifying disclosures**'. They include when someone reports:

- That someone's health and safety is in danger
- Damage to the environment
- A criminal offence
- That the company isn't obeying the law (like not having the right insurance)
- That someone's covering up wrongdoing

25.3.3 Who is protected?

The following people are protected:

- Employees
- Agency workers
- People that are training with an employer, but not employed
- Self-employed workers, if supervised or working off-site.

25.3.4 Who's not protected?

Workers aren't protected from dismissal if:

- They break the law when they report something (e.g. they signed the Official Secrets Act)

- They found out about the wrongdoing when someone wanted legal advice ('legal professional privilege') – e.g. if they're a solicitor.

25.3.5 Tribunals

If a worker is dismissed for whistleblowing, they can go to an Employment Tribunal.

If the tribunal decides the employee has been unfairly dismissed, it will order that they are:

- Reinstated (get their job back)
- Paid compensation

25.3.6 Whistleblowing abroad

Workers are protected from unfair treatment even they blow the whistle on something that happened abroad. This includes when a different country's law has been or will be broken.

25.3.7 Whistleblowing Policies

Practical Guidance on Whistleblowing in the NHS from Public Concern at Work.

Week in and week out doctors blow the whistle across the NHS. Few of these doctors will think of themselves as whistle-blowers, insisting that they are just doing their job.

This is understandable as, for many, the perceived characteristic of whistleblowing remains that the message is not heard, the messenger gets crucified and it all ends in tears. Essentially what this means is that only when the message is unwelcome is it considered to be whistleblowing.

However, the culture is changing and people up and down the NHS are much more aware today that they may have to account for their actions. This helps inject an element of self-discipline and circumspection when people are presented with difficult choices. Recent initiatives mean that many, if not most, NHS Trusts are committed to promoting responsible whistleblowing as an essential aspect of good clinical governance. Whistleblowing in today's NHS need not end in tears.

Before you blow the whistle, it's always a good idea to be very clear about the limits of your own responsibility. First, a whistle-blower is a witness, not a complainant. Secondly, a likely consequence of not blowing the whistle is the Chief Executive or Chair saying "Why didn't anybody tell us?" or "If only we had known…" The treatment, then, should be to let the facts speak for themselves and allow those responsible to take an informed decision.

The Public Interest Disclosure Act 1998 (PIDA) was introduced to protect employees who are worried about wrongdoing in their place of work and want to 'blow the whistle'.

The act applies to all NHS employees and includes all self-employed NHS professionals (i.e. doctors, dentists, opticians, optometrists, and pharmacists). For the purposes of the Act, the employer of self-employed NHS professionals is deemed to be the relevant primary care trust or health authority.

An employee who is victimised or penalised for making a protected disclosure can bring an action for compensation against the employer at an Employment Tribunal. Some 1,200 employees have taken their employer to Employment Tribunals since the Act came into force and it is estimated that employers in compensation every year pay out some £10 million. The largest single award to date was £805,000.

25.3.8 Suggestions

My sincere advice to all, particularly to all non-clinical staff:

1. Read the references given on whistleblowing carefully.

2. Non-clinical staff do not have any cover from powerful external organisations as GPs and nurses have. CAB is helpful but you are on your own – in terms of lost time, aggro, stress, loss of job and earnings.

3. There may be many government legislations to protect staff etc. but in the final count you will be left in limbo.

4. For an individual, the best protection is to keep quiet (unless a murder takes place!) and get on with one's work, oblivious of the surroundings.

5. Observe and learn – should be the two key objectives, and soak up all the knowledge that practice experience would give you.

On contentious issues, there are no friends, and do not confide your worries to any colleague or mates. In the end you would be the loser and become bitter.

Do let these perception issues affect your personality.

25.4 Clinical Care

Good clinical care:

Most surgeries have practitioners who have been in the NHS for several years, including General Practice experience. The nurses may also be qualified and trained and have several years' experience. Consequently, the general patient care is of a high quality. They all should go for regular training courses or seminars organised by HTPCT.

The areas to improve would be in data input due to some practitioners not being fast enough in the use of computers. Consequently, some surgeries may still have a dual system of computers and records.

1. Maintaining good clinical practice:

More informal and formal discussions by the practitioners and nurses would improve the clinical practice further. The practitioners need to be aware of new guidelines, which come very frequently and with exhaustive protocols. Continual upgrading of skills and knowledge base is crucial to maintain good clinical care.

2. Teaching and Training:

There should be an induction period for GPs, nurses and admin staff, and procedures are in file. All staff should go through in-house and PCT courses to improve their skills. Appraisals should be done once a year for all staff in the practice. External personnel do GP assessments. Some practices may not be a teaching practice and GP Registrars are not employed.

3. Relationship with patients

The surgery should have very good relationship with the patients and should have very few complaints.

Patient surveys should be conducted each year and improvements made from the comments made.

Dealing with problems arising should be in a most professional manner. This includes dealing with irate patients. The practice manager should respond in a cool and calm manner even under intense provocation.

4. Working with colleagues

The practice should have a good team concept and the staff motivated to get on well with each other. The staff, mostly young ones, who leave, should be very few and even in those cases, due to college or home pressures, they should be advised to come back to re-join. The same applies for the nurses and the GPs.

25.5 Clinical Governance

Practice Managers should be very aware of clinical governance procedures as these become crucial when a practice has to endure remedial issues and adverse actions usually taken by PCTs. Most managers and the GPs have a 'blind spot' for these procedures.

It is a framework through which NHS organisations are accountable for continually:

- Improving the quality of their services
- Safeguarding high standards of care

Three key attributes:

- High standards of care,
- Transparent responsibility and accountability for those standards,
- A constant dynamic of improvement

Clinical governance is composed of at least the following elements:

- Education and Training – continual professional development of clinicians
- Clinical audit
- Clinical effectiveness
- Research and development
- Openness
- Risk management – for patients, for practitioners and for the practice
- Information Management – keeping all records accurately.

Clinical governance aims to integrate the various systems for quality improvement and professional development and to ensure that everyone in the practice team becomes involved. Indeed, an underlying challenge for clinical governance in primary care is to move away from professional development based on uni-disciplinary education towards multidisciplinary, team-based learning. However, there are also potential problems with multidisciplinary learning in general practice. These include issues of hierarchy, gender, and varied educational achievements in team members, all of which may act as barriers to effective learning.

Problems with underperformance might become evident through the review of care for continuing professional development, performance monitoring, annual appraisal, patient surveys, complaints, or revalidation. However, once underperformance is identified, the individual clinician, the practice, and the leader for clinical governance should act to ensure that care is improved.

Actions should include an assessment of the doctors or nurses in the context in which they work. Some underperformance is due to local deprivation and health inequities, some is due to poor systems of care, and some may be due to under-resourcing. Where it is due to an individual, the cause may be a health problem or problems with competency or behaviour.

Whichever it is, there needs to be an accurate and agreed 'diagnosis' and a 'management plan'. The latter must, in time, include the capacity to remove a doctor or nurse from active practice, if appropriate, while they are retrained. A locum will be needed to cover patients while a failing clinician is rescued.

Effective clinical practice requires access to and use of evidence-based guidance on cost effective care. To implement national service frameworks and local health improvement priorities, staff will need to understand what these priorities are and monitor progress towards agreed standards.

Many primary care practitioners even now remain unsure about the meaning of clinical governance and about the changes needed within a practice to implement it.

All should look at the websites of RCGP, BMA, Pulse, GP commissioning, NICE etc. to become aware of the details of the clinical governance and what it means for the practice.

Clinical Governance is the way surgery ensures it has in place the right people and right systems so that it continues to provide patients/customers with the highest standards of care. Clinical Governance is implemented through a framework, which promotes consumer participation, clinical effectiveness, as an effective workforce and risk management.

- **Infection Prevention and Control** is an important unit that is responsible for monitoring infection prevention and risks to patients and staff, to ensure a safe hospital environment. The surgery should implement measures to reduce infections and the impact of those infections on patients. Surgery staff are encouraged to develop guidelines and policies that guide clinical practice, educate, support and monitor staff in infection control practices including hand hygiene and staff immunisation.

- The **Mortality, Morbidity and Major Review** to be carried out on patient safety issues. The Committee reviews sentinel events, serious adverse events and deaths with the assistance of independent audit undertaken by an external medical expert.

- **Patient Safety** is everyone's responsibility and fully investigates types of events to improve practice.

- The surgery is responsible for responding to complaints and concerns. These should be viewed as providing an opportunity to better understand how best to improve its services.

Some examples are given to illustrate the nature of quality improvement for clinical governance:

1. Activities:

a. Repeat prescription:

A patient wanted more than 3 repeat prescriptions.

The issue was stopped and patient was called to come for an appointment. A medication review took place and only then was the prescription given.

GPs must see all patients if more than 3 repeats are requested – exceptions are for mental health patients.

b. New Registration:

A patient needed urgent hospital referral due to severe pain. Despite his temporary registration, action was taken by the GP to send the patient to hospital due to the urgent nature of the illness. Normal procedures for accepting registration to the list or sending to walk-in centre were ignored due to special circumstances.

2. Critical Event Recording

i. Patient A – Referral to hospital when HB values less than 5

- Arrange for blood transfusion referral, if required.
- Immediate appointment should mean same day or next morning consultation and not clinic appointment.

ii. Patient B

When a patient's fasting glucose is very high, then arrange for medication immediately. Refer to hospital if necessary for monitoring.

3. Audit

Clopidogrel audit conducted audit for 13 patients following prescription adviser's visit. Either stopped or changed medication to aspirin, after reviewing each patient.

25.6 Clinical Supervision

Clinical supervision provides an opportunity for staff to:

- Reflect on and review their practice.
- Discuss individual cases in depth.
- Change or modify their practice and identify training and continuing development needs.

Clinical supervision is often primarily aimed at registered professionals (for example, nurses, doctors, social workers and allied health professionals).

1. Has highlighted the need to enforce more vigorously the clinical supervision procedures to ensure a similar slip up does not occur.
2. The clinical supervision would involve all staff – clinical and admin.
3. The doctors, new and existing, would be supervised quarterly by Partners on various cases of patients handled by the doctor concerned to ensure the procedures and protocols are followed.
4. Nurses and admin, the Partners and Practice Manager would supervise nurses and staff respectively, again at quarterly intervals.
5. Lessons learnt would be discussed in the monthly meetings to highlight areas of concern and where remedial actions were taken to correct it.
6. CDM (Clinical Decision Making) procedures and particular attention to mental health and cancer patients would be focused to ensure conformity to guidelines.

Prescribing and repeat prescriptions, not collecting prescriptions etc., would be areas where a receptionist can alert the Practice Manager, the partners.

26. PBC

Practice Based Commissioning (PBC)

PBC is a United Kingdom Department of Health initiative, introduced in 2005, designed to target financial drivers, general practitioners, nurses and other primary care professionals the power to decide how NHS money is spent in their local area.

PBC is about engaging practices and other primary care professionals with the NHS (National Health Service) commissioning of services.

Through PBC, front line clinicians are being provided with the resources and support to become more involved in commissioning decisions.

PBC aims to provide high quality services for patients in local and convenient settings. GPs, nurses and other primary care professionals are in the prime position to translate patient needs into redesigned services that best deliver what local people want.

GP practices will be supported by the PCTs (Primary Care Trusts) so that they may buy in (commission) services for their patients based upon cost and quality of care. This process is expected to generate financial savings of which 7/10ths may be retained by the practice for further investment while the remainder is passed back to the PCT.

In 2006 on sites in England a study was instituted focusing on the implementation and impact of practice-based commissioning (PBC) and assessed progress against the policy's three main objectives – better clinical engagement, better locally-provided services for patients and better use of resources – and identified barriers that were limiting its success.

Evaluation of practice-based commissioning indicated that it has had little impact in terms of improving use of resources or providing better services, and examples of initiatives attributed to PBC tend to be small-scale local pilots. GPs have found it hard to find time to engage with PBC, and one survey of GPs found that 80 per cent felt they lacked some or all of the necessary skills to be an effective commissioner.

Slow progress has been attributed to a lack of clear financial incentives and cumbersome bureaucracy in PCTs' approval of business cases.

PBC never took off in the UK and was replaced by Clinical Commissioning Groups who now fulfil the role. This was a part of the Health and Social Care Act 2012.

27. Impending Changes

Changes in NHS affecting GP Practices

NHS is the biggest employer in the UK and it is a pride of Britain when healthcare systems around the world are compared. The features and benefits it offers to all people in Britain and the visitors are immense and not provided in any country, particularly USA. Canada does have a very good system like UK in most areas.

The government, since 1993, has been doing a lot tinkering with the way the GP system in the main is operating and also the Hospitals. They had allowed administrative staff to multiply without reason in trying to check and control the care provided by the GPs and hospital doctors to the patients.

There were lot changes that were welcome like use of computers and moving away from paper records, which still a lot of surgeries use; in fact they operate a dual system. Treating patients as customers, the demands on the GPs were very severe and often unrealistic.

A patient can be seen anywhere in UK, which was happening before these changes; now it is expected that the new GP should have the records available via his computer. This has not yet happened due to the immensity of technical problems and there is also a major element of fraud in such transfer of data.

Patient confidentiality cannot be guaranteed but Ministers decree that safeguard should be built in. Even large banks face hacking problems and NHS with its limited funding would never be able to provide such safeguards.

The companies, which were to provide IT support, have failed immensely with large wastage of money. Still as new Minsters take up their jobs, the main task is to tinker with the NHS GP system. A lot of time King Canute philosophy is still applied with utmost vigour.

Not a day will pass by without some criticism of NHS neglecting patients but what the Ministers would not realise is that due to overspending in some areas, mostly on exorbitant salaries to top level administrative staff, they have decimated the jobs of lower grade crucial supporting staff to balance the books and in many cases closed several hospitals by opening new improved ones. Then the complaints come in the form of lack of beds, transporting patients to hospitals at a great distance from their area to find beds incurring heavy costs in the process.

There is no philosophy of how to improve the old hospital but to close it and make a new one with modern facilities, which only appeals to creature comforts but not in more beds, convenience of access, more clinical and support staff etc.

Despite all these tinkering, NHS is still the best healthcare available in the world.

Just like in the poem '**Men may come and may go but I go on forever**. A PMgr has to keep up with the new changes and developments in the NHS GP practices. PMgr is required constantly to reading publications like Pulse, GP Commissioning, Online, Diabetes UK, BMA, RCN and others to keep abreast of changes and be alert to know when these changes would come into practice and how it would affect the services the Practice has to provide.

GPs are usually briefed at their weekly meetings about impending changes; the above publications also highlight the good and bad of the changes; their interactions with other GPs in other practices; and contacts in PCTs and GP friends in other areas to mention a few. They will also have separate communications about these from PCT, MPS and MDU. Still they may not read in detail or remember in detail the various aspects except when it refers to their contract payments and terms.

PMgr has therefore should be alert to the impending changes and notify the GPs by raising these issues in the monthly meetings so that these are not forgotten and then one fine day they may find that they have to institute the changes immediately. If the surgery has a writing board, PMgr should leave points in bullet form for GPs to read during break hours for tea and lunch. This should be done continually about all impending changes.

NHS has always been in a constant state of flux. More so, when a new Minister takes over or the government changes. The changes are not just cosmetic but usually too fundamental; and involves a lot of consultative stages making the working life of the Doctors and staff very difficult.

Sometimes one wonders whether there is a fault finding secret agenda on NHS. Always one of the aspects of care or disease would be highlighted to show NHS is not functioning as well as intended; thereby justifying the principle of changes are needed continually.

Some of the changes that are imminent are given below:

1. From April 2015, every patient would have a named GP, who would be responsible for his or her care. The change will definitely affect GPs, practices and patients.

2. There is a move to have GP coverage 24/7; this change would involve substantial lay out of money for the practices and how effective this change would be on patient services has to be monitored.

3. APMS (Alternative Provider Medical Services) contracts can play growing primary care role. Primary care commissioners to allow providers to run GP practices have increasingly used APMS contracts. This is partially due as a response to the

recruitment problems the surgeries are faced with. APMS does not provide a universal solution, but it is an option and one that CCGs are likely to increasingly explore when they begin taking responsibility for primary care budgets. APMS contracts are time-limited and the contracts need to be of longer duration with less risk of a provider being 'turfed out' even if they are performing well. APMS practices, many in deprived areas of England, face funding cuts or closure as NHS officials complete a wave of contract reviews.

4. Practices may consider boycotting a scheme that would pay them £55 per patient diagnosed with dementia.

5. Primary care funding will rise sharply over the next five years as part of a 'new deal for GPs' that will merge primary and acute care in parts of the country but maintain valued existing practices.

6. The number of QOF points for 2015/16 will remain at 559, with some changes to indicators, the GPC and NHS Employers have confirmed. Five indicators have been retired and others amended in what the GPC hailed as 'important, clinically appropriate changes to QOF'. Changes have been applied to indicators for AF, CHD, dementia and CKD.

All patients in England will have a named GP who is responsible for coordinating their care from next April and practices will be forced to publish average GP earnings as part of changes to the GMS contract agreed for 2015/16.

Incorrect coding may mean the prevalence of particular diseases within your practice is not accurately represented - and this could have a significant impact on your QOF income.

Boost QOF income by improving data accuracy.

1. GPs should consider working with other practices to 'increase the scale of delivery of GP services', the CQC has said in its annual review of health and care services in England.

2. More of Co-commissioning to bring a holistic approach to commissioning services for a specific population; achieving greater integration of health and care services, in particular more cohesive systems of out-of-hospital care that bring together general practice, community health services, mental health services and social care to provide more joined-up services and improve outcomes.

3. Military-style restrictions could be placed on medical training to tie newly qualified GPs to the NHS and stop them moving abroad, the government's primary care minister has said. One solution to the 'brain drain' was to make training funding conditional on remaining in the country and serving the NHS for a set period.

4. GPs should be able to form expanded group practices, which also directly employ hospital consultants.

5. Labour proposals to remove GPs' independent contractor status and take away their commissioning powers. Labour plans for GPs to become salaried employees of hospital-led integrated care organisations and to downgrade their CCG responsibilities.

6. NHS pensions will change from 1 April 2015 and will impact on members of the scheme.

7. GPs will not control primary care commissioning when CCGs are handed expanded powers under new CCG reforms proposed.

8. All GP practices in England have to carry out the Friends and Family test from 1 December 2014 as part of their contract.

The Friends and Family test is continuous rather than a one-off traditional survey. Patients must be able to give feedback after every interaction with the practice, and anyone on the practice list should be able to complete the test at any time. It is up to the practice how it promotes the test and how it collects responses.

The key GMS contract changes from 2003 to 2015, starting with the first three-year GMS contract, which was introduced in 2003/04, are well covered in the web site

On 30 September 2014, NHS Employers and the General Practitioners Committee of the BMA announced changes to the GMS contract in England for 2015/16.

The focus of the changes is on providing a named, accountable GP for all patients, publication of GPs' average net earnings and a further commitment to expand and improve patient online services.

GPC and NHS England would separately submit evidence to the Doctors' and Dentists' Review Body (DDRB) in relation to the 2015/16 uplift to the GMS Contract. The Government will consider the DDRB recommendations before making a final decision.

28 Fraud

Guidance to GP practices on GP patient registration fraud

The NHS CFS has responsibility for all policy and operational matters relating to the prevention, detection and investigation of fraud and corruption in the NHS.

It offers guidance to GP practices on how to identify and manage suspicions of patient registration fraud and how to prevent this type of activity occurring in the future.

Patient registration fraud

There have been a number of cases where patients (both temporary and newly registered) have registered at GP practices (often at multiple practices) using their own or false details and fraudulently obtained prescription drugs without providing evidence of their identity or giving details of their most recent GP. They have obtained prescription drugs for personal use and/or to sell and this is resulting in a financial loss to the NHS.

Minimising patient registration fraud

Taking the following steps will ensure that patient registration fraud in practice is minimised.

1. Request identification

It is important to ask all new patients (whether registering permanently or temporarily) to provide identification upon registering.

A combination of the following can be accepted as identification (it is preferable that one item of photo ID is seen, along with one document like an utility bill containing the patient's address):

- Birth certificate
- Marriage certificate
- Medical card
- Driving licence
- Passport
- Local authority rent card
- Paid utility bills
- Bank/building society cards/statements
- National Insurance number card
- Pay slip
- Letter from Benefits Agency/benefit book/signing on card
- Papers from the home office
- P45. This list is not exhaustive.

The following documents are easily obtained and **should not** be accepted as proof of identity if presented in isolation:

- Library card
- Video rental card
- Health club card
- Private rent book.

If the patient provides identification, a note of this should be made on their record and they should be treated as normal.

If the patient does not provide identification, the registration should still be accepted but a note should be made on the patient's records to say that no identification has been seen and they should be asked to bring something next time they attend the surgery.

2. Request proof of address

Permanent patients should also be asked to provide evidence of their address.

3. Contact your Local Counter Fraud Specialist

GP practices should report suspected false registrations to their Local Counter Fraud Specialist (LCFS), giving as much detail as possible. Details of these patients can then be circulated and all related incidents can be collated by the NHS CFS to identify serial offenders.

Prescription fraud

It is not unusual for some surgeries to have a too close a relationship with the local pharmacists; the senior receptionists may have such relationship bordering on unethical practices.

The senior receptionists may some times ask pharmacists to supply the usual prescription medicines and promise to give the repeat prescription soon. Due to pressure of work and forgetfulness these promised prescriptions may not been sent to the pharmacy. At the month end the pharmacist may submit a long list of repeat prescriptions that are due to him so as to claim money for medicines supplied. These would also result in surgeries prescribing less medication for those periods when the true situation is just the opposite.

The potential weaknesses in the prescription processes are ones well known to the NHS counter fraud service. In two recent cases practice receptionists have exploited these weaknesses. In each case the receptionists, both long term members of staff, had fraudulently used the computerised patient notes' system to access records and create fraudulent repeat prescriptions, which were then unwittingly signed by the prescribing GP.

Surgery practice managers and 'fixers' have been secretly filmed selling access to doctors, enabling foreign nationals who have no legal right to free hospital treatment to be seen without paying.

Hospitals should check if foreign patients are entitled to free NHS hospital care but in many these patients are not entitled to as per checks.

Fraud can happen in all areas of the NHS and can be committed by staff of all levels. The various cases involving fraud and resulting in punishment are given below:

- There have been cases where one NHS practice manager sold patient registrations at a health centre to an undercover reporter for up to £800 a time.

- The reporter went on to obtain an MRI scan to which the patient was not legally entitled, which would have cost £800 privately.

- A practice manager entered her son, who was not employed by the practice, onto the practice payroll.

- A GP worked privately while off sick from the NHS. He claimed payment for locum cover for his NHS practice from the primary care trust.

- A patient used aliases and false addresses to fraudulently obtain prescriptions.
- Two GPs claimed an improvement grant for their practice but transferred a third of the grant to their personal accounts.
- A GP submitted prescriptions to a pharmacist in the name of one of his partners to gain drugs for himself.
- A bogus nurse who carried out vaccinations and cervical smears on more than 1,400 patients in Kent has admitted deception, fraud and forgery.
- Patient travel claim fraud.
- Staff nurse imprisoned for timesheet fraud.
- Patient sentenced for prescription fraud.
- Salisbury man jailed for conning Dorset GPs.
- Trust gives stark warning as worker is sentenced for theft after joint security operation.
- Bank Nurse Fraud.
- Two cases of obtaining drugs by deception.
- Poole nurse sentenced to 150 hours community punishment.
- Agency Operating Department Assistant jailed for 16 months.
- Somerset GP convicted of impersonating patients in drug fraud.
- Deferred Sentence used to control drug addicts behaviour.
- Former employee of Dorset PCT admits sickness fraud.
- Nursing & Midwifery Council removes nurse from Register.
- Manager fined £5,000

Not all fraud, though, is to do with money. Some cases of fraud, such as faking qualifications, could be considered less serious, but it can have much more serious consequences when patients' lives are put at risk.

There are many examples of this occurring in the press where people have got positions as practice nurses without having actually qualified. In these cases, references and certificates were not followed up and checked to see if they were legitimate.

The most common sign that a financial fraud has taken place will be a drop in the amounts held in the bank account from the usual monthly levels that the partners and practice manager will be familiar with.

This drop will also appear in the accounts as a reduction in bottom line profit and partners' current account balances. This should prompt further inspection of the accounts to see if there are any other tell-tale signs that a fraud has taken place. These include:

- Unexplained increases in costs
- Unexplained drops in income
- Unusual explanations for missing items
- Regular payments falling out of sequence
- Unexplained delays in income.

In order to protect the practice, it is important to identify and put controls in place in the key risk areas, such as:

- Receipts of cash/cheques
- Access to the cheque book or payment process
- Access to drugs
- Sending of signed cheques
- Authorisation of claim forms and supplier payments
- Authorisation of the payroll.

However, the most effective deterrent from fraud is to create a culture where no one would think they could perpetrate a fraud without serious consequences. Implementing controls in the above risk areas is a good way to start.

However, not all GP practice frauds are the result of rogue staff. Sometimes, one or more of the partners themselves may be the fraudsters. These cases are harder to spot, as controls and identification processes may have been bypassed.

An example of this is a case when a GP partner was falsifying his patient lists, including 23 patients living in a one bedroom flat owned by the doctor and adding them to the PCT returns in order to achieve higher payments. These were picked up by PCT audits and the case was referred to the NHS Counter Fraud Service (now NHS Protect).

In these cases, the money would have been paid into the practice and then would have to be extracted by the fraudsters, so this could also be picked up by some of the internal methods that we have already looked at.

In order to put some control over these areas, it is important not to give any one partner too much control over the practice. For example, ensure that large value cheques have to be countersigned by more than one partner and those administrative tasks are shared out or rotated among partners.

If one has concerns about a possible fraud then, firstly, one should follow your standard internal reporting procedure. However, if one does not have one in place, or one suspects that the fraud may involve these individuals, then one can report in confidence to NHS Protect on 0800 028 40 60, or report on-line at www.reportnhsfraud.nhs.uk. Most of the examples about fraud were obtained from NHS sites in addition to details obtained by net working with the surgeries in earlier years.

29. Practice Booklets

There are two formats for a Practice Booklet:

29.1 Standard Format

Typical format for most of the surgeries will be a Booklet - the usual size 210x150 mm - listing the various details with lots of adverts (see Modified Format). The adverts usually pay for the cost of printing and would be collected by the printers. The practice would get FREE copies to cover roughly twice the practice patient list.

29.2 Modified Format (29.2a)

The above shows the cover page - front and back for the surgery the author has worked for a short time.

This format is preferred as the size 135x95 mm is slightly smaller than the UK passport and can be kept in the shirt pocket.

Patients are advised to bring the book each time for each of the patient when they visit the GP. It has pages where the receptionists mark next appointments. This eliminates errors of date and time for the appointments with computer records. This is an 'aggro' issue in all inner city surgeries. Also, it has the facility to check names and addresses on each appointments page to ensure the patients details of name, address, Dob are updated. Patients usually forget to update changes in marital status, addresses etc.

The parent or guardian has to bring booklet for each child being seen by the GP. Each patient would have a dedicated booklet, which they are encouraged to bring and it would have all the details contained in the Standard format. The details will include opening hours, clinics and dates and most importantly their next appointment date and time, which would match with the computer booking. It also enables them to know more about the surgery, as these are easier to carry than the Standard Format booklet and refer to it frequently, even when they are waiting for their appointments.

The next illustration is a 32-page booklet and copied with pages spread out (See 29.2b); these are then folded and stapled in the middle to form the booklet. The information contained in is 'dated' and the practice can change to their current details to produce their booklet. The pages are numbered, as they appear in the photos, as a guide. There are 8 pages in each copy x 4 making it 32 in total.

I have identified from left to right giving detail or page number as appropriate.

1st set Top 4:   pages 30, 3, 6, 27

1st set Bottom 4:   Back cover 32; Front cover 1; 26, 7. The GP had 8 peacocks with 3 chicks, sometimes riding on the mum's back!

2nd set Top 4:   2, Inside Back cover 31; 28, 5

2nd set Bottom 4:   pages 4, 29, 8, 25

3rd set Top 4:   pages 10, 23, 20, 13

3rd set Bottom 4:   pages 16, 17, 12, 21

4th set Top 4:   pages 24, 9, 14, 19

4th set Bottom 4:   pages 18, 15, 22,11

Suggestion - increase the number of pages to 40

- 6 pages for additional appointments.

- 2 pages for 1/4 page - say 3-4 line adverts - 8 adverts total, priced to recover the cost of producing the booklet by the printers who would deal with the money side of it - surgery has to do nothing other than give the draft to the printers.

Practice Boundary

HOBtPCT decides the Practice Boundary not surgery. GPs are required to service patients within the practice boundary. All ancillary services are provided for within the practice boundary – teams of Community Nurses, District nurses, CPNs, Health Visitors etc. If a patient is registered outside the area then the ancillary teams and GP would not be able to do home visits. When Post Codes change, and it is outside our practice boundary, then please register with a GP in the new area. You should notify the address to us and once we change in the computer system you would be automatically removed from our list.

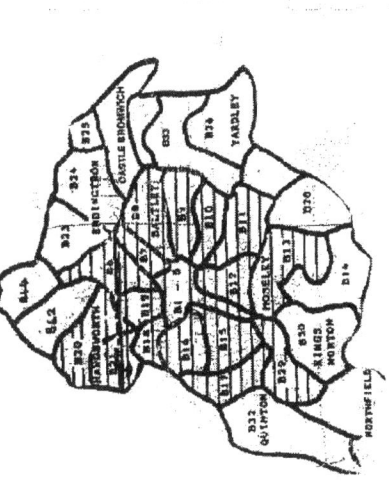

B1 – B13, B15 – B21, B29
B20 Handsworth, B8 Saltley, B13 Moseley

Surgery – Hours

Receptionists:
Mon, Tue, Wed, Fri   8.30AM to 6.30 PM
Thu   8.30AM to 1.00 PM

Appointments: (for patients)
Mon, Tue, Wed, Thu   10.00 AM to 12.30 PM
   3.00 PM to 6.00 PM
Thu   10.00 AM to 12.30 PM
   Half day morning only
PLT days: 3rd Tue of each month
   From 1.00 PM Surgery closed

Appointments (10 min):
First two hours: Mornings only
1/3 - prior booking by GP/Nurses/patients
2/3 - walk-in on the day
Last Hour - emergencies
Evenings (10min):
1st hour - prior bookings
Last hour - emergencies
Triage: 3 hours in the afternoon most days
Home Visits: By Community Nurse team, District Nurses and by GP (only if Triage indicates visit by GP) Only for patients home bound or in serious condition affecting mobility

Out of Hours: by Badger
Weekdays: 6.30 PM to 8.30 AM
Wednesdays: 1.00 to 4.00 PM
PLT days: 1.00 to 4.00 PM
Sat, Sun, Bank Holidays – by Badger
One call to surgery –   0845 074 0451
NHS Direct: 0845 4647
NHS Walk in Centre: 7AM to 8PM; 7 days/week
Lower ground floor, Boots the Chemist, 66 High Street, (opposite M&S) – 0121 255 4500

Old Mill Surgery

22 Speedwell Road, Edgbaston, Birmingham, B5 7QA
Tel: 0845 074 0451　　　　Fax: 0121 446 4302

Family of 9 Peacocks with 3 new chicks (11 to hatch)

July 2005

Flu / Pneumococcal Vaccinations

Flu – for over 65 and those suffering from CHD/Stroke/Diabetes/Asthma/COPD Given from Sept to March.
For patients, not in the above DoH approved Category, who want Flu vaccines, a charge would be made.
Pneumoccocal – over 65 years.

Child Immunisations Schedules:

At 2, 3 and 4 mo: DTP, Hib, Menin C, Polio oral
12-15 mo: MMR (single dose)
13 mo to 4 years: Hib (if not immunised before)
Before school or nursery school entry: DTP, MMR /boosters
Routine Development checks: 8 weeks; 18 and 39 month

Cervical Cytology (Smears): All female patients between the ages 24 and 65 are invited for a smear every 3 years – exceptions:
a) those who had total abdominal hysterectomy (t.a.h.) for benign reasons;
b) those who had t.a.h. with malignant histology but have had negative smears for 5 years or as advised by national protocol. There are procedures for Recall system and Non-attenders (DNA).

Family Planning Clinics: Planning to start this clinic by autumn for in-house and other surgery patients. Discussions with PCT are proceeding.

Choose and Book: By the end of 2005, through the GP or primary care worker, patients would be able to choose their preferred hospital / specialist in hospital and book an appointment to suit them. This will only apply to the first appointment. For revisits, hospitals will arrange in the usual way.

Out of normal surgery hours, all Doctors have an answering machine message referring you to out-of-hours telephone numbers or **NHS Direct on 0845 4647**.

Do you need to visit a Minor Injuries Unit?

Minor Injuries Units: Many people continue to go to A&E even when they could be treated just as professionally and usually more quickly at a Minor Injuries Unit. Minor Injuries Units are for patients with less serious injuries, such as sprains, cuts and grazes. The waiting times are usually much shorter than those in A&E, as staff must give priority to serious and life-threatening conditions. You do not need an appointment to visit a Minor Injuries Unit. Minor Injuries Units are led by highly qualified nurse practitioners with more experience and expertise than many doctors in this kind of treatment.

Minor Injuries Units can treat a wide variety of problems including:
- Cuts/grazes and lacerations
- Sprains and strains
- Broken bones (fractures)
- Bites and stings (including human/animal bites)
- Infected wounds
- Minor head injuries
- Minor eye infections, foreign bodies & scratches

If you are not sure whether your injury is minor and can be treated in a Minor Injuries Unit, telephone **NHS Direct on 0845 4647**, who can advise you and direct you to the most appropriate place for your care.

➢ Self-help or support organisations
* Calls are charged at local rates. For patients' safety, all calls are recorded.

For deaf people or those hard of hearing there is a **textphone service available on 0845 606 46 47**. For those whose preferred language is not English, there is the choice of a **confidential translation service**.

Have you tried your local NHS Walk-in Centre? There are now 49 NHS Walk-in Centres throughout England. They offer fast and convenient access to healthcare advice and treatment for minor injuries and illnesses. They are open from early morning to late evening, seven days a week. They are run by experienced NHS nurses, and you don't need to make an appointment.

Do you need to visit your Doctors surgery? Doctors surgeries: Your local Doctors surgery provides a range of services, including general medical advice and treatment; prescriptions; referral to a specialist or hospital (where appropriate); jabs and tests (such as immunisations, blood tests or cervical smears). Find your local Doctors surgery.

Remember to tell your doctor if you have tried or are still taking self-care treatment. Surgeries are always busy, so be sure to keep to your appointment time and cancel it if you need to; missed appointments waste precious time and resources. Out of normal surgery hours, all Doctors have an emergency service. This service is only for urgent medical problems that cannot wait until the next day to be treated.

Local Enhanced Services: Provided for minor surgery, wound management and Goserelin injections for all in-house patients. May provide for other surgery patients as well later this year.

Other areas like CHD, Diabetes, COPD, Asthma, IUCD's, Glucose Tolerance tests, Insulin Initiation, Family Planning etc. as local enhanced services are under discussion with PCT.

Health Clinics: CHD/IHD/Stroke/Hypertension/Diabetes/ Hypothyroidism/Cancer/Asthma/COPD/ Epilepsy/Mental Health

At least once a year; 3 or 6 monthly intervals as decided by GP/Nurses.

Well Person Clinics: under 75 — once in 3 years
75 and over — once a year

Community Psychiatric Nurse: – usually by referral

Dietician: being arranged on a regular basis with PCT

Others: ear syringing, removal of stitches, blood samples, dressing as required – all by appointments only.

Education: Surgery has major periodicals pertaining to Health Care; leaflets on various health issues are also displayed for patients to take away.

Patients Comments: We welcome comments from patients; participation in Practice Meetings – 3rd Wed. of each month – 1.30 to 2.30 PM; able to see Practice Manager for all issues to discuss including **Complaints**;

Services: Travel vaccinations, insurance work and health checks/examinations, passport application forms, employment medicals and a host of other services including Private patients, Flu vaccination for patients not in approved category, copy of records would be charged and details can be obtained from reception. Fees to be paid prior to work being carried out.

OLD MILL SURGERY

Dr. Badri Narayan (Male, S/H GP)
22 Speedwell Road, Edgbaston
Birmingham B5 7QA
Tel: 0845 074 0451 (contacting surgery)
Fax: 0121 446 4302
Badri.Narayan@hobtpct.nhs.uk

Heart of Birmingham Primary Care Trust

The Surgery Team

Principal GP:	Dr. B S Narayan MMBS (India) '67
Locum GP:	Dr. S. Varadharajan
Nurses:	Mrs Kay Coldicott
	Mrs Linda Anderson
Practice Manager:	Dr. V S Mani
Admin. Manager:	Miss Azmah Qurban
Medical Secretary/	
Receptionist:	Miss Shakila Bi
Receptionists:	Mrs Fozia Begum
	Mrs Julie Cleaver
	Mrs. Ishrat Bibi
	Mrs. Lata Singh
Health Visitor:	Mrs. Meryl Nee
CPN:	Mr. Sat Singh
District Nurse:	Ms Pauline Broadbent et al.
Midwife:	Mrs Christine Innes
Domestic:	Mrs. Catherine Chariery
HobtPCT Co-ord:	Mrs Jyoti Srikanta

SURGERY STAFF

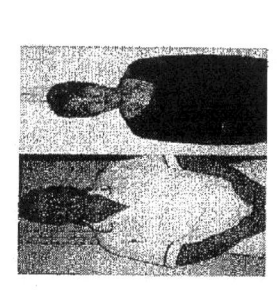

USEFUL TELEPHONE NUMBERS

Hospitals/Clinics:
Birmingham Chest Clinic	0121 424 2000
B'ham & Midland Eye Centre	554 3801
B'ham Women's Hospital	472 1377
Children's Hospital	333 9999
City Hospital	554 3801
Heartlands	424 2000
Queen Elizabeth	472 1311
Queen Elizabeth Psychiatric	678 2000
Royal Orthopaedic	627 1627
Selly Oak	627 1627
NHS Direct	0845 4647
Out of Hours (surgery/Badger)	0845 0740451

Emergency
	999
Heart of Birmingham Teaching PCT	224 4600
HOBtPCT – Complaints Manager	224 4640
HOBtPCT – Health Promotion	627 8688
HOBtPCT – Older People	224 4627
HOBtPCT – PALS (M-F 9AM to 5 PM)	224 4725

Out of Hours Health Care:
Dental NHS clinic	237 2752
Social Care and Health	457 4806
Balsall Heath Health Centre	446 2300
Family Planning	446 1010
Whittall Street Clinic (Genito-Urinary)	237 5700
West Midlands Ambulance Service	01384 215555
Stop Smoking Advice (M-F 9AM to 7PM)	0800 917 9199

Emergency Appointments
Reserved for children, old people, sick notes (no back dating), pregnancy and those seriously ill
Not for cough and cold or ailments lasting over 48 hours.

Normal Appointments: GP/Nurse
GP/Nurses need reason for all appointments
Reason to be given to receptionists when asked
GP may decide that it is adequate for the patient to be seen by a nurse only.
Multiple appointments – please give names of each patients e.g. mother with two children all needing appointments – 3 in total.
Parental consent to see children under 16 with or without guardians.

Private Patients: Fee to be paid in advance
30 min. appointments to see GP/Nurse (as reqd.).

Registration: We have an open list and will register new patients. Appointment may not be given till their registration is accepted by PCT. New patients are required to bring in for identification purposes – passport for checking first, second and given names, date of birth; bank statement or utility bill for checking address for residence and post code within the practice boundary; admission to a college course in case of students; home office or other government body headed letter to the person in the absence of passport. A form has to be filled in at the reception for GP and Nurses to decide on registration.

Medical Cards: These are issued by PCT *not surgery*.
Newly registered patients will have to wait a few weeks to get Medical cards – contact PCT
Always bring medial card for appointments and give to receptionists to book you in.

Do you or a family member need emergency hospital treatment?

Accident & Emergency (A&E) or 999:

It is often very obvious when emergency care is needed for serious injury or illness. You should get medical attention by either taking the patient to the nearest Accident & Emergency (A & E) department or by phoning 999 for an emergency ambulance.

An emergency is a critical or life threatening situation such as:

- Loss of consciousness
- Heavy blood loss
- Suspected broken bones
- Persistent chest pain for 15 minutes or more
- Difficulty breathing
- Overdose, ingestion or poisoning

Remember to keep calm, do everything you can to help the person, but don't put yourself in danger and don't give the person anything to eat, drink or smoke.

Unless you need emergency medical attention avoid local A&E departments. Doctors and nurses there are equipped to deal with serious cases of injury and illness, not routine and minor ailments. Calling an ambulance won't necessarily mean you are seen any quicker at A&E as the most serious cases are prioritised. Find your local A&E unit.

Insurance/DWP/Passport etc.
Afternoon appointments only to see GP.

Repeat Prescriptions:
Always give the white copy of previous prescription. On rare occasions the medicine packet or hand written details of medicines with dosage may be accepted. Do not wait till medicines have run out. 48 working hours need to be given for repeats. Repeats given only for previously issued drugs. Antibiotics, changed medication/ dosage, steroids
- to be approved by GP after an appointment.
Due to malpractice prescriptions will not be posted
- personal collection, nominee or to pharmacist.

Test Results:
Will only be given by GP/Nurses to the patient.

Clinics by Nurses (GP in surgery)
Mon PM Diabetes (8)
Tue AM Hypertension (9)
     AM/PM Asthma (5+8)
Wed PM Cervical Cytology/Smear
     PM COPD/Hypothyroidism/Epilepsy (8)
Thu AM Stroke (5)
Fri AM Child Immunisations (GP/Nurses/ Health Visitor)
     PM CHD/IHD/TVA/Hypertension (8)

Clinics by Health Visitor:
Fri only Child Health Surveillance/ Home visits

Minor Surgery: done by Dr. Narayan for surgical Procedures e.g. minor skin operations, wart, skin tag removals; joint injections (e.g. Depo-medrone) by GP/Nurses

Maternity Services: (Antenatal/Postnatal)
Mon AN 1.00 – 4.00 PM Midwife / Dr Narayan

Premises: Wheelchair access has been provided and assistance provided. Consulting rooms for GP and Nurses and special WC are available on ground floor.

Languages: Staff able to converse in English, Urdu, Gujarati, Hindi, Punjabi and Bengali. For other languages advance notice is needed for arranging interpreter but availability is not guaranteed. Better to bring a friend or relative who is able to speak in English.

Self Treatment of Common Illnesses and Accidents

Many common aches and pain can be treated at home without the need to consult a GP.

Back Pain: Because of the complex nature of the spine, consult the GP if pain persists for more than a few days. If caused by lifting or pushing heavy weights etc, be sensible and take things easy. Take care to sit as upright as possible with a support for the small of the back. Take aspirin (if not allergic) or paracetamol, which not only relieve pain but also help to relieve inflammation.

Bed Sores: caused by prolonged pressure to certain parts of the body while lying in bed for long periods. Try to shift position as often as possible. Take care to smooth out creases in the bottom sheet to avoid irritation. If red marks appear at the pressure points such as heels, elbows, buttocks and hips, inform the GP before they get worse.

Burns: Apply large quantities of cold water/ice to the affected area as soon as possible and maintain this until the pain subsides – usually 15 min. If the skin is unbroken but blistered, apply a loose, dry dressing. If the burn is larger than 4-5 inches in diameter or if the skin is broken, consult the GP as soon as possible.

Head Lice: Affects clean hair as well. Medicated head lotion from the chemist without prescription can be used.

Can you treat yourself at home?

Self care: A well stocked medicine chest will help you treat many everyday illnesses and minor ailments at home. For example, a small supply of paracetamol or ibuprofen (available as syrup for children) and other remedies will help you treat common ailments such as coughs, colds, sore throats, indigestion, toothache, headaches and constipation. If you have children, don't forget to include appropriate medicines for them. The NHS Direct Online Self-Help Guide can also help you identify common symptoms. If symptoms persist or worsen you should contact **NHS Direct** on **0845 4647** or your GP.

Have you been to the pharmacist?

Ask your pharmacist: Pharmacists (sometimes called Chemists) are experts on medicines and how they work. They can also offer advice on common complaints such as coughs, colds, aches and pains and other health issues, such as healthy eating and giving up smoking. They can help you decide whether you need to see a doctor. You can talk to your pharmacists in confidence - even about the most personal symptoms and you don't need to make an appointment. Find your local pharmacy.

Have you called NHS Direct?

Call NHS Direct: You can call **NHS Direct** on **0845 4647*** for confidential health advice and information 24-hours a day, 365 days a year. The lines are staffed by nurses and professional advisors. NHS Direct has become a first point of contact for patients seeking medical help outside normal surgery hours. NHS Direct can offer you information on:
What to do if you or a family member feels ill
Particular health conditions

Sprains: Treat with a cold compress, containing ice if possible, for 15030 min to reduce swelling. Then apply firmly a crepe bandage and give the sprain plenty of rest until the discomfort has subsided. Further strain will inevitably lead to further swelling and a longer recovery period.

Minor Cuts and Grazes: Wash the wound thoroughly with water and a little soap. To stop bleeding apply a clean handkerchief or dressing firmly to the wound for 5 min. Cover with a clean dressing

Sunburn: Treat as for other burns with cold water to remove the heat. Calamine lotion will relieve the irritation whilst paracetamol will also help. Children are particularly susceptible to sunburn and great care should be taken to avoid ever-exposure to the harmful effects of the sun.

Insect Bites and Stings: Antihistamine tablets can be obtained from the chemist without prescription and will usually relieve most symptoms. **Note**: Bee stings should be scraped-away rather than 'plucked' in order to avoid squeezing the contents of the venom sac into the wound.

Chickenpox: On the 1st day a rash appears as small red patches about 3-4mm across. Within a few hours of these developing, small blisters appear in the centre of these patches. During the next 3 or 4 days further patches will appear and the earlier ones will turn 'crusty' and fall off. Calamine lotion may be applied to soothe the often severe itching. Cold baths may also help. **The most infectious period is from 2 or 3 days before the rash appears and up to 5 days after this date.** Children may return to school as soon as the last 'crusts' have dropped off.

When might I need to find a new Doctor?

You may need to find a new doctor for various reasons. For example:
- You have just moved into a new area
- You have moved outside the catchment area of your current surgery
- There is a problem with your relationship with your current Doctor
- Your current Doctor has removed you from his or her list

Use the nhs.uk Doctor searches to find a new Doctor.

Doctors.

Your local Doctor surgery (or GP practice) provides a wide range of family health services, including:
- advice on health problems
- vaccinations
- examinations and treatment
- prescriptions for medicines
- referrals to other health services and social services

Most surgeries can also provide family planning/contraception services, care during pregnancy, child health checks and immunisations, health promotion/health screening services, such as smear tests and well person checks and minor operations and procedures.

It is important to attend for appointments, or notify the surgery if you have to cancel or change it.

APPOINTMENTS

Ref	Day	Date	Time

APPOINTMENTS

Ref	Day	Date	Time

Practice Booklet – please read and follow. If in doubt ask about our services offered. Always bring medical card with you for all appointments. An appointment is for one person only – not multiple. Always allow 48 hours (working days) for repeats. Hospital appointments – contact the hospital not surgery.

SOME MESSAGES FROM THE JX BOARD

➢ Please always bring your medical card
➢ Any forms and letters to be given to the receptionist
➢ Condoms are available from the nurse please ask
➢ Feel free to make comments or suggestions to the Practice Manager
➢ Feel free to attend the practice meeting held 3rd Wednesday of every month
➢ Do not phone for repeat prescription requests
➢ Always use your tick sheet for repeat medication
➢ Aged 20-24? Ask for Meningitis C vaccination
➢ Any private work is chargeable in advance
➢ Cannot attend? Please ring to cancel
➢ Surgery is closed between 1-4 Wednesdays
➢ Take regular medication? Bring it with you
➢ Please check your prescription before you leave the surgery
➢ You may not be seen if you are more than 15mins late
➢ Our commitment is to give appointment with a GP or Nurse as deemed necessary

General Information:

What Can I expect from my Doctor?

Doctors (who are also called GPs) look after the health of people in their local community and deal with a whole range of health problems. They also give health education and advice on things like smoking and diet, run clinics, give vaccinations and carry out simple surgical operations. Doctors usually work with a team including nurses, health visitors and midwives, as well as a range of other health professionals such as physiotherapists and occupational therapists. If a Doctor cannot deal with your problem themselves, they'll usually refer you to a hospital for tests, treatment or to see a consultant with specialised knowledge. Every individual living lawfully and on a settled basis in the UK has a right to be registered with a local Doctors surgery and visits to the surgery are free. Find your local practice using the nhs.uk Doctor searches.

It is important to be registered with a surgery as they refer you for specialist hospital and community treatment services if needed. The services provided by the surgery can be found in the Practice / Surgery Leaflet available from the surgery

Do I need to register with my chosen surgery?

Yes. Once you have chosen a Doctors surgery that is most appropriate for you (nearby location, easy to get to etc), contact the surgery and ask to be registered.
If the surgery is able to add you to their patient list, you will need to fill out some registration forms.

PRACTICE CHARTER

Practice Responsibilities:

Name: People involved in your care will give their names and ensure that you know how to contact them. Surgery will be well sign posted and doctors' and nurses names are indicted on their consulting rooms.

Waiting Time: We run appointment/walk-in system in this practice. You will be given a time for doctor / nurse to see you. You should not wait more than 30 min. in the waiting room without receiving an explanation for the delay. Receptionists have no control on the delay.

Access: You will have access to a Doctor/nurse:
Rapidly in case of extreme emergency
Normal appointments (walk-in) within 2-3 days
Home visits if Triage determines the need.

Telephone: Usually response will be prompt. With only 2 lines and with receptionists attending to other duties, you may have exercise patience in getting a reply. Triage system will enable you to talk to Doctor/nurse in the afternoon.

Test results: For tests or X-rays ordered by the practice we will inform you of the results at your next appointment or earlier, if situations demands. Usually we may not contact you if the results are normal or not serious.

Respect: Patients will be treated as 'customers' and 'partners' in health care irrespective of their ethnic origin, religious or cultural beliefs, or language and communication deficiencies.

Information: Every effort will be made to ensure that you receive all pertinent information that affects your health and the care being offered.

Can a surgery refuse to accept me as a patient?

Yes. A surgery may refuse an application to join its list of patients, if for example you do not reside in its surgery area or it has formally closed its list of patients. Where a surgery does refuse to accept you, then it must have reasonable grounds for doing so, which do not relate to race, gender, social class, age, religion, sexual orientation, appearance, disability or medical condition, and it must give you in writing, reasons for its decision.

How can I get a NHS card?

An NHS medical card is issued when a patient is first registered with a Doctor. It contains your NHS number and other personal details such as your name, address and date of birth.

When you register with a new Doctor, you will be asked for your NHS medical card. If you do not have one, the receptionist will give you a form to fill in (GMS1).

When you have completed and returned the form, your local Primary Care Trust (PCT) will transfer your medical records to your new Doctor. Your medical card will be sent by post, to your home address.

What can I do if I cannot find a local doctor will not accept me as a patient?

Contact your local Primary Care Trust (PCT) if you are having problems registering with a nearby Doctor. Your PCT will normally be able to help you find a Doctor quite quickly.

DR. V. SUBRAMANIAN

No Appointment Needed
To make the most of NHS health services and to get the best possible treatment, you should choose the option that is right for your needs, saving yourself time and inconvenience.
To get the right treatment, follow our useful **check list**:

Self care →	Can you treat yourself at home?
Pharmacist →	Have you been to the pharmacist?
NHS Direct →	Have you called NHS Direct?
NHS Walk-in Centre →	Have you tried your local NHS Walk-In Centre?
Doctor's surgery →	Do you need to visit your Doctors surgery?
Minor Injuries Unit →	Do you need to visit a Minor Injuries Unit?
A&E / 999 →	Do you or a family member need emergency hospital treatment?

Diarrhoea and vomiting in children: Buy Dioralyte from the chemist and feed to the child the first 24 hours at least. On the 2nd day start light, solid feed or very diluted milk. On the 3rd day back to normal feeding. Any anxiety consult GP.

Nosebleeds: Sit in a chair, lean forward with your mouth open, and pinch your nose just below the bone for approximately 10 min. by which time the bleeding should have stopped. Avoid hot drinks or hot food for 24 hours. If symptoms persist consult GP.

Flu: For children under 5 buy Calpol; for over 5 paracetamol. Monitor temperature and give sponging with tepid water to keep temperature down. Keep child in a cool room and give plenty of fluids and rest. Lighten bed linen or clothing. If the child has a high temperature and refuses to take fluid orally then consult GP.

Gastroenteritis: A group of diseases affecting the stomach or part of the intestine. Symptoms are often diarrhoea, sickness and stomach ache. Because the lining of the stomach is likely to be inflamed, medicines are often immediately vomited up. Large quantities of water, orange juice, milk or thin soup should be taken to counter the effects of dehydration. Consult your GP if symptom persists for more than a day, or in the case of babies or young children, 6 hours.

Stomach ache: Most attacks not serious and are usually caused by indigestion or wind. A hot water bottle will often relieve the symptoms and in the case of indigestion, a teaspoon of bicarbonate of soda in half a glass of water will help. If the pain lasts longer than 8 hours or increases in intensity please consult GP.

Colds: No cure has been found yet. Rest in bed, take plenty of hot drinks (soft). If having headache or feverish, take aspirin (if not allergic) or paracetamol. Antibiotics will not have any effect on viral infections!.

APPOINTMENTS

Ref	Day	Date	Time

APPOINTMENTS

Ref	Day	Date	Time

When you register with a new surgery, it would be helpful to take your NHS medical card along if you have one. When you have completed and returned the forms, your local Primary Care Trust (PCT) will transfer your medical records to your new surgery. If it issues them, your PCT will send your medical card to your home address and will write to confirm your registration as a patient with the surgery.

Can I go to a different doctor in the same surgery?
Yes. You can normally see any Doctor within your surgery, this is quite normal, especially if you need an appointment quickly.
A patient no longer registers with an individual Doctor but with a Doctors surgery. When registering, a patient has the right to say which healthcare professional they receive primary medical services from.

What do I do if I have to see a Doctor out of normal surgery hours?
Out of normal surgery hours, all Doctors have an emergency service. This service is only for urgent medical problems that cannot wait until the next day to be treated.
Most surgeries have an answering machine message referring you to out-of-hours telephone numbers or **NHS Direct** on **0845 4647**.

Health Promotion: The practice will offer patients advice and information on steps they can take to promote good health and avoid illness. Self-help which can be undertaken without reference to a doctor in the case of minor ailments.

Health Records: You have the right to see your health records, subject to limitations in the law, in the surgery at times convenient to the receptionists but we may charge you for copies of records. The details will be kept confidential at all times.

Complaints: All complaints will be handled as per procedure and with utmost sensitivity.

Patient Responsibilities:

Help us to help you
Notify change in name, address, telephone numbers etc. immediately (will affect home visits)
Please try to keep appointments. Inform in advance about cancellations. 3 DNA's may mean removal from the list.
Home visits only when you are too ill to visit the surgery. Test results take time – we will call you only if not normal and serious.
Treat Doctors, Nurses and other staff with courtesy and respect.
Telephone calls – please keep it brief. Call between 10.00AM and 12 PM. For Triage i.e. taking to GP/nurses call between 2 and 4 PM (M, Tu, W, F)
For insurance/DWP forms/ Referrals etc. Med. Sec between 11.30 AM and 12.30 PM.

Measles: The rash is blotchy and red and appears on the face and body around the 4th day of illness. It is at its most infectious from 2 or 3 days before the rash appears until 8 or 10 days after that date.
Immunisation can prevent this disease.

Mumps: Symptoms are swelling of the gland in front of one ear often followed, after a couple of days, by swelling in front of the other ear. It is infectious from 2 or 3 days before the swelling appears until 8 or 10 days after that time. If the pain is severe you should consult the GP.
Immunisation can prevent this disease.

German Measles (Rubella): The rash appears during the 1st day and usually covers the body, arms and legs in small pink patches about 2-4 mm across and doesn't itch. No other symptoms are usually present apart from occasional aching joints. It is infectious from 2 days before the rash appears until the rash disappears in about 4 or 5 days from that date. **The only danger is to unborn babies.** All contacts should be informed so that any one pregnant can consult their GP immediately.
Immunisation can prevent this disease.

You can locate your PCT via the nhs.uk PCT search

Can I get travel inoculations in my Doctor's surgery?

Normally yes. Some inoculations may be free under the NHS, though there may be a charge for others. Consult your Doctor preferably at least 2 months before you plan to travel for advice and to arrange any inoculations that you may need.

This is because some inoculations take time to become effective. You can also get travel inoculations at specialist travel clinics.

For further health advice for travellers, use the Department of Health Travel Advice Guide.

How do I get a Dotor to visit me at home?

Normally you should go to your surgery to see a Doctor. However if you are too ill to do this, you can ask your Doctor to visit you at home.

You should contact your surgery as early as possible to arrange a home visit.

Can I change my Doctor?

You have the right to change your Doctor without having to give a reason. The process of finding a new Doctor is similar to registering. However, it would be extremely helpful (for administrative purposes) to notify the surgery that you are leaving.

- On top of each addition page - type 1st line Name - first, middle and last name; 2nd line DOB, 3rd line address. Only fill in when any details have changed after ensuring the computer is updated of these changes.

- Put the name and details of the patient in the first appointments page before handing the booklet to the patient.

- Print 2x the number in patient list.

30. The List of Attachments

No	Section	Details	Pages
1	2.3.5a	List of errors in service to GPs by receptionists	1
2	2.3.8a	Receptionists job rota	1
3	2.6.4a	Registration - Telephone / Direct Communication	6
4	2.7.3a	Registration Training Module General Procedures	2
5	2.7.5a	Weekly report	1
6	2.8.4a	Branded and Generic Drugs - selected common drugs	1
7	2.9.8a	Continuous Practice Development - meeting minutes	1
8	2.9.9a	PMgr - List of things to do and check continnually	2
9	3.1a	Tasks to perform - IMT assistant	1
10	8.10a	Petty Cash Expenses	1
11	8.10a	Petty Cash Income / Expenses Layout	1
12	18.1.4a	Surgery Accounts	4
13	18.1.4b	Staff Budget	1
14	18.1.5a	Surgery Accounts	4
15	18.1.5b	Net Worth Template Financial Summary	1
16	24.2a	BP Chart	1
17	24.4a	GI-GL Chart	4
18	24.4b	Food Values	2
19	29.2a	Front & Back cover pages	1
20	29.2b	Practice Booklet Details	8

References

1. Abbreviations Used:

ACAS – Advisory, Conciliation and Arbitration Service

ASAP – As soon as possible

BMA – British Medical Association

BP – Blood Pressure

CAB – Citizens Advice Bureau

CCG – Clinical Commissioning Group

CQC – Care Quality Commission

DWP – Department for Work and Pensions

EDI – Electronic Data Interchange

GMC – General Medical Council

GMS – General Medical Service (most GPs in GMS Contract with PCTs)

GMSQP – General Medical Services Quarterly Payments)

GP – General Practitioner

GPFC – General Practice Finance Corporation (for all finance e.g. rents)

HA – Health Authority

HCA – Healthcare Assistants

HCP – Healthcare Professionals

HMRC – Her Majesty Revenue and Customs

HR – Human Relations

IMT – Information Management and Technology (IT specialists)

IOS – items of Service (for making claims for payments)

LMCs – Local Medical Committees – www.lmc.org.uk

MDDUS – Medical and Dental Defence Union of Scotland

MDO – Medical Defence Organisations

MDU – Medical Defence Union

MPIG – Minimum Practice Income Guarantee

MPS – Medical Protection Society

NCAS – National Clinical Assessment Service

NHS – National Health Service

NHSNET – NHS communicating via private network service – controlled.

NI – National Insurance

PAG – Performance Advisory Group

PAYE – Pay as you earn (for Tax and NI)

PBC – Practice Based Commissioning

PCO – Primary Care Organisation

PCT – Primary Care Trusts (Now CCG – Clinical Commissioning Group)

PFI – Private Financial Incentives

PMgr – Practice Manager

PMS – Personal Medical Service (some GPs are in this contact with PCTs)

PPA – Prescription Pricing Authority

QMAS – Quality Management Analysis System (for QOF payments)

QOF – Quality and Outcomes Framework (for extra income for procedures)

RCGP – Royal College of General Practitioners

RCN – Royal College of Nursing

VAT – Value Added Tax (for HMRC Tax payments)

2. References

The eBook is based mostly from my notes while working – with PCT and other organisations, which gave periodic information of changes and how to process them.

The references given below are for the users of the eBook – for current practices and more detailed descriptions of each of the sections.

1. Google – for searching the relevant sites – https://www.google.co.uk/
2. Wikipedia – A good site as well
3. BMA – British Medical Association – https://www.bma.org.uk/
4. NICE – National Institute for Health and Clinical Excellence – www.nice.org.uk/
5. RCGP – Royal College of General Practitioners – www.rcgp.org.uk/
6. GMC – General Medical Council – www.gmc-uk.org/

7. CQC – Care Quality Commission – www.ukqcs.co.uk/CQC

8. MPS – Medical Practitioners Society – www.medicalprotection.org/uk/

9. MDSU – Medical Defence Union – www.themdu.com/

10. PCTs – Various Primary Care Trusts – en.wikipedia.org/wiki/NHS_primary_care_trust

11. HMRC – Her Majesty Revenue and Customs – www.hmrc.gov.uk/

12. ACAS – Advisory, Conciliation and Arbitration service – www.acas.org.uk/

13. Councils – All local councils – https://www.gov.uk/find-your-local-council

14. CAB – Citizen's Advice Bureau – various regions in the country – www.citizensadvice.org.uk/

15. NHS Patients' Rights – http://www.adviceguide.org.uk/nireland/healthcare_ni/healthcare_nhs_healthcare e/nhspatients_rights.htm

16. Administration in General Practice by Helen Owen 1975 – I spotted it only 2 years ago.

17. NHS111 – www.nhs.uk/NHSEngland/AboutNHSservices/.../Pages/NHS-111.aspx

18. http://www.nhs.uk/

19. QOF – Quality and Outcomes Framework – www.hscic.gov.uk/qof

20. chooseandbook.nhs.uk

21. connectingforhealth.nhs.uk

22. NHS complaints procedure.

23. prsmusic.com

24. cla.co.uk

25. Get anyone to do anything – David J Lieberman PhD 2000.

26. PULSE – www.pulsetoday.co.uk/

27. GPonline – www.gponline.com/news

28. First Practice Management – www.firstpracticemanagement.co.uk/

29. Medeconomics – www.medeconomics.co.uk/

30. For QOF refer to – http://www.nhsemployers.org

31. Job Descriptions – http://job-descriptions.careerplanner.com/Medical-Secretaries-5.cfm

32. Claims, procedures etc. – www.systems.hscic.gov.uk/

33. IOS Links – HA-PCT/GP Links IOS Reference Manual. (http://systems.hscic.gov.uk/)

34. Customer service – http://www.ncbi.nlm.nih.gov/

35. Customer service – http://voices.yahoo.com/

36. Customer service – html http://en.wikipedia.org/

37. Premises – http://rcgp-innovait.oxfordjournals.org

38. training checklist and overview of operations – http://www.unison.org.uk

39. http://www.nhsemployers.org

40. Journey to perfect Mayo clinic – James A. Dilling, Associate Administrator – Systems Quality, Mayo Clinic

41. PCT/CCGs/CQC notifications and guidance

42. The Health and Social Care Act 2008

43. Mental Health Act 1983 CHAPTER 20 – An Act to consolidate the law relating to mentally disordered persons.

44. For more details relating to GPES, please see the NHS HSCIC website: http://www.hscic.gov.uk/gpes

45. Health and Safety at Work Act 1974 revised.

46. Management of Health and Safety at Work Regulations 1999

47. Display Screen Equipment Regulations 1993, 2002 amendment

48. Manual Handling Operations Regulations 1992, 1993

49. Personal Protective Equipment at Work Regulations 1993, revised 2005

50. Workplace Health, Safety and Welfare Regulations 1993

51. Fire Safety HSC 1993/191

52. Control of Substances Hazardous to Health (COSHH) regulations

53. Environmental Protections Act 1990

54. http://www.bhf.org.uk/bmi/home.html

55. http://www.bloodpressureuk.org/

56. BloodPressureandyou/Thebasics/Bloodpressurechart

57. http://www.diabetes.org.uk

58. http://www.the-gi-diet.org/lowgifoods/

59. http://www.mendosa.com/gilists.html

60. http://www.patient.co.uk

61. carersfederation.co.uk/icas

62. nmc-uk.org

63. ombudsman.org.uk

64. pals.nhs.uk – Locating your local services, commenting on your practice, making a complaint

65. Department of Health 68-71 Patient registration, GPs, hospitals etc.

66. National Association for Patient Participation
67. NHS Choices
68. Patient Association
69. Princess Royal Trust for Carers
70. NHS Care Records Service
71. bma.org.ukwww.nhscarerecords.nhs.uk – 0300 123 3020
72. www.direct.gov.uk – Patients' rights to accessing patient records and fees charged
73. The new Summary Care Records initiative in England
74. How to organise a Lasting Power of Attorney in England and Wales via the Office of the Public Guardian – Independent Complaints Advocacy Service
75. Nursing and Midwifery Council

Patient Opinion.

Contact Us

For any comments or to contact for anything else, please send an email to: vsmani8604@gmail.com

I will endeavour to reply ASAP.

Thanks

My gratitude for this book is mainly to the surgeries where I worked and visited, the GP partners and other GPs, the staff, the very helpful HAs, PCTs and their staff, pharmacists and the accountant friend, Mr G. Viswanathan, in London, who initially pushed me to join the surgery in London as the Practice Manager.

I started this new career at a very late stage in my life but I enjoyed it the most in my working life.

I also gained valuable experiences in the surgeries I worked at in Birmingham and Manchester, with very talented GPs and supporting staff. PCT staff in the respective places were extremely helpful and ready to support when requested.

I thank Dr. Shiva Devaraj and Dr. Sujoy Jaiswal for continued support and giving motivation to complete the task. I also thank Mr Karthik Raghavan, a specialist on WordPress to check the format of the final presentation and for giving it the 'kiss of life' in getting the right format for publication. His support was like a **'shot in the arm'** for me.

I am very grateful to the late Mr R. V. Ramachandran (ex-chairman of Cummins India and South East, and a great industrialist), who **'spoon-fed'** me on the principles of **'patients as customers'** and how the UK GP practices have to change and adapt. He had sent me papers on various management issues and I greatly benefitted from his **'Top Down'** approach on dealing with people and issues.

My gratitude is also due to Mr Dev Ganesan, a great entrepreneur in Washington D.C., for his constant encouragement to make this into an eBook ASAP. His enthusiasm and zeal motivated me to pursue the publication of the eBook.

Finally, I must thank my family for continued support and encouragement:

Bala, my wife, for helping with any assistance on **'fire fighting'** tasks when the computer gave me problems.

My elder son Sanjay, in Washington D.C., for pushing me to embark on this venture and to make sure that I did not give my email ID or telephone to anyone (maybe to avoid being inundated with complaints about my eBook).

His wife Meera, who is a whiz kid on computers and had hands-on experience for various aspects including Microsoft packages.

My second son Deepak, Medical Doctor, Respiratory Consultant in Derby, who was highly and constructively critical of this venture but always pushed me to change the course, when needed, for better response.

And, his wife Kashmira, as hospital pharmacist, chipping in on various occasions in areas pertaining to medication and related aspects.

Finally, my elder brother, V. Jagannathan in Chennai, who taught me company accounts, which I adapted to do surgery accounts.

Postscript

Having read the eBook, it would be expected of all to have a good idea of not only GP surgery management, but also management principles in a small company or even in a large corporate world.

Any newcomer, not necessarily a fresh school leaver or graduate, even experienced people in senior management, who might not have had GP surgery experience, should find the book immensely useful. It introduces the topics in a simple way and lists the areas to know, even beforehand, which would be useful at the interview.

Training in surgeries and in PCTs is given for new and existing staff but please do not depend on this alone for your personal development. Surgeries are very busy and training may not be structured; training is mostly by standing '**next to Nelly**' now called '**shadowing**'. For experienced people this type of '**shadowing**' may still be very useful. For a new person, with little or no experience, the training has to be interactive with a trainer, who is able to listen and answer the many queries the new staff may have.

One must always remember that internal motivation is crucial and more effective than external, e.g. like having a mentor. One has to read and train oneself, if one wants to better oneself in a job, and being ambitious has to be matched by putting in a lot of effort.

Do not rely on external training alone – sometimes that may not be available or training might not be given in time, when the staff needs it most. So always read this eBook and use the references to find details and make copious notes. There are no substitutes for self-help and self-motivation.

As a non-clinical staff member, do not ever get involved in areas other than learning and observing. Never take sides or be critical or judgmental or ridicule colleagues or clinical staff or patients.

Patients are the main source of surgery income and never forget that one's salary depends on it. Just learn and do the job and strive to do it well.

Never get involved with whistle blowing as the route is too horrendous and one is bound to lose in the end. If one does not like the environment, then plan to leave, but always find an escape route first and not resign to show off to others that one is very principled. Do not forget that graveyards are full of 'principled' people.

Good behaviour is the only saviour in retaining and growing in the job.

Remember always that '**Talent is knowledge, Tact is skill; Talent knows what to do but Tact knows how to do it**'. Knowledge and talent alone are not enough for survival; ability to have the tact and skill to deal with people without antagonising is a very great asset.

Also, be aware that '**it is the Attitude and not the Aptitude that determines one's Altitude**'. It is not the number of times you fall down, but if the number of times you get up is one more than the times you fall down, then you have the right attitude to survive.

GP surgeries are wonderful places to work for, and PCTs and others are there to help. No kudos for PCTs to punish or discredit a surgery as they get discredited too! PCTs have a crucial role to play and always respect and appreciate their roles. Criticising is easy but appreciating requires a lot of understanding and skill.

Whatever level you join and whichever place you decide to work, always have the right attitude. Never be '**an accumulator of bad memories**' but be positive and keep smiling even when facing adversity.

Wherever you intend starting work, always imagine this objective – as it is going to be the same, as working in a surgery.

Buy:

1   An A4 3-inch thick good folder (not box file)
2   Coloured separator sheets (for the 10 sections in the sidebar).
3   1 to 31 separator sheets (for the 31 sections).
4   How to write in simple English – most sentences should have no more than 20 words, typically 15 at maximum.
5   A simple book of synonyms and antonyms.

Print out each section in the eBook and put it in the folder.

Replace my CV with your current CV. Always update your CV every 6 months.

As one gains experience in the surgery, one should make new notes and either add, amend or remove the original ones in various sections, so that the details are always current.

When making notes, avoid jargon or long words and sentences. Medical terms are unavoidable but in brackets put it in words that a non-clinical person would understand.

Notice and study patients and others coming to the surgery and any experience gained in interacting with them, please note it down. Do not mention names, race or colour or any judgmental attributes but note it as an experience with, say, case 1 or 2.

Read a lot of books, especially on psychology, particularly, social psychology and communications; working in a surgery is working for a '**people industry**' and both types of books would be most useful.

Over a 1-2 year period one would have enough details to write one's own 'blogs' or 'book'.

You are your own motivator. Doing the job creditably is very good but always look beyond. You do not have to wait till a ripe old age, like me, to publish blogs or write an eBook.

All of you, when joining a GP surgery, should be aware it is a healthcare industry.

Surgeries will have limited facilities and there will be a lot of restraints on staff and facilities.

The caretaker for the surgery may only come for 2 hours in the morning to open the surgery and 2 hours in the evening for closing. Cleaners would come for 4 hours max during lunch breaks so that the GPs and nurses' consultation rooms would be free for cleaning.

People come to the surgery mostly because they are unwell and may not be in the best of their temperaments. Children may run around eating food and sometimes may cause damage to sofas, mark the walls etc. But the testing times come when they empty their bladders or 'throw up'.

Faced with this, cleaning of these becomes imminent due to people moving around and health & safety issues. It is totally dependent on the receptionists and the PMgr to deal with the issue.

The PMgr has to take his jacket off, roll up the sleeves, put on a dirty overall, take a pan and brush and mop and bucket – the key tools to have – and deal with those issues.

Do not regard any job in the surgery as menial or below one's dignity; staff must treat surgery as a **'home'** within a special workplace. At times, attention to WCs may also be needed. PMgr may be admin head but he is also the 'caretaker' for the surgery and should fix the problems immediately.

There are several issues that all non-clinical staff should be aware of. GP Surgery is purely a clinical environment and importance would always be given to people with clinical qualifications. Non-clinical staffs are there just to help the clinical staff. **That focus should never be lost**. Despite all the HR rules, procedures and practices, when non-clinical staffs have a serious issue with a clinical staff, he/she is the one, who is bound to lose.

Never try to go on a moral crusade while working in a GP surgery. One is there to learn the procedures and help the GPs, Nurses, HCAs and other clinical staff. It is not a place to wage wars with GPs and raise issues pertaining to **'whistleblowing'**. It would always be a losing battle.

Also, it is not a place for **'fashion attire'** or **'heavy makeup'** or **'nail decorations'**. Proper dress code, simple manners and the main decoration needed is **'a pleasant smile'** when dealing with patients.

All religions in the world preach the same things – **leading a righteous life following simple principles**. The head, be it a single person or multitude of people, have all decreed in very simple terms what to do and what not to do. Just like the Ten Commandments, the language is simple – **'Thou shall not steal"** – nothing could be a simpler expression than that. All religious leaders have used simple understandable and unambiguous terms. There were no hidden meanings, no innuendoes, and no need for elaborate explanations of what they have said to all of us to follow.

All the leaders of the various religions have also given exemptions / amnesty to the following people, from not required to follow the strict religious codes of behaviour:

All children and young people;
All old people;
All pregnant women;
All sick people; and
All those who, attend and take care of the sick people or pregnant women, old people or children and young people.

I remember being taught when I was 10 years old, in Calcutta, India a wonderful poem:

Abou Ben Adhem
BY LEIGH HUNT

Abou Ben Adhem (may his tribe increase!)
Awoke one night from a deep dream of peace,
And saw, within the moonlight in his room,
Making it rich, and like a lily in bloom,
An angel writing in a book of gold:—
Exceeding peace had made Ben Adhem bold,
And to the presence in the room he said,
"What writest thou?"—The vision raised its head,
And with a look made of all sweet accord,
Answered, "The names of those who love the Lord."
"And is mine one?" said Abou. "Nay, not so,"
Replied the angel. Abou spoke more low,
But cheerly still; and said, "I pray thee, then,
Write me as one that loves his fellow men."

The angel wrote, and vanished. The next night
It came again with a great wakening light,
And showed the names whom love of God had blest,
And lo! Ben Adhem's name led all the rest.

There may be times when service to the community would be placed at a higher level than following the religious strictures to the detriment of overlooking serving the humanity.

The above should apply to all those who work in GP surgeries, in Hospitals, in Out-patients centre and various health clinics.

I do remember our tutor for training in an insurance industry telling all of us a story on the last day before we all left, fortified with all the knowledge he imparted to us on how to succeed (I never made it in that industry!).

It was about a '**bird in the hand**' different to the conventional one.

A very famous and reputed sage was in his cabin on top of a hill and vast numbers of people were queuing to see and talk to him. Usually it took about 4 hours or so of queuing to be in front of him. The sage always had his eyes closed all the time, even while talking to others.

Two boys were seeing this crowd every day for some days. One was a perpetual doubter and a troublemaker (let us call him 'John'). His friend, Jack, was like most of us – afraid to go against his close friend John.

John said the sage was a phony and he would prove it in no time.

Jack said, 'Yes you may be right; however, all these people couldn't be wrong to assume the sage is real and famous.'

John said people were like sheep and follow each other, and large crowds did not prove anything.

Jack said, 'You might be right,' but he was not happy.

John caught a small bird, given birth to a few minutes before in a nest from the branch of a tree and he held it in his palm, covering his fingers but not crushing the bird. Jack said, 'What are you doing?'

John said, 'Let us see the sage and I will ask him whether he could guess what I have in my right hand.'

Jack said, 'What if he says it is a bird?'

John said, 'The sage might have his eyes deceptively open, without us noticing. But I will ask him whether the bird is alive or dead.'

Jack said, 'What would you do?'

John said, 'Very simple – if he says it is dead, I will open my fingers and show the live bird. If he says it is alive, I will tighten my fingers and crush it to death and show him.'

Jack said that it may be clever but fooling him is not what he liked and was very apprehensive.

Still they waited in the queue and John was in front of the sage who had his eyes closed and asked, 'What would you like young man?'

John asked whether the sage could say what he had in his right hand.

Sage replied with closed eyes, 'It must be a young bird, given birth to 4-5 hours ago.'

Jack was stunned and looked at John, who was thinking of his glory to come.

John asked whether the bird was alive or dead.

The sage then opened his eyes and said, 'Young man the bird is in your hand. It is all up to you; you can make it live or crush it to death. I can do nothing about it.'

Our tutor then said, 'Our career and success is all entirely dependent on us and not on the tutor. We all have the bird in our hands – at various stages in our lives – studies, exams, jobs, marriage, etc. it is all up to us to demonstrate and succeed.

I feel like that tutor, all your careers depend on you as individuals, not on others. I hope you make a thumping success of your careers with the eBook beside you!

I do not expect the eBook to be like **'next to sliced bread'** for a career in this industry but if it helps even 10 people I would consider my effort, over the last few years to produce the eBook, and my mission, well accomplished.

About Me

I am Mani (Dr. V Subramanian). I have had varied experience, from Engineering industry to Import/Export, insurance, teaching, managing own companies and as Practice Manager in GP surgeries.

After retirement, I worked for my wife's company as Company Secretary, Accountant, and as an all 'odd jobs' person. Now she has also retired.

I have done voluntary work for Thames Valley Police and for the NHS hospital in Amersham, but I discontinued this and spent my time writing this book over the last 2-3 years.

I must admit that when I joined the surgery for the first time, I did not know anything about surgery management, but I had years of experience in senior management in several companies in the UK, India, and USA.

When I visit flower gardens in the UK, I have no clue about many of the types of plants or flowers surrounding me. My know-how at the time of joining the surgery was akin to my knowledge of plants. However, I built up the surgery know-how and experience quickly over a short period. Unfortunately I cannot say that my knowledge of plants and flowers has improved one bit even today.

Printed in Great Britain
by Amazon